The State and Women in the Economy

SUNY Series,
WOMEN AND WORK

Joan Smith, Editor

The State and Women in the Economy

Lessons from Sex Discrimination
in the Republic of Ireland

JEAN LARSON PYLE

STATE UNIVERSITY OF NEW YORK PRESS

Photo on the front cover is the Four Courts on Inns
Quay, Dublin, which now houses the Supreme and High
Courts. (Courtesy of the Irish Tourist Board)

Published by
State University of New York Press, Albany

© 1990   State University of New York

For information, address State University of New York
Press, State University Plaza, Albany, N.Y. 12246

Library of Congress Cataloging-in-Publication Data

Pyle, Jean Larson, 1944–
   The state and women in the economy: lessons from sex
discrimination in the Republic of Ireland / Jean Larson Pyle.
      p.   cm. — (SUNY series on women and work)
   Includes bibliographical references.
   ISBN 0-7914-0379-3. — ISBN 0-7914-0380-7 (pbk.)
   1. Women—Employment—Ireland.   2. Labor policy—Ireland.
3. Family policy—Ireland.   4. Sex discrimination against women—
Ireland.   I. Title.   II. Series.
HD6138.P95   1990
331.4'09415—dc20

For

Lloyd L. Larson

and

the memory of
Jean A. Larson

with love and admiration

Contents

Figures

Tables

Preface

WHERE: Republic of Ireland
WHEN: 1961 to 1981
WHAT: Measures of female labor force participation remained surprisingly low and unchanging during export-led development and shifts of employment from agriculture into industry and service sectors—two types of growth which typically incorporate women into the labor force.
WHY: Why did this occur?
Why is this case study of importance now for a wide range of social scientists interested in understanding the subordinate role of women in the economy and feminists analyzing the foundations of male domination?

This book examines the interrelationship between gender, economic development and employment, and state policy. The relevance of this research to us as social scientists is explored on three levels of analysis: first, on the concrete level by analyzing why women's participation in the labor force in the Republic of Ireland from 1961 to 1981 remained surprisingly low during export-led growth; secondly, on a more general plane by discussing what the main findings contribute to the interdisciplinary literatures on women in the labor market or women in development; and lastly, by outlining the implications for two broader areas of scholarly research, feminist theory and the theory of the state.

The Republic of Ireland offers the researcher an invaluable case study with respect to the role of women in the labor market during economic development or growth. Because its economic experiences in these decades exhibited many similarities to those of both industrialized and some developing countries and because of the blatancy of sex discrimination, a study of the role of women in the Irish development process has relevance for those studying women in both types of situations.

The Irish case, which offers new perspectives on the interrelated processes of economic development, state policy formation and women's labor force participation, has been essentially overlooked by the literatures examining the export-led development strategy and the roles of women in the economy. This book is devoted to alleviating that omission and to presenting an analysis of women in Irish export-led development and the insights it offers to academics and policymakers in other industrialized and developing countries.

At the concrete level this study shows that, contrary to the expectations of traditional theoretical approaches and in contrast to what occurred elsewhere during similar types of growth, the expected increases in measures of Irish female labor force participation were precluded during this period because of the role of the state in conjunction with other social institutions in maintaining gender inequality. The expected labor market outcomes for Irish women did not materialize because of the impact of discriminatory state policies — employment policies *and* reproductive rights and family policies — on decision-making in the firm and in the household.

This situation is an eye-opener. Discrimination against women in Ireland has been so widespread and the manner in which it has been reinforced by government policies so distinct that it is easy to see. The way in which it has worked is also simple to understand. Therefore, a major benefit derived from a study of the Irish case is that it shows us how women can be dominated elsewhere in similar ways that may be much less obvious. Because of this, the study of women in Ireland has implications that extend well beyond the country itself and the particular dimension of female economic activity examined, labor force participation.

The Irish study suggests an approach that can be utilized in understanding women's subordinate economic positions elsewhere. The main lesson—that we cannot understand the role of women in the economy without utilizing a theory of gender inequality which incorporates the role of the state and assesses the impact of a broad range of state policies (employment policies along with reproductive rights and family policies)— has relevance at a more general level for the literatures analyzing women's roles in industrialized or developing countries.

This approach can also be applied to other aspects of women's economic lives such as occupational segregation, relative earnings, unemployment rates, and access to training, full-time versus part-time jobs or other economic resources. Studies based on this type of analysis can show us what changes must be made to facilitate equality between men and women in the economy.

In addition, broader implications for feminist theory and the theory of the state spring from the results of this research. This study not only indicates that a feminist approach to gender inequality must be utilized but, by revealing the way state policy affects gender inequality in the household, firm, and society at large, it substantially expands our understanding of the social dimensions such an approach must incorporate. I argue that this suggests the usefulness and timeliness of a substantially revised and revitalized structural approach to male domination. Similarly, recognition that the objectives of state personnel can involve maintenance of traditional gender relations (male domination) as well as the stimulation of economic development and growth (and the complications that result when these goals are contradictory) can contribute to the theory of the state.

Development of this book has involved years of research, analysis, discussion, and writing. The process is not finished, but rather is entering a new phase. I have found the Irish case enormously interesting and enlightening, rich with important insights and implications. It is now my task to try to share these findings with a wider interdisciplinary audience.

Over the years various parts of this manuscript have been read and discussed by economists, sociologists, political scientists, anthropologists, and gender specialists. I have valued this interaction and the resulting inputs greatly. It is my hope that this process will continue: that based on the Irish case study and its implications, further debate regarding the impact of state policy, as it interacts with social relations in the household and firm, on women's economic roles during economic growth or development will be stimulated. I hope that in this way our understanding of women's disadvantaged economic position and what may be necessary to alleviate it, as well as our understanding of the dimensions of male domination and how it can be changed will be enhanced.

I am immeasurably grateful to more people than can be named in the space of a preface for their assistance, support, and encouragement as I pursued this research and analysed its contributions.

I have benefitted from the extensive work of researchers in a number of fields — political economy, feminist theory, women in the economy, and women and development — and the tremendous strides they have made in developing our understanding of women's roles in the political economy and gender oppression. Special thanks go to Samuel Bowles, Richard Edwards, and Ann Ferguson for reading earlier drafts, for many challenging discussions, and for encouragement and advice.

Without exception, my innumerable contacts in Ireland were generous with resources and provision of data. I am particularly grateful to John Blackwell and to personnel at the Industrial Development Authority and the Department of Labour for information I could not have otherwise obtained.

The staffs at the University of Massachusetts and University of Lowell libraries have made extensive efforts on my behalf. Personnel in bibliographic materials and interlibrary loan willingly and untiringly obtained what must have appeared to be an unending flow of requests for documents or hard-to-find articles.

I have appreciated comments of participants in a number of conferences, study groups, and classroom situations in which portions of this research have been presented.

The contributions of these resources have been enormous, and the support of family and friends essential. The results of this research are heavily dependent on them all, although any errors remain solely my responsibility.

Chapter One

Women in the Economy, the State and Development: An Overview

Introduction

The analysis of women in the labor market or women in the economy is a critical issue in both the labor market literature for industrialized countries and the economic development literature. With respect to the former, it has been widely acknowledged that the topic of women in the labor market is currently of central importance and that the single most important development in the labor market in the last four decades has been the dramatically increasing labor force participation of women, especially married women (Gunderson, 1989; Lazear, 1989). It is assumed that female labor force participation rates in industrialized countries have substantially risen in a manner that is not temporary. However, women are clearly not equal to men in the labor force, and research has focused primarily on uncovering causes of such dimensions of inequality as relative wage differentials and occupational segregation. Increasingly, policies developed in the past to alleviate these sex differences are being reevaluated and the efficacy of these and potential new ones is being debated.

With respect to the development literature, there has been increasing recognition that in most countries, except export-led economies, women have not been integrated into the development process. Furthermore, it has been found that women have been increasingly disadvantaged by development, and that the failure to incorporate them has in some cases fundamentally undermined economic development and augmented crises (Sen and Grown, 1987; Ward, 1987). The main concerns in this literature are (1) understanding under what conditions women are integrated rather than marginalized by development; (2)

why, if they are integrated, it is usually on a disadvantaged basis; and (3) what can be done about this (Tiano, 1987).

Therefore, the issues of whether women are incorporated into the labor force during development and growth and if so, how, are of primary importance in these literatures. Much attention from a number of theoretical perspectives has been devoted to understanding the factors that affect the roles women obtain in the labor force and the larger economy.

Because the Irish economic development process has dimensions that make it comparable to both industrialized and developing countries and because of the explicitness of sex discrimination and the manner in which it was maintained, the situation of women in Ireland can assist in furthering our general understanding of the factors that influence women's labor force participation and shape other dimensions of their experience in the paid labor force and economy.

Expectations versus Reality in the Republic of Ireland

The Republic of Ireland is a small country on the western edge of Europe with a population that rose from 2.8 million to 3.4 million in 1981. It consists of the 26 southern counties of the island of Ireland, which achieved independence from Great Britain in 1921–1922. It is to be distinguished from Northern Ireland, the northern six counties of which remain part of the United Kingdom.[1] For simplification, the Republic of Ireland will be referred to hereafter as Ireland.

Ireland occupied a unique position on the continuum of industrialized/developing countries during the years from 1961 to 1981. On the one hand, it was categorized as a member of the set of industrialized nations; on the other hand, it was also considered a developing country, being one of the original and most active sites of export-led development. Because of this, its development process and the role of Irish women can be related to both the experiences of women in other industrialized countries or small export-led economies.

Ireland has been classified by the World Bank and the United Nations as an industrialized nation. Its receipt of Marshall aid after World War II, its memberships in a variety of First World organizations such as the Organization for Economic Cooperation and Development (OECD), its long historical association with Great Britain, and its integration with the European Economic Community (EEC) in 1973 all result in its being viewed as an integral part of Western Europe and the community of developed nations.[2]

However, although tied with Western Europe, the Irish development process had many similarities with those of several other countries developing during this same period, especially in East and Southeast Asia. Although virtually overlooked in the literatures and case studies examining export-led growth, and the economic roles of women during it, Ireland was the first country to initiate this type of development strategy by establishing an export-processing zone at Shannon. By the 1970s, it was acknowledged as having formulated one of the most sophisticated export-led promotional strategies in the world. It was classified by the EEC, upon entry into that organization, as an underdeveloped industrial region.

Ireland's experience in development is neither fully that of the industrialized countries nor that of the Third World export-led economies but rather combines features of both. Ireland's growth was linked to its outward-looking development strategy and also, via its economic and social affiliations, to trends in Western Europe and the United States.[3] It can perhaps be most accurately characterized as an industrializing nation within the community of industrialized countries or as a semiperipheral nation (Coughlan, 1980; Stanton, 1979).

As shown in Chapter 2 (Table 2.3), Irish women's labor force participation was below the average for the Western European OECD countries in 1961. Given this low level of women's activity in the formal economy and the circumstances of Irish economic development (export-led development with increasing integration into the community of Western European OECD nations), several of the major theoretical frameworks — the integrationist/modernization view, the neoclassical economic school of thought and the Marxist approach — suggest that the expected trend in Irish women's labor force participation during the period 1961–1981 would be substantially upward.

The integrationist/modernization approach has been used chiefly in the context of developing countries but is also relevant to the recent historical experience of industrialized countries. It argues that women become more fundamentally involved in the formal economy as development proceeds (Tiano, 1987: 217).[4] It builds upon earlier modernization theory, which embodies the liberal view that, with the replacement of traditional value systems and forms of social organization by "modern" values and social roles, the status and well-being of all are enhanced. Because this process is assumed to be gender-neutral, the implication is that women will benefit more than men, as their options were more severely constrained in earlier societies (Jacquette, 1982:268 –69; Tiano, 1981:2). This suggests that equality for women will occur due to enlightenment.

This view is reinforced by neoclassical economic analyses that argue that any statistical discrimination or discrimination based on tastes, whether racial or sexual, will be eradicated in the long run by competitive forces (Lloyd and Niemi, 1979:201). All other things equal, better informed producers without tastes for discrimination will be able to profit relative to other employers, resulting in wage and employment equality. This suggests that enhancement of women's position in the economy will occur through competition.[5]

Orthodox Marxian theory recognized that, in the words of Engels (1942/1972), the "emancipation of women will only be possible when women can take part in production on a large, social scale, and domestic work no longer claims anything but an insignificant amount of her time." He argued in 1884 that this now had "become possible through modern large-scale industry, which does not merely permit the employment of female labor over a wide range, but positively demands it, while it also tends toward ending private domestic labor by changing it more and more into a public industry" (221). In other words, incorporation of women accompanies the rise of social production.

These arguments regarding the experience of women in development have been empirically supported by research in industrialized nations and export-led developing countries. With respect to industrialized countries, the rise in women's labor force participation rates has been broadly based and one of the most striking changes in the postwar years (Gunderson, 1989; Hagen and Jenson, 1988).[6] Research by the OECD shows that women's participation rates in industrialized countries during the postwar period have risen as proportionately more of the labor force were employed in the industrial and service sectors (Organization for Economic Cooperation and Development, 1980).

Other research has revealed the positive impact of export-led development on women's participation in the labor force. Quite in contrast to import-substitution development, export-led or outward-looking development favors the use of female workers (Ward, 1987). According to Jones (1984a), women's share of the manufacturing workforce in five Asian export-led economies was greater than in western countries. Salaff's (1986) research reveals that the proportion of women in the total registered labor force in Hong Kong, Taiwan, and Singapore increased dramatically during export-led development.[7] The participation of women is thought to have made a key contribution to the achievement of the high growth rates of eight East and Southeast Asian nations (Jones, 1984a and b).

The rationale underlying this phenomenon of heavy participation of women in export-led development is that this type of development is based on the attraction of foreign direct investment in labor-intensive industries. Multinational corporations locate in developing countries primarily because they are labor-intensive industries seeking low-wage workers.[8] Because it was common practice to pay women substantially lower wages than men, women constituted the major proportion of the work force of the multinationals (Fuentes and Ehrenreich, 1983; Heyzer, 1986; Jones, 1984a and b).[9]

Therefore, to the extent a country experienced both of these types of structural change — a shift from agriculture to industry and service sectors, and export-led growth — it would be considered highly likely that the participation of women in the labor force would increase.

This study reveals that although both of these types of structural change in the economy occurred in the Republic of Ireland, 1961–1981, the expected increase in women's labor force participation did not materialize and measures of female economic activity remained low relative to countries experiencing similar types of economic change and/or with which Ireland was increasingly economically and socially integrated.

Observation of two types of data describing women's changing roles in the labor force—the female labor force participation rate and the female share of total employment—indicate that Irish women were not able to substantially enhance their aggregate position in the labor force during the growth associated with the outward-looking development strategy. As shown in Chapter 2, both of these measures of the position of Irish women in the labor force became among the lowest in the Western European Organization for Economic Cooperation and Development (OECD) during this period and showed a startling lack of response to the dramatic social and economic change experienced in Ireland during this period.

Two further observations regarding an analysis of labor force participation data must be made. First, measures of women's participation in the official labor force constitute only one type of indicator of women's position in the economy and only one of the ways to examine how women have shared in the development process.[10] Nevertheless, it is a critical indicator. Because employment generation is typically a goal of the economic development or growth strategies, a logical starting point in analyzing how women shared in this process is to examine their changing access to jobs. If women do not have access to employment in the official labor force, their range of income-generating activities is restricted and they clearly are not equal participants. Being able to obtain paid employment is one of the first steps in moving toward economic equality.

Second, an increase of women in the labor force is a necessary but not sufficient condition for an improved economic position for women.

That women have equal access to employment is essential in order for them to obtain economic parity with men, but it is only a first step. Access to employment may not result in equality if women are clustered in low-level, low-paid jobs and still have primary responsibility for domestic duties.

Although measures of labor force activity are only part of the profile of women's position in the economy, analysis of factors that influence them can provide insight into processes that constrain women's economic opportunities. In this case, examination of the surprisingly lackluster change in Irish women's labor force participation can be insightful for analyzing this and other dimensions of women's economic life in industrialized and developing countries and formulating strategies to improve their position.

The Basic Lesson: Its Importance for the Labor Market Literature

Explanations based upon traditional approaches are not able to explain the relatively unchanging female labor force activity during the first two decades of export-led growth. The results of further research indicate that labor market outcomes for women in Ireland, 1961–1981, cannot be understood without analyzing the state and the way in which its employment and family policies reinforced gender inequality in firms and households, constraining the labor market decisions of both regarding women. Female subordination and unresponsive measures of labor force activity continued because of this reinforcement despite the erosive power of both export-led development and the shift of employment from agriculture to industry and services. The main insight of the Irish case is that understanding women's role in the economy requires use of an approach that focuses on unequal gender relations in social institutions such as the firm and household and incorporates the impact of a broad range of state policies on decision-making regarding women's economic activity in each.

This conclusion contributes directly to a number of current and often controversial issues that have emerged in the labor market and policy literatures in the course of the continuing endeavor to understand factors influencing women's subordinate economic roles. There is still debate over the causes of women's continuing subordinate status in the labor market and considerable controversy over how best to address or alleviate it. This part of the chapter outlines three of the main trends of analysis that have been developing in the labor market literature examining women's roles and suggests the contribution the Irish case can make to each. This section also previews how understanding women's labor force participation in Ireland provides an alternative approach for examining women's subordinate status elsewhere and what may be necessary to redress it.[11]

Issues that have become increasingly evident in the literatures analyzing women's subordinate roles in the economy are (1) broader theoretical recognition that discrimination can underlie much of what occurs on both demand and supply sides of the labor market; (2) increasing realization that women's disproportionate home and childcare duties affect their roles in the labor market; and (3) growing evaluation and reconsideration of policies established earlier to help alleviate unequal labor market positions of women.

First, there has been increasing movement toward approaches that recognize discrimination in various social institutions and structural barriers to women's free movement in the economy in understanding all aspects of women's roles, whether labor force participation, relative wages, occupational segregation, or their lack of full integration into all levels of job hierarchies. For example, economists Blau and Ferber (1986), in their comprehensive introduction to the study of women in the labor market, relate that both neoclassical supply-side and demand-side explanations of women's roles in the economy are likely to involve discrimination. On the supply side, the human capital individuals choose to accumulate can be affected by societal discrimination. Demand-side explanations are more fundamentally rooted in economic discrimination, whether statistical or based on tastes (of employers, workers, or consumers). These types of discrimination can in turn have feedback effects on people's human capital decisions and perpetuate a vicious cycle.[12] This means that, recognizing they will not be able to gain entry into certain jobs because of discrimination, potential applicants will not obtain the education or skills required for these jobs.

Similarly, England and McCreary (1987) write that discrimination in hiring and promotion is one of the factors underlying sex differences in jobs and pay. Other contributing factors are socialization and human capital characteristics, which they also suggest may be distorted by gender inequality. In addition, Gunderson's (1989) review of the literature on male – female earnings differentials reports that most studies find some residual wage gap that they attribute to discrimination. He argues, that in cases where the wage gap is close to zero, it is because of the inclusion of control variables that reflect discrimination (i.e., if discrimination is built into the model, the wage gap can disappear). Reskin and Hartmann (1986), in their comprehensive study of sex segregation, say "the scientific evidence we reviewed ... fails to support the argument that women's occupational outcomes result primarily from free choices that they make in an open market. It suggests rather that women face discrimination and institutional barriers in their education, training, and employment" (125).

Secondly, it has been increasingly recognized that women's position in the labor market is adversely affected by their disproportionately large responsibilities for household and child-care duties. According to England and McCreary (1987), most women employed full-time still do the largest proportion of housework, which hinders their progress toward equality in jobs and pay (314). Fuchs (1989) says that "in contemporary America, the greatest barrier to economic equality [for women] is children" (39), because women's concern for the welfare of their children appears to be stronger on average than men's. Reimers (1988) argues that the work of Mincer, Polacheck, and Becker shows the traditional division of labor in the family is the ultimate source of women's disadvantaged position in the labor market. Gunderson (1989) reports that factors originating outside the labor market such as household responsibilities are an important source of the overall earnings gap.

However, in spite of the constraint that household duties have on women's labor force activity, there has been very little change since 1950 in the proportion of the total housework done by males in the United States even though there has been a dramatic increase in the labor force participation of married women during this period (England and Farkas, 1986: 94 – 99). Bergmann (1986) reports virtually no difference in time spent on household duties by husbands with wives employed full-time versus husbands with wives working only in the home (263).

Clearly, for women to share equally in the labor market, this disproportionate responsibility for home duties must change. In light of the failure of individuals in households to share tasks, state policies are an alternate way to address this problem (Bergmann, 1986; Bose and Spitze, 1987; and Fuchs, 1989).[13]

Lastly, evaluations and assessments of existing public policies designed earlier to provide equal opportunity and ameliorate gender inequality are taking place, many in countries where political environments have grown increasingly conservative in the 1980s (Hagen and Jenson, 1988). In these countries, anti-regulatory interests have exerted considerable influence on policy-making, funds may be lacking for enforcement, and there has been an erosion of past well-established policies (for example, in the United States, affirmative action and abortion rights policies were weakened in 1989 by Supreme Court decisions).

Debate over appropriate policy spans a wide range of fundamental questions. Some ask if policy is necessary or whether the situation is now becoming self-correcting (Lazear, 1989). Others, believing that the subordinate economic status of women warrants action to alleviate it, attempt to assess which policies are effective and what new policies may be needed for the future. Policies are largely evaluated on a one-by-one basis. Although in many cases at least some measure of effectiveness is shown (Gunderson, 1989; Reskin and Hartmann, 1986), the necessity for present policies and the advisability of legislating more are nevertheless actively questioned.

We are at an important juncture in our understanding of women's subordinate status in the labor market and the economy. It has been increasingly recognized that women's disadvantaged economic positions involve both discrimination on the demand and supply sides of the labor market and women's disproportionate responsibility for household duties. There is much debate over what can and should be done about it. The debate is made even more critical by the trend toward conservatism and interest in market solutions that could undermine existing and potential gains from policy formation.

Because sex discrimination has been so explicit in Ireland, the Irish case not only contributes to each of these issues but permits a broader view of the way unequal labor market outcomes are caused by gender inequality in the firm and household and the role of the state in perpetuating it. The Irish case provides a clear perspective and further input into each of these issues: it affirms the need for a theory of gender inequality that recognizes structural barriers and unequal relations of power between men and women as obstacles to women's achievement of economic equality; it verifies the importance of unequal social relations in the household as a determinant of women's position in the labor force; and it makes the very strong point that a broad range of appropriate state policies are needed, in combination, to facilitate women's labor force activity.

However, this main lesson from the Irish study is more than just further support for each of these issues. It builds on these extensive bodies of knowledge about employers, households, and state policy in a synergistic way that extends our understanding of how female subordination is perpetuated in a distinctly new manner. It suggests the usefulness of a feminist approach to understanding gender inequality that includes the role of the state and shows how the state can interact with the firm and/or household to maintain gender domination.[14] It reveals that to understand the nature of the process fully both family and reproductive rights policies as well as employment policies must be examined.

The Irish case puts into sharp relief how the state can be involved in reinforcing male domination. In so doing, it sheds light on ways in which different types of state policy can be altered in a coordinated manner to assist in alleviating gender inequality. That the Irish case provides these insights is revealed in the following chapters.

In Chapter 3 we shall learn that potential explanations based upon the traditional approaches are not able to explain the reason for relatively unchanging female labor force activity during the first two decades of export-led growth. It is only when we begin exploring two analyses that recognize the existence of barriers to gender equality that we find relevance to the Irish case. One such approach is a culturally based argument that, given a traditional sexual division of labor, men obtain the jobs in a job-scarce economy. The other is a feminist analysis that would explain the lack of increase in Irish women's labor force participation by their subordination in the household (or possibly the firm). However, although having much relevance to the situation in Ireland, these two approaches have one critical problem: they cannot explain how gender inequality is maintained in the presence of forces, such as export-led development, which tend to undermine it by hiring workforces which are substantially female. The alternative explanation developed in Chapter 4 is based on evidence that Irish employment and family policies affected the structure of female participation in the labor force by reinforcing male domination in firms and households and restraining the labor market decisions of both regarding women.

This book shows that state personnel can have objectives in addition to that of economic growth. Elected legislators in Ireland were concerned with maintaining traditional relationships between the sexes as well as spurring the development process; they formulated government policies that sought to achieve both objectives. Moreover, the situation in Ireland illustrates how the effect of state policy on the labor market can be complicated if conflicts arise between the major objectives of government policy. Policies designed to implement one major goal of government policy (economic growth) may undermine attainment of the other (maintenance of traditional relationships between men and women). This can occur, for example, if foreign firms, attracted by the state-promoted development strategy hire substantial numbers of women, altering the traditional division of labor between the sexes. Labor market outcomes depend, therefore, on the relative strength of government objectives, the policies designed to achieve them, and the manner in which conflicts between them are resolved.

State policies must be comprehensively examined, both employment and family and reproductive rights policies. This book shows that focusing on changing employment policies as a means to eliminate discrimination and to incorporate women fully into the labor force is simply not going to produce the desired results if restrictive family and reproductive rights policies remain in effect. Elimination of discriminatory employment policies is indeed necessary, but it is not sufficient. Also needed are changes in family policies and reproductive rights policies that reduce gender inequality in the household and permit women to move closer toward the same labor market choices men encounter.

Although the situation for Irish women improved slightly when explicitly discriminatory employment policies were altered in Ireland in the mid-1970s, and this dimension of gender inequality was reduced, there was little change in labor force participation. Women's labor market options remained constrained, hampered by gender inequality in the household which was (and is) well fortified by family and reproductive rights policies. For the potential benefit of eliminating such employment policies to be realized, gains in other arenas of social policy needed to be made. The constraints on women shifted and lay more with restrictive family and reproductive rights policies than with employment policies. This shows how, as in Ireland, gender domination can remain robust even though changes are made in some aspects of it.

However, two caveats are in order. First, highlighting the manner in which Irish state policy reinforced gender inequality in the household and firm during export-led development and restrained the employment of women. This is not to suggest that other social institutions and their practices (for example, religious and educational systems) were not also contributing to the perpetuation of male domination in Ireland at this time. It is to focus, rather, given the complexity of social life, on the processes that were clearly the dominant constraints during this period. (For a broader perspective regarding the nature of Irish women's lives and the constraining effect of other institutions such as the Catholic Church and the educational system on them, the following sources are useful: Beale, 1987; Mahon, 1987; and the special issue of *Women's Studies International Forum* (1988, Vol. 11, No. 4) on "Feminism in Ireland." In addition, the reader can consult Brady (1988), a comprehensive annotated bibliography of materials on Irish women and Smyth (1983), a detailed guide to women's rights in Ireland.)

Second, the conclusions from this study are not to be interpreted to mean that if these constraining policies were removed and replaced by others that did not reinforce male domination in the household and firm, women would then be able to achieve equality in the economy. Such changes in state policy are necessary and would clearly assist in eradicating gender inequality, but they are not the total solution to the problem. Further changes in social relations in the firm and household which cannot be legislated and/or enforced are also clearly necessary.

To assess the usefulness of a theory of gender inequality further and examine the validity of traditional approaches, I examine their applicability at a regional level, using data from the Western European OECD countries for this same period, 1961–1981. In Chapter 5 regression analysis is used to explore whether there is evidence for these 17 countries that their increased labor force activity for women occurred in accordance with the factors emphasized by modernization, neoclassical, or Marxian approaches, or whether an alternative focusing on structural changes in the economy as growth and development proceed and the role of gender inequality in mediating their impact might be more applicable.

This type of approach — a theory of gender inequality which recognizes that the state, in addition to and interactively with the household and firm, is a social institution that can place women in disadvantaged positions via a wide range of policies — can assist in understanding a variety of other situations. The insights it provides are not only useful in understanding women's labor force participation rates, but also for analyzing a variety of other issues such as occupational segregation, women's presence in upper-level jobs, and relative earnings. Government policies cannot only shape labor force participation but can also influence the type of jobs women are able to obtain, the positions to which they can rise, and the earnings received.

The Relevance of the Main Insight for Development Literature

The extensive literature exploring diverse experiences of women in developing countries (social lives that diverge along the lines of class, ethnicity, religion, type of development strategy, kinship, and household relations) has been chiefly concerned with assessing whether women are integrated or marginalized by development and, if integrated, whether in an exploitative manner (Tiano, 1987).[15] Considerable attention has been directed to understanding the factors influencing these outcomes and how women can be integrated more equitably.

It is widely thought that in most developing countries, women have been increasingly disadvantaged and marginalized by economic development. This is not simply an issue for the women involved; rather, it is a problem for the entire society because it is a misallocation of available resources. The seriousness of this underutilization of human resources can be critical, even devastating, for the country's economic development process. According to Dwight Perkins, Director of the Harvard Institute for International Development, "Concern with issues of gender, of course, involves more than how gender affects distribution. Understanding the role played by gender in development can also make a substantial difference as to whether growth-oriented projects succeed or fail" (Overholt, Anderson, Cloud, and Austin, 1985:x). Sara Tinsley, Director of the Office of Women in Development for the United States Agency for International Development, says "gender roles constitute a key variable in the socio-economic condition of any country — one that can be decisive in the success or failure of development plans" (Overholt, Anderson, Cloud, and Austin, 1985:xi). This is particularly the case, for example, in many African nations where the failure to recognize women as the major food producers led to their exclusion from many critical aspects of agricultural development programs and has been widely acknowledged as a primary cause of Africa's food crisis (Charlton, 1984; Whitaker, 1988).

The major exception to the marginalization of women is in the export-led countries where women have been a primary source of workers for labor-intensive export industries. In these cases, the concern regarding women is over whether the employment opportunities provided women were to their overall advantage or disadvantage (*Multinational Monitor,* 1983; Lim, 1983). Although it has been argued that employment in the multinational firms has provided an income-earning option for women who otherwise had few possibilities, the dominant analysis concludes that these women have been exploited via low wages, poor working and living conditions, and high turnover and job insecurity.

This leads to the conclusion that women in developing countries have largely been marginalized or exploited. The question of why this is so remains. The insights of the Irish case suggest a general framework of analysis—use of a theory of gender inequality that incorporates the effect of a broad range of state policies on gender relations in social institutions such as the household or workplace—that can be adapted to understanding why women are not equitably integrated in developing countries and what might be done to redress the situation.

The way the state contributes to women's disadvantaged economic position can be even more obvious and broad-based in developing countries. To begin with, the economic development process, a major focus of Third World countries, is planned by the state, often in conjunction with international organizations and agencies. The manner in which women are or are not involved in the planning process and the effects of the broad range of development and social policies on equality of gender relations in the household, community, and workplace critically affect the choices women can make in their economic lives.

Women in developing countries, however, have largely been excluded from the planning process. In an even more extensive manner than in industrialized countries, the state in many Third World countries directly influences women's access to resources or paid labor and the terms on which access, if any, exists. For example, with respect to agrarian activities, not only did colonial governments in Africa distribute land titles only to males during land reform but, more recently, it has been widely documented that access to newer technologies and credit facilities was channeled to men by government development agencies (Beneria and Sen, 1982). Regarding industrial employment, Enloe (1983) examines the use of police and military control of female textile workers in Southeast Asia that was designed to maintain workplace discipline even under the adverse working conditions in multinationals and their subcontractors mentioned above.

Because government personnel hold particular views regarding the role of women in the family and household, many policies are shaped with this in mind and in turn reinforce the subordination of women. Research results presented in a volume edited by Agarwal (1988) reveal the variety of complex ways that the state, in conjunction with the household and community, have maintained patriarchal relations in Asia, via agricultural and industrial policies, discriminatory health-care and food programs, and by supporting particular ethnic, religious, and class interests. Another volume, edited by Afshar (1987), examines the way state policies concerning population, family, and household affect women's subordination and paid employment in Africa and Asia.

Since there is such wide evidence that women as an economic resource are bypassed by development, and since economic development is planned and influenced by the state, a full grasp of how state policy affects women is vital to understanding women's subordinate economic position. This is particularly critical in the cases where it is acknowledged that the failure to incorporate women has, in turn, contributed to crises and a lack of development. On the basis of both efficiency and equity, it is necessary to understand the causes of women's subordination in the economy, how a wide range of state policies contribute to it, and how policies might be adjusted to alleviate it.

In many of these countries the main lesson of the Irish case is applicable: that to understand the roles of women in the economy (in this case their marginalization and exploitation) we need an approach that focuses on gender inequality in various social institutions and examines how state policy reinforces it and constrains women's roles. However, because of the great diversity of experience in these countries, it may be necessary to extend the approach suggested by the Irish case to examine how state policy influences gender inequality in a wider range of social institutions (the household, workplace, educational and religious systems) via a broader spectrum of policy.

Further Implications

The previous two sections of this chapter outlined the ways this case study and the approach developed in analyzing it can be vitally important to our understanding of a variety of contemporary issues regarding women in the labor market in many industrialized countries and the roles of women in the economies of developing countries.

However, in Chapter 6 I conclude by suggesting its further implications for two broader bodies of thought: feminist theory and the theory of the state. This research is relevant for feminist theory and practice in a number of ways. First, the Irish case and data analysis at the regional level provide solid support for the necessity of a fundamentally feminist approach to understanding gender inequality. In other words, that to understand women's disadvantaged economic position we must focus primarily on the sources of male power and how it is maintained in society. This is an important finding since feminist approaches have often been marginalized by mainstream literatures. Second, it shows that the state, in addition to and interactively with the workplace and the household, is an institution which can maintain male domination. It details how a broad range of state policies can reinforce gender inequality in these sites even in the presence of forces (for example, export-led development) which would tend to erode it.

Lastly, I shall argue that the Irish case demonstrates the insights to be gained from a revitalized structural approach to feminist analysis, an approach that has been broadened to incorporate the state as it interacts with both the household and firm in maintaining unequal gender relations. Earlier structural analyses of male domination, which were based on social relations in the household or firm, have been set aside during most of the past decade as other feminist approaches, such as psychoanalytical and deconstructionist modes of thought, were explored and gained preeminence.[16] This study shows male domination exists in both the household and the firm, and that it can be reinforced by the state. It reveals why we cannot ignore the ways in which gender inequality is maintained by patterns of social relations in various institutional sites in society and why we must build on and extend the rich feminist literatures examining male domination in the household or firm and the growing feminist research on the role of the state.

A broader structural approach to understanding male domination is needed than has been developed in the past. Based upon this insight from the Irish case, I suggest an alternate approach to understanding structures of male domination which I call the social structure of patriarchy. I outline the dimensions the social structure of patriarchy approach might include and how it could facilitate our understanding of women's roles and the manner in which they differ over time and cross-culturally.

I also briefly note the implications the Irish case provides for the theory of the state. Conclusions from this study suggest the theory of the state must fundamentally integrate the dimension of gender into its analysis and that it must then recognize the contradictions and complexities that arise with the addition of this aspect of social life. The maintenance of traditional gender relations can be as much of an objective of state policy as economic development or growth. Contradictions between these objectives can readily arise. For example, in choosing to promote export-led development, the Irish government found it was beginning to undermine its other major objective: reproduction of traditional relations between the genders. This undermining occurred because industries locating in Ireland as part of the development strategy were typically employers of large proportions of women. The conclusions also reveal that the way state policy affects gender relations occurs over a broad range of policy which must be fully understood so that implications of policy changes can be accurately assessed.

Although much beyond the scope of this book, a theory of the state developed with these insights in mind would not only integrate gender as a basic category of analysis but would indeed examine contradictions between major objectives of the state and would include the impact of a broad spectrum of policy in its analysis. This richer theory of the state could move us forward substantially in understanding how outcomes in the political economy can differ from those expected by traditional social science literatures and how they can be positively influenced in the future. Outcomes can depend in a complex fashion on state goals, their relative strength, the contradictions between them, the manner in which contradictions are resolved, and the way policies reinforce inequality in other institutions.

Chapter Two

Economic Development and Women
in Ireland, 1961 – 1981

Introduction

Ireland's economic development process from 1961 to 1981 exhibited two distinguishing features. On the one hand, it followed a development pattern that has now become typical of many industrializing countries, vigorous pursuit of export-led development after earlier decades of disappointing results with an import-substitution strategy.[1] On the other hand, this pattern occurred in conjunction with its increasing integration with the social and economic life of the other Western European nations and a distinct shift of economic activity from agriculture to industry and service sectors.

Both of these structural changes in the economy — export-led development and a shift to industry and services — were changes that conventional economic and social theory argued would result in increased participation of women in the labor force. Export-led development is based on attraction of foreign direct investment in labor intensive industries. According to the theory of factor proportions, assuming equal productivity, labor-intensive industries seek low-wage workers, which have been found to be female. In addition, as shown in Chapter 1, each of the major approaches (integrationist/modernization, neoclassical or Marxist) argues, although from different theoretical frameworks and diverse sets of reasons, that women would be increasingly incorporated in the economy with the shift of production toward industry and service sectors.

Therefore, it would be considered highly likely that the participation of Irish women in the labor force would increase. However, this did not occur. The experience of women in Ireland, 1961 – 1981, not only contradicts the expectations of the traditional approaches regarding the

17

effect of economic development on women but also contrasts to empirical results occurring under similar economic situations.

Why did this happen? The first steps are to examine the nature of
the development process and to analyze changes in measures of wom-
en's labor force participation. Comparisons must be drawn to similar
measures in other countries experiencing these types of structural
change and with which Ireland was increasingly linked economically
and socially to ascertain how the labor force profiles of Irish women di-
verged from the others and to begin to uncover what factors shaped
these strikingly different labor market outcomes.

Economic Development in Ireland, 1961–1981

The first decades of the Irish export-led development strategy for which
labor market data are available, 1961–1981, marked a period of extensive
social and economic change.[2] The economy changed dramatically in
terms of its institutional structure, the sectoral components of economic
activity, the extent of foreign investment, performance levels, and integration with Western Europe.

Institutionally, the Irish economy was substantially altered by the
augmented role of the state and the increased presence of foreign firms.
A gradual evolution from import-substitution policies toward an export-led development strategy had been occurring in Ireland in the
1950s. This change was formalized by two 1958 government documents,
Economic Development and the first *Programme for Economic Expansion*,
which presented the main objectives of the export-led strategy.

The role of the state in the economy expanded as it implemented
the development program by gradually widening free-trade agreements and by establishing a program of financial incentives to attract
foreign direct investment.[3] Some tariff reductions and an Anglo–Irish
trade agreement were enacted in the mid-1960s, and Ireland became a
member of the EEC in 1973.

The Irish government aggressively pursued foreign direct investment via the energetic promotional activities of the Industrial Development Authority (IDA), a semi-autonomous state body that had considerable discretionary use of funds in attracting foreign investment. It
implemented a highly attractive incentives package whose major components were export profits tax relief (effective until 1990 for firms entering Ireland through 1980), the reduction of the corporate profits tax
rate to 10% for all firms as of 1981, liberal depreciation allowances, and
a package of nonrepayable cash grants (of 35 percent to 50 percent of assets based on regional location). Via offices in ten countries, the IDA ac-

tively approached carefully selected target firms in industrialized countries it considered likely to meet the social and economic criteria desired in a potential investor.[4] According to Eoin O'Malley, the Irish industrial promotion effort in the 1970s was "one of the most highly intensive and organized of its type among competing countries" (National Economic and Social Council 1980: 12–13).

Incoming foreign corporations represented a wide range of industries, most of which at the time were growth industries, relatively new to the international scene, and set up chiefly with low-skill, relatively small production units. A typical pattern in the 1970s was for a multinational corporation to establish multiplant operations in Ireland, often in decentralized locations, because of the structure of the incentives packages (Jackson, 1983).

The main source of foreign direct investment was the United States. U.S. Department of Commerce data show that, worldwide, Ireland was one of the locations experiencing the fastest rate of growth of U.S. foreign direct investment during the period 1966–1977. Ireland was third only to Singapore and South Korea, two Asian countries widely known for their export-led development, high growth rates and their status as Newly Industrializing Countries (NICs). Ireland had a compound annual growth rate of total assets of U.S. foreign direct investment of 27 percent for the 1966–1977 period (Howenstine, 1982).

Although there was an influx of firms in the 1960s, the largest proportion of total foreign investment for the period 1961–1981 came after 1973, because of two changed aspects of the outward-looking strategy. First, EEC membership in 1973 allowed the IDA to offer potential investors tariff-free access to a market of 270 million people. Second, the IDA specifically targeted a few industries as growth industries (electronics, pharmaceuticals, and health care) and vigorously courted them. According to IDA data in the early 1980s, Ireland ranked eighth and fourteenth worldwide in the production of electronics and pharmaceuticals by the end of the 1970s.[5]

Many of the firms locating in Ireland were in manufacturing industries that elsewhere had hired predominantly female work forces. For example, incoming electronics firms were known to have production workforces that were over 80 percent female elsewhere in the industrializing world.[6] This contrasts sharply to the average share of women in the manufacturing labor force in Ireland (30 percent in 1970).

Ireland was considered an attractive site for foreign direct investment and has been characterized as having created an "environment in which capital can thrive" (Minard, 1982). The financial and trade incentives listed above combined with a wide range of other subsidies,[7] relatively lower labor costs, political stability, and a well-educated work-

Table 2.1

Percent of Employment Generated by Sector, Ireland, 1961 and 1981

	1961	1981
Agriculture	36	17
Industry	25	31
Services	39	52

Sources: *Census of Population of Ireland*, various years.

force, made Ireland an attractive competitor for foreign direct investment. U.S. Department of Commerce data support this contention, revealing that U.S. firms in Ireland from 1977 to 1980 earned an average 33.7 percent yearly rate of return on manufacturing investment, more than twice the average rate of return on U.S. investment in the EEC (16.8 percent) or in all countries (14 percent).

Sectorally, as shown in Table 2.1, Ireland changed as the proportion of employment in the agricultural sector fell and that in industry and services rose. In 1961, over a third of the labor force was engaged in agriculture; by 1981, 83 percent were involved in industry and service sectors.

Ireland became a much more open economy. Exports rose from 37 percent of gross national product (GNP) in 1962 to 55 percent in 1981 while imports increased from 40 percent to 68 percent. These measures of openness substantially exceeded the EEC averages: exports and imports were each 29 percent of GNP for the community as a whole (White, 1981). Not surprisingly, the sectoral composition of exports shifted from agricultural to industrial.[8]

This period constituted a marked break with the economic performance of the past. The average annual growth rate of real gross domestic product (GDP) doubled initially, rising from a level of 2 percent for 1949 to 1961 to 4.1 percent for 1961 to 1973 (Nolan, 1981:154). Ireland's average rate of growth of GDP of 3.8 percent for the period 1961 –1979 was among the highest in the OECD (Long, 1976). Manufactured exports grew at over four times this rate (Long, 1976). This was a sharp reversal of Ireland's economic performance vis-à-vis other Western European countries. In the 1950s, Ireland's stagnation, high unemployment, and excessive emigration contrasted to the economic recovery and growth that most of Western Europe was experiencing.[9]

There is widespread agreement among Irish scholars that this sharp change in economic performance was correlated with the adoption of the export-led strategy and the influx of foreign direct investment[10] (Coughlan, 1980; FitzGerald, 1968; Jacobsen, 1978, 1980; Kennedy and Dowling, 1975; Long, 1976; McAleese, 1977a; National Economic and Social Council, 1980: 23–27, 29–34; Stanton, 1978/1981; Wickham, 1980).

A substantial part of the growth in GDP, investment and exports during this period can be linked to the presence of foreign direct investment.[11] The GDP growth rates were led by 6 percent annual growth rates in the output of the industrial sector; in turn, three-quarters of the industrial expansion of the 1960s was due to foreign firms (Long, 1976). Similarly, export growth of 12 percent a year from 1960 to 1970 was led by the growth in industrial exports of 14 percent; two-thirds of this increase in industrial exports was due to foreign-owned firms[12] (Long, 1976; Coughlin, 1980). In addition, foreign firms became an increasingly important source of employment, employing one-third of the manufacturing workforce (Industrial Development Authority of Ireland *Annual Report,* 1982).[13]

During these two decades Ireland vigorously pursued export-led development and shifted toward a more industrial and service economy —two types of structural change which economic theory implies will be accompanied by substantial increases in women's participation in the labor force. In addition, an integral part of the Irish export-led development strategy was attainment of membership in the EEC. Membership was important in attracting foreign direct investment because it offered foreign firms an export-production platform in Ireland with tariff-free access to markets in the EEC. However, membership in the European Economic Community required that Ireland reform social policy to conform with EEC directives on equal pay (1975) and equal treatment with regard to access to employment, vocational training, promotion, and working conditions (1976). This increased economic and social integration with European nations simply added to the likelihood that women's labor force participation would rise.

Surprisingly, this increase did not occur. The female labor force participation rate and the female share of the labor force both remained relatively low and unchanging throughout the first twenty years of export-led development. Although information on female employment in Ireland has been presented in a variety of Irish sources, some covering substantial amounts of this period (Blackwell, 1982, 1983; Garvey, 1983; McLernon, 1980; Walsh, 1982; Working Party on Women's Affairs and Family Law Reform, 1985), Ireland's export-led strategy has not been examined or questioned with respect to its effect on the employment of women. This contrasts to the considerable analysis of the role of women in export-led development elsewhere (Agarwal, 1988; Fuentes and Ehrenreich, 1983; Heyzer, 1986; Jones, 1984a, 1984b). Although a few Irish writers draw comparisons of Irish women's employment patterns with those of other EEC and Western European OECD countries, they were made only for a particular year rather than over time (e.g., see Garvey, 1983). No one explores similarities or differences with other export-led countries. As will be shown in the next section, it is comparisons over time between Ireland and these other countries that leads to a more striking perspective on the lack of change in Ireland.

Women's Participation in the Irish Labor Force, 1961–1981, in Comparison to Other Western European OECD Countries and Singapore

The weak responses and low levels of these two measures of women's labor force participation in Ireland contrast sharply to similar data for the sixteen other Western European OECD countries and a nation chosen as representative of other small, export-led economies: Singapore.

Both measures are explored, using aggregate and disaggregate data, because they offer different perspectives on women's experience in the labor market and provide insight into factors that can influence it.[14] On the one hand, a labor force participation rate measures the percentage of a specifically defined group of women who are gainfully occupied (at work or unemployed). It describes the female workforce by ascriptive characteristics such as age and/or marital status. On the other hand, the female share is the proportion of the work force, categorized by industrial sector, occupation, or both, which is female.[15] Second, data on the female share directly presents intergender information (and therefore reflects women's employment position relative to men) whereas the labor force participation statistic contains intragender information, looking at a subgroup of a specifically defined category of women.[16]

Last, they are related to two different points of view regarding the key factors structuring the sex composition of the labor force. On the one hand, labor force participation rates are often utilized by economists analyzing factors that influence the supply of labor decision. Demand-side factors enter this type of analysis in a limited manner, as wages or unemployment rates. Structural factors that shape the sex composition of the demand for labor are not considered directly. On the other hand, labor market approaches that study the importance of factors shaping the demand for labor (and, in turn, their impact on the composition of the labor force) look at the share of a particular gender (or racial or ethnic group) in the work force of various sectors and/or occupations.

Labor force participation decisions are made in the household; demand for labor decisions are made in the firm. However, demand- and supply-side factors are not independent because, for example, over time individuals will cease to prepare and supply themselves where there is little to no demand (Blau and Ferber, 1986; England and McCreary, 1987; Lloyd and Niemi, 1979). Nevertheless, in spite of the lack of independence between them, analysis of female shares provides some insight into what is happening in the firm; examination of labor force participation rates similarly presents information regarding what may be occurring in the household.

Both types of information are useful. Examination of one or the other describes only one dimension of women's participation in the labor force and therefore focuses primarily on one set of factors shaping the composition of the labor force.[17] It cannot be ascertained *a priori* which factors may be more insightful in explaining women's labor force activity.

Aggregate Labor Force Participation Rate and Share of Women in the Labor Force

Table 2.2 shows that the labor force participation rate for Irish women was virtually unchanged, 1961 – 1981, remaining at just under 30 percent. Tables 2.3 and 2.4 provide a broader perspective with the use of data from countries with which Ireland had similarities, whether com-

Table 2.2

Measures of Women's Participation in the Labor Force, Ireland, 1961 – 1981

	1961	1966	1971	1975	1979	1981
Labor Force Participation Rate[1], women aged 15 and over	29.4*	29.1*	28.0*	28.5	28.7	29.7
Female Share of the Labor Force[2]	26.4	26.3	26.4	27.8	28.9	29.1

Sources: Calculated from tables in *Census of Population in Ireland*, various years; *Labour Force Survey 1979*.

*Rates for these years were calculated from ratios in which the datum in the numerator was for ages 14 and over.

[1]"Gainfully occupied" women aged 15 and over as a percentage of all women aged 15 and over, where "gainfully occupied" includes those "at work" and "unemployed," having lost or given up previous job.

[2]The percent of total employment which is female.

Table 2.3

Female Labor Force Participation Rate, Aged 15 and Over,
Western European OECD Countries, 1960/61–1980/81

	1960/61	1980/81	Change
weighted mean*	31.5	37.6	5.2
Austria	44.8	37.4	−7.4
Belgium	25.5	28.9	3.4
Denmark	36.5	57.0	20.5
Finland	48.5	55.6	7.1
France	36.2	41.3	5.1
Germany	41.1	39.8	−1.3
Greece	35.5	29.6	−5.9
Ireland	**28.9**	**30.3**	**1.4**
Italy	24.9	32.3	7.4
Luxembourg	27.6	33.3	5.7
Netherlands	22.6	29.2	6.6
Norway	23.8	52.8	29.0
Portugal	17.0	46.5	29.5
Spain	17.7	22.1	4.4
Sweden	32.0	53.6	21.6
Switzerland	35.3	42.1	6.8
United Kingdom	37.6	42.9	5.3

Source: ILO Yearbook of Labour Statistics, various years.
*In calculating the mean labor force participation rate of women, the female labor force
  participation rate of each country is weighted by that nation's proportion of the total
  population of women aged 15 and over in these seventeen countries.

parable structural changes such as export-led growth, a continuing shift
from agriculture to industry and services, or an increasingly common
regional economic and social environment.

With regard to the level of female labor force participation, Table
2.3 reveals that by 1981 the labor force participation rate of women in
Ireland had become one of the lowest in the seventeen Western European OECD countries, slipping from a ranking of tenth in 1961 to fourteenth and falling well below the (weighted) average of 37.6 percent.
The increase in the female labor force participation rate in Ireland was
only 27 percent of the average change for these countries.[18] All other
countries which had a female labor force participation rate below 33 percent in 1961 experienced larger increases.

The contrast is even sharper when a comparison is made to another small export-led economy for which data is available for a comparable period, Singapore. This city-republic of 2.3 million inhabitants

Table 2.4

Measures of Women's Participation in the Labor Force, Singapore, 1957–1979

	1957	1970	1975	1979
Labor Force Participation Rate[1]	21.6	29.5	34.9	41.9
Female Share of the Labor Force[2]	17.5	23.5	29.6	33.6

Source: Aline K. Wong, "Planned Development, Social Stratification, and the Sexual Division of Labor in Singapore," Signs 7, 2 (Winter, 1981), p. 440.
[1]Economically active women as proportion of total female population aged 15 and over.
[2]Economically active women as proportion of total number of women and men employed.

did not establish its export-led strategy until the early 1970s, somewhat later than Ireland. It also offered features attractive to foreign capital: tax incentives, factory sites and infrastructure, as well as a strictly controlled labor force. Its growth rates were impressive and the role of women in its development strategy has been both analyzed and acknowledged (Jones, 1984a; Wong, 1981). Table 2.4 shows that women's labor force participation in Singapore nearly doubled, 1957 – 1979, rising to 41.9 percent, a level 45 percent higher than that in Ireland (see Table 2.2).

With respect to the female share of the Irish labor force, Table 2.2 shows that it rose from 26.4 percent in 1961 to 29.1 percent in 1981.[19] That this was a relatively weak response can also be shown by comparisons. Table 2.5 reveals (1) that the female share in Ireland became the lowest in the Western European OECD by 1981, falling well below the (weighted) average of 37 percent; and (2) that the increase in the female share in Ireland was only 36 percent of the average change for these seventeen countries. In addition, as shown in Table 2.4, the female share of the labor force in Singapore nearly doubled, rising to one-third in 1979. This large rise in female labor force activity in Singapore was also characteristic of other Asian export-led economies. For example, Salaff (1986) reports that the proportion of women in the labor force in Taiwan rose from 19 percent in 1956 to 34 percent by 1970.

The lack of change in these two measures of female labor force activity is striking when viewed in the context of average levels of female labor force participation and/or female share of the labor force (and the average changes in each of them) for both Western European OECD countries and Singapore. The levels in Ireland were less than Western European averages in 1961; these differences not only persisted during this period but widened. In addition, although Irish levels of female par-

Table 2.5

Female Share of the Labor Force, Western European OECD Countries, 1960/61 – 1980/81

	1960/61	1980/81	Change
weighted mean*	28.9	37.0	6.9
Austria	40.4	38.5	−1.9
Belgium	26.6	37.2	10.6
Denmark	30.9	44.4	13.5
Finland	39.4	46.3	6.9
France	33.4	38.9	5.5
Germany	36.7	38.2	1.5
Greece	32.8	31.2	−1.6
Ireland	**25.9**	**28.4**	**2.5**
Italy	24.9	33.3	8.4
Luxembourg	27.0	33.3	6.3
Netherlands	22.3	31.8	9.5
Norway	22.9	41.7	18.8
Portugal	17.7	41.5	23.8
Spain	18.2	29.5	11.3
Sweden	29.8	45.2	15.4
Switzerland	30.1	36.3	6.2
United Kingdom	32.4	39.1	6.7

Source: ILO Yearbook of Labour Statistics, various years.
*In calculating the mean female share of the labor force, the female share of each country is weighted by that nation's proportion of the total labor force of these seventeen countries.

ticipation had exceeded those in Singapore around 1960, the response during export-led growth differed dramatically, resulting in a reversal of their relative positions by 1979.

Disaggregated Female Labor Force Participation Rates

The labor force participation rates can be disaggregated by age and/or marital status, the female share data by major industrial sectors/subsectors. This provides a detailed profile of women's participation in the labor force in Ireland and delineates the components of the relatively unresponsive aggregate labor force participation of women and female share of the labor force, 1961 – 1981. It establishes a basis for assessing how they differed from similar measures of women's labor force participation in other Western European countries or Singapore.

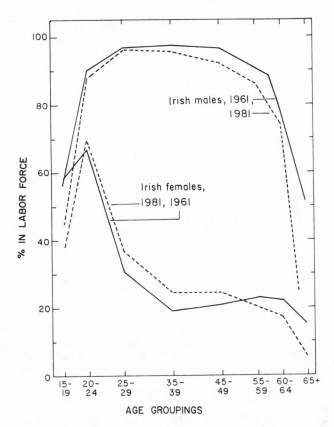

Figure 2.1 Male and Female Age-Participation Profiles, Ireland, 1961 and 1981 (Source: *Census of Population,* various years, 1961–1981)

The age-specific labor force participation profile presented in Figure 2.1 suggests that the female labor force in Ireland throughout this period was young.[20] Rates were highest for the 20–24-year-old age group, and dropped off sharply thereafter. This profile changed in only minor ways during these two decades[21] and, therefore, the youthfulness of the female labor force was not altered: In 1961, 41 percent of the female labor force was under 25 years of age; in 1981, 42 percent.

This pattern differed sharply from that of Irish men, women in other EEC countries, and women in Singapore. Figure 2.1 also shows that Irish males had higher labor force participation rates for all ages, with strikingly different participation rates after age 25.[22] Comparison with age-participation profiles of women in other EEC countries for 1974

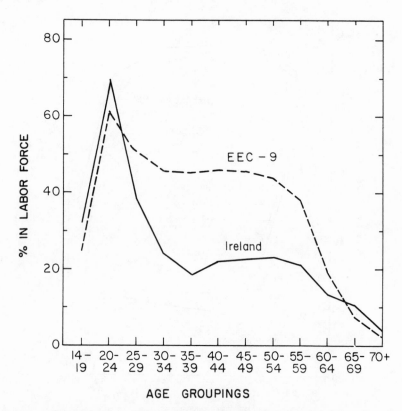

Figure 2.2 Female Age-Participation Profiles, Ireland and EEC Average, 1975   (Source: Composed from information in Brendan Walsh. *The Unemployment Problem in Ireland* (Dublin: Kincora Press) 1978, p. 18)

(Figure 2.2) shows that activity rates for Irish women aged 25–64 were substantially below the Community average.[23] Further, the age-participation pattern changed dramatically in Singapore, 1957–1979 (Figure 2.3), in sharp contrast to the small modifications in the Irish pattern. By 1979, activity rates for all women under 50 in Singapore exceeded those for Irish women.

Labor force participation rates of Irish women by marital status are presented in Table 2.6 for three categories: married, single and widowed. In contrast to census data collection procedures in many other countries, data has not been collected in Ireland for the category "separated and/or divorced." The growing number of women who mark themselves on census forms as "other" (i.e., not married, single or widowed) have been lumped with the "married."[24] Because of this, the labor force participation rate of married women is a somewhat inflated figure.[25]

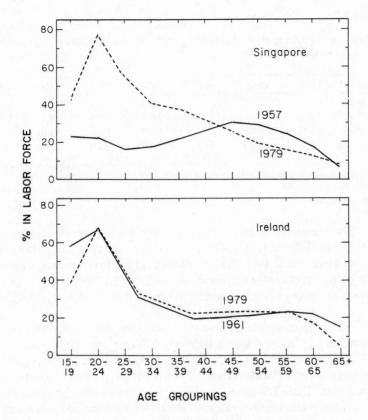

Figure 2.3 Female Age-Participation Profiles, Ireland 1961–1979, and Singapore, 1957–1979 (Sources: Ireland: *Census of Population,* various years; Singapore: Wong, 1981)

Table 2.6

Labor Force Participation Rates of Women Aged 15 and Over in Ireland by Marital Status, 1961–1981

MARITAL STATUS	1961*	1966*	1971*	1975	1979	1981
Single	60.5	62.0	59.8	57.1	55.0	54.9
Married	5.2	5.3	7.5	14.5	15.2	17.4
Widowed	26.2	22.2	19.3	14.7	12.8	11.4

Sources: Calculated from tables in *Census of Population of Ireland,* various years; *Labour Force Survey 1979.*
*ages 14 and over.

Table 2.7

Labor Force Participation Rates of Men Aged 15 and Over in Ireland by Marital Status, 1961–1981

MARITAL STATUS	1961*	1966*	1971*	1975	1979	1981
Single	77.5	75.8	70.8	70.4	68.3	67.4
Married	90.8	90.2	89.9	85.6	85.0	84.8
Widowed	51.7	47.6	45.0	35.8	28.9	30.2

Sources: Calculated from tables in *Census of Population of Ireland,* various years; *Labour Force Survey 1979.*
*ages 14 and over.

The female labor force was primarily single throughout this period. The participation rate of married women was very low, although it rose suddenly from 1971 to 1975.[26] This profile also contrasts dramatically with that of Irish men, as shown in Table 2.7. Men's rates exceed women's in every category during this period, with the largest differentials occurring in the category "married."

Although complete data were not available for labor force participation rates by marital status in Western European OECD countries, 1961–1981, information from several sources indicates that a major difference between Ireland and the Western European OECD countries occurred here. Table 2.8, based on data from around 1970, shows that although the participation rates for single and widowed Irish women were comparable to those of other Western European OECD countries, that of married Irish women was strikingly low. This disparity continued through the end of the two decades under examination. In 1980 the labor force participation rate of married Irish women was about 15 percent, less than half the EEC average of 37 percent (*Working Party on Child Care Facilities for Working Parents,* 1983:19).[27]

Comparison with changes in Singapore (Table 2.9) during this period reveals that rates of single, married, and widowed women in Singapore rose to levels exceeding those in Ireland. In 1979, 26.8 percent of married women in Singapore were employed, whereas only 15.2 percent (57 percent of the Singapore rate) were in Ireland (see Table 2.6).

This suggests that much of the difference between the average labor force participation rates of women in the EEC and those of Irish women aged 25–64 can be attributed to the very low labor force participation of married women in Ireland in these age brackets. In turn, it can be inferred that this is the major reason for the comparatively low aggregate labor force participation rate of Irish women.

Table 2.8

Female Activity Rates by Age and Marital Status, Selected OECD Countries, 1970 (percentages)

	Total 15+	15–19	20–24	25–34	35–44	45–54	55–64	65+
Single								
Austria	63	60	84	89	88	83	40	7
Belgium	46	34	71	78	72	67	38	5
Finland	50	32	64	84	83	80	53	5
France	56	35	69	84	81	78	61	14
Germany	66	65	85	89	88	85	55	11
IRELAND	56	39	87	85	72	64	51	22
Italy	44	38	57	63	57	51	25	7
Spain	43	38	53	55	51	47	38	12
Sweden	44	29	58	72	73	71	53	5
Switzerland	70	59	90	93	91	85	69	21
Married								
Austria	38	58	53	45	46	45	23	4
Belgium	27	44	54	40	30	25	11	2
Finland	53	47	60	63	64	56	35	5
France	40	50	62	53	45	43	28	4
Germany	35	58	55	41	41	39	22	6
IRELAND	7	11	15	9	7	7	7	3
Italy	21	20	29	27	25	24	12	3
Spain	7	11	10	7	7	8	7	2
Sweden	37	35	45	40	48	48	28	3
Switzerland	31	54	48	35	35	34	23	6
Widowed								
Austria	10	*	*	42	46	42	17	2
Finland	24	*	*	75	80	72	39	3
France	15	*	*	70	71	67	40	3
IRELAND	19	*	*	44	47	42	31	11
Spain	10	*	*	37	39	28	16	3
Sweden	13	*	*	42	56	57	32	2
Switzerland	21	*	*	61	66	63	42	8

Source: United Nations. *The Economic Role of Women in the ECE Region.* (New York: United Nations, 1980):15, Table II.4.
*signifies less than one thousand in each category.

Table 2.9

Labor Force Participation Rates of Women by Marital Status, in Singapore, 1957–1979

Marital Status	1957	1970	1975	1979
Single	24.8	35.6	39.1	66.5
Married	14.0	14.7	22.1	26.8
Widowed	25.8	15.5	14.8	21.4
Divorced	46.5	47.6	50.0	68.5

Source: Aline K. Wong, "Planned Development, Social Stratification, and the Sexual Division of Labor in Singapore," *Signs* 7, 2 (Winter 1981), p. 440.

Disaggregated Female Share of the Labor Force

A detailed profile of the female share in sectors of the Irish economy and changes occurring from 1961 to 1981 is provided in Table 2.10.[28] Women's share of employment varied widely by sector: They comprised over half the work force in textiles/clothing/footwear/leather but under 5% in building and construction. Variation of this sort is not unusual; on a cross-country basis the percent female in certain industries (textiles, clothing, food) is usually relatively larger than their share in industries such as building and construction or mining. The former industries are considered traditional "female" industries while the latter are thought to be "male" industries.[29]

Using this type of data one can observe: (1) what happened during this period to the percent female in sectors that (numerically) were the largest employers of Irish women in 1961; and (2) how the percent female in subsectors of the Irish economy compared to the female share in similar sectors of other Western European countries.[30]

Table 2.11 shows the trends over the first two decades of the export-led development program in the sectors that were the major employers of women in 1961. The ten major employers of women in 1961 remained eight of the ten largest in 1981.[31] Looking at the five largest employers, which accounted for 80 percent of the employment of women in 1961, the female share decreased in four and only rose slightly in one. Extending this to the ten largest employers of women in 1961 (encompassing 94 percent of female employment), the female share fell in seven and increased in only three.[32] Women lost ground relative to men in a substantial proportion of the major sectors employing women, 1961–1981.

With regard to international comparisons, some indication of how female shares in Ireland contrast to the average for Western European

Table 2.10

Females as a Percent of Total Employees by Industry, Ireland,
1961–1981

	1961	1966	1971	1975	1979	1981
Agriculture, Forestry, Fishing	11.1	10.0	9.3	9.1	9.2	6.2
Industry	23.9	22.2	21.1	20.7	19.5	19.5
Mining, Quarrying, Turf Production	2.1	2.2	2.9	2.0	3.3	*
Manufacturing	33.4	31.8	30.5	29.5	27.4	27.2
Food, beverage, tobacco	27.3	25.8	26.0	23.5	21.2	22.4
Textiles, clothing, footwear, leather	58.3	57.9	56.8	56.2	52.0	54.0
Wood and wood products	6.0	8.5	8.2	6.4	6.5	7.8
Paper, paper products, printing and publishing	34.4	33.9	29.3	35.3	29.6	29.6
Chemical, rubber, and plastic products	29.2	28.5	25.7	27.2	24.7	23.3
Glass, pottery and cement	12.9	12.0	11.2	14.4	19.4	14.9
Metal, metal products & machinery	17.1	19.6	20.1	21.4	23.0	24.7
Other mfg. (incl. transport equipment)	14.6	14.5	16.0	19.2	27.8	22.0
Electricity, gas, water supply	5.9	5.9	7.0	12.3	12.9	11.5
Building and construction	1.7	1.8	2.0	2.2	3.2	3.7
Services	42.0	41.5	40.2	41.4	41.2	42.0
Commerce	33.9	33.1	31.3	33.7	32.9	33.1
Insurance, finance, business services	32.4	34.6	40.0	46.4	46.4	49.5
Transport, communication and storage	12.7	14.5	15.8	18.0	17.7	17.1
Public administration and defence	19.5	21.8	23.5	24.2	26.1	29.1
Professional services	59.3	59.9	59.1	62.1	59.2	60.0
Personal Services	78.2	75.0	69.3	66.9	62.5	60.9
Other industry or industry not stated	43.7	37.3	38.0	35.6	38.1	35.3
All Sectors	26.4	26.3	26.4	27.8	28.0	29.1

Sources: *Census of Population of Ireland*, various years; *Labour Force Survey*.
*The percent was not calculated in 1981 because there were less than 1000 women.

Table 2.11

Changes in Female Share in Sectors Employing Largest Numbers of
Women, Ireland, 1961–1981

MAJOR SECTORS EMPLOYING WOMEN (ORDINAL RANKING BY NUMBERS EMPLOYED)			CHANGE IN FEMALE SHARE, 1961–1981
	1961	1981	(percentage points)
Professional Services	1	1	.7
Personal Services	2	3	−17.3
Commerce	3	2	−.8
Agriculture	4	9	−4.9
Textiles, Clothing, etc.	5	6	−4.3
Food, Beverage, etc.	6	8	−4.9
Public Administration and Defence	7	4	10.6
Transport, Communication	8	10	4.4
Other Industry	9	11	−8.4
Paper, Paper Products	10	13	−4.8
Insurance, Finance, etc.	11	5	17.2
Metals	12	7	7.6

Source: Census of Population of Ireland, various years.

countries can be provided by EEC data on the percent female for manufacturing categories, 1974 – 1980, and for selected service categories
(distribution, banking, and insurance) in 1974.[33]

According to Table 2.12, the female share in Irish manufacturing
was below the average for the EEC throughout this period in every category except three. (These were industrial categories in which there had
been substantial foreign direct investment in Ireland: manufacture of
office machinery and data processing, electrical engineering, and in-
strument engineering.[34] The probability that the level in Ireland would
be lower than the EEC average in twelve of the fifteen categories (if for
any individual category it was equally probable that Ireland's level
would be above the average) is .014 — a highly unlikely outcome.

Similarly, Table 2.13, constructed for wholesale and retail distribution, banking, and insurance sectors in Ireland and the EEC in 1974,
shows that the percent female was lower in Ireland than average EEC
levels in all but three subcategories. These detailed analyses of the proportion female by sector show that the gender structure of employment
in Ireland differs across the board from the average profile of the EEC as
a whole.

Table 2.12

Proportion of Female Employees in Manufacturing Industries by NACE Classification, Ireland and EEC, 1974–1980

	1974		1977		1980	
	IRL	EEC	IRL	EEC	IRL	EEC
Chemicals	23.9	27.6	22.3	25.9	22.8	26.2
Metals/Engineering						
Metal articles	13.8	21.1	13.1	19.0	12.4	18.9
Mech. Engineering	10.0	15.0	10.4	15.0	9.9	14.3
Office Machinery	61.0	NA	56.5	NA	54.3	26.6
Elec. Engineering	41.0	40.4	41.8	38.0	42.2	37.5
Motor Vehicles	9.2	14.1	11.0	14.3	12.2	13.5
Other Transport	4.2	NA	3.7	NA	4.7	10.6
Instrument Eng.	34.1	39.7	39.0	39.3	48.5	39.0
Food, Drink, Tobacco	25.6	37.1	24.4	36.1	23.5	37.1
Textiles	46.5	56.0	43.4	50.0	41.5	54.1
Leather/Leather goods	27.0	NA	21.1	NA	22.3	54.7
Footwear/Clothing	71.9	76.3	73.9	76.9	74.7	78.5
Timber/Wood Furn.	11.4	20.8	11.1	21.4	10.8	20.4
Paper/Printing	29.7	33.7	27.7	31.8	28.4	32.4
Rubber and Plastics	21.1	32.8	22.4	30.8	22.1	29.9

Sources: Data on Ireland was taken from the Industrial Development Authority *Annual Employment Survey.* Data for the EEC for 1974 and 1977 were from *Economic and Social Position of Women in the Community* (Luxembourg: Office of Official Publications of the European Community) 1981, Table 37. Data for the EEC 1980 was from John Blackwell, "Digest of Statistics on Women in the Labour Force," Table 4.5.
NA = not available.

Conclusions

The development of the Irish economy, 1961–1981, involved several types of structural change thought by traditional economic theory to lead to increased participation of women in the labor force: export-led growth, based on foreign direct investment and the influx of multinational corporations which elsewhere hired large proportions of female workers, the shift from agriculture to industry and services, and the increased economic and social integration with other European nations. Examination of the aggregate female labor force participation rate and the female share of the labor force shows that not only did these expected increases not occur in Ireland, but that the differentials that ex-

Table 2.13

Proportion of Female Employees to All Employees in Wholesale and Retail Distribution, Banking and Insurance, Full-Time Employees, Ireland and EEC, 1974

	IRELAND	EEC
Wholesale Distribution		
Top management personnel	*	6.0
Management personnel and senior managers	*	5.1
Executives and management staff	5.0	9.2
Highly skilled junior personnel	8.3	20.4
Skilled junior personnel	32.5	33.9
Unskilled junior personnel	15.1	33.7
Retail Distribution		
Top management personnel	*	8.5
Management personnel and senior executives	*	11.6
Executives and management staff	17.6	24.8
Highly skilled junior personnel	23.7	41.4
Skilled junior personnel	63.4	64.5
Unskilled junior personnel	43.8	58.2
Credit institutions		
Directors, top management	*	0.8
Senior executives	*	3.9
Executives (junior management)	4.5	24.0
Highly qualified clerical staff	60.6	41.0
Qualified clerical staff	70.7	61.0
Other employees	25.0	57.7
Insurance		
Managers and senior management executives	*	0.0
Middle-management executives	*	5.5
Junior executives and personnel with equivalent qualifications	*	15.7
Highly skilled employees	53.3	40.1
Skilled employees	65.4	65.5
Other employees	*	58.8

Source: John Blackwell, "Digest of Statistics on Women in the Labour Force," Table 4.10.
*data not available.

isted between the Irish levels in 1961 and the (higher) average Western European OECD levels widened by 1981. Comparable statistics for Singapore reveal very different responses in measures of female participation in the labor force; both measures doubled in Singapore during export-led development, ending at levels substantially higher than in Ireland.

A look at more detailed female labor force participation data and female share statistics shows that (1) the low labor force participation of married women in Ireland was the major determinant of its low aggregate participation rate, and (2) not only were female shares in subsectors lower across the board in Ireland vis-à-vis the EEC average but that, during this period, Irish women lost ground relative to men in seven of the ten largest employers of females, gaining in only two.

Why were the labor force participation rates of married women in Ireland so low? Why were the female shares in most sectors lower in Ireland than in the EEC? Why weren't they both rising to levels comparable with the other Western European OECD countries and Singapore? Were there factors in either the workplace or the household which could have adversely affected either the demand for labor or the supply of labor or both and, in turn, produced such relatively low participation even in light of these dimensions of economic change thought likely to result in higher female participation? I shall begin to answer these questions in the next chapter.

Chapter Three

What Went Wrong?
Possible Traditional and Feminist Explanations

Introduction

A number of arguments often advanced by social scientists can be examined for their usefulness in explaining the relatively unchanging labor force activity of women in Ireland during the period of growth considered likely to increase it, 1961 – 1981. First, changes in the sectoral composition of the economy are commonly examined by researchers to determine if the demand for female labor has been altered by shifts toward sectors that hired larger proportions of males. Second, the factor-substitution hypothesis of economists investigates whether an increase in women's wages relative to men's may have adversely affected the demand for women workers.

More broadly, others could reason that, if jobs are scarce and if the society has traditional cultural norms regarding appropriate sex roles in the economy, men will be disproportionately provided employment. Last, there is a feminist approach that would argue that these measures of women's participation in the labor force were unchanging and relatively low in Ireland because it was fundamentally a male-dominated or patriarchal society. In particular, the large body of feminist theory that locates gender inequality in household relations would suggest that women's access to the labor force was constrained by their subordinate position in the household.

These explanations move from a more circumscribed and technical view of structural changes in the economy or in relative wages to a broader vision of the social determinants of women's labor force activity. All four will be explored in this chapter for their applicability to the general question (why measures of women's labor force participation remained so low during changes in the economy thought likely to increase it) and for their insight into social relations and labor market decision making in the workplace or the household or society in general.

Adverse Sectoral Change Explanation

It is often argued that women's participation in the economy is affected by changes in the sectoral structure of the economy (i.e., by changes in the relative importance of agricultural, industrial, and service sectors and their respective subsectors in the total economy). Given that the workforce of certain sectors may be proportionately more male (or female) than others, changes in the structure of the economy accompanying economic development can alter the pattern of the demand for female labor and in turn impact on the female share.

A number of studies have analyzed the changes in the female share of the labor force along these lines. For example, OECD publications typically argue that female employment has increased in member countries relative to male because of the expansion of the service sector, an area where women predominate (OECD, 1984:47; OECD, 1979:32 – 33). Ward (1987) contrasts the preference for males in import-substitution development, which were based on heavy industry, to labor-intensive export-led industries, which favored the employment of women.

In particular, Brazil is an economy to which this type of analysis has been repeatedly applied. Humphrey's (1984) work investigates the hypothesis that there was a change in industrial structure in Brazil in the 1970s that increased the relative demand for female workers. He was testing the hypothesis of Hirata that female employment shares were rising because of the growth of industries, such as electronics, which employed large proportions of women and because of technical change which led to the feminization of the labor force by deskilling jobs.[1] Earlier, Vasques de Miranda (1977) suggested that women's declining share of the industrial labor force during Brazil's early industrialization was attributable to a shift of industrial structure toward manufacturing sectors, which employed largely men.[2]

With respect to Ireland, this line of reasoning would suggest that, export-led growth notwithstanding, increases in the demand for female labor were circumscribed by a shift in the structure of the Irish economy toward sectors that hired larger proportions of males.[3] Initial examination of the data presents a somewhat mixed picture, necessitating further analysis. On the one hand, in looking at changes in employment among the three major sectors (agriculture, industry, and services), it seems unlikely that the shift in the sectoral composition of employment

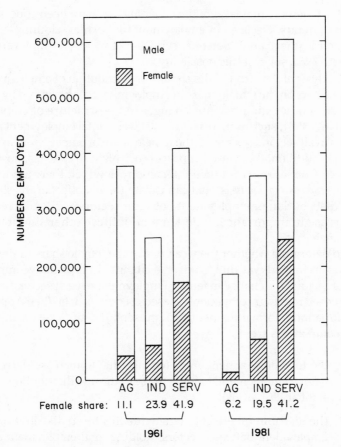

Figure 3.1 Total Employment, Republic of Ireland, 1961 and 1981 (Source: *Census of Population,* 1961 and 1981)

in the Irish economy could account for the lack of change in the female labor force participation rate or the weak change in the female share. It appears from Figure 3.1 that changes in distribution of total employment in Ireland between the major sectors 1961–1981 were favorable for women. There was a marked movement of total employment from agriculture, which was 11 percent female, to industry and services which were 24 percent and 43 percent female, respectively, in 1961. As Figure 3.1 also shows, this movement was accompanied by a shift in female employment toward the nonagricultural sectors (the cross-hatched portions of the sectoral employment bars represent female employment). On the other hand, it is possible that structural changes favoring industries that employed larger proportions of males could have occurred at a more detailed sectoral level of the economy and have been concealed by overall trends. Declines in employment in "textiles, clothing, footwear, and leather" and "personal services," two major employers of women in 1961, suggest this possibility.

Analysis of the effect of the change in distribution of employment among sectors on the female share of employment is complicated by the presence of other simultaneous changes in the structure of employment, 1961–1981, such as increases in the level of total employment and changes in all sectoral sex ratios (the female share of employment in the sector). In addition, the "pure" impact of each of these changes must be separated from the effect of their interaction. However, there is a technique, *decomposition analysis,* that can isolate the net effect of the shifts in the distribution of employment between sectors as they increase or decrease in importance, independent of these other simultaneous changes.[4]

To determine whether the weak rise in the female share of the labor force in Ireland was due to adverse changes in the relative importance of sectors, the change in female employment in each sector can be decomposed into four components, based on census data. (See Appendix A for a more formal mathematical presentation of these changes.) These components are:

1. the total employment effect (change due to increase/decrease in total employment, holding the sex ratio and distribution constant at 1961 levels);

2. the distribution effect (change due to altered distribution of employment between sectors, holding total employment and sex ratios constant at 1961 levels)

3. the sex-ratio effect (change due to increase/decrease in sex ratios in individual sectors holding total employment and distribution constant at 1961 levels)

4. interactions between these effects. (There are four interaction effects, all of which are specified in Appendix A. For example, one is the interaction between the change in total employment and the change in distribution of employment among sectors, holding sex ratios constant at the 1961 level.)

Complete results of this analysis are presented in Table 3.1. They show that, although the change in female employment consisted of a variety of diverse changes in the distribution and sex-ratio effects among the sectors, certain clear tendencies prevailed overall. For example, the diversity can be illustrated by changes in two sectors, "metal, metal products and machinery" and "textiles, clothing, footwear, leather." This table shows that the increase of female employment in the metals sector of 11,140 jobs was composed of a substantial positive distributional effect of 5,790 jobs but a relatively small increase due to the change in sex ratio of 1,580. The decrease in employment in textiles of 11,420 women was due to a very large negative distributional effect (− 11,680) in conjunction with a negative sex-ratio effect (− 2,320), which were not offset by a positive change in total employment effect.

Summing each component over all sectors permits an analysis on an economywide basis of overall trends and the relative importance of these four components of the change in female employment, 1961–1981. It reveals that the overall increase of 57,000 women employed consisted of (1) a positive "change in total employment effect" of 26,000 jobs; (2) a positive "change in distribution of employment among sectors" effect of 28,000 jobs; (3) a loss of 24,000 jobs due to adverse changes in the sex ratios of employment in sectors; and (4) the addition of 27,000 jobs by the effects of the four interactions.

Two conclusions emerge from these results. First, this analysis dispels the validity of the adverse sectoral-change argument, which investigated the possibility that changes in distribution of employment to those sectors that hired larger proportions of males may have been the cause of the relatively unresponsive female share. The decomposition confirms what Figure 3.1 had suggested: that on an economywide basis, distributional changes of employment among sectors were favorable for females. Women gained 27,800 jobs from the "pure" distributional effect. A set of similar calculations reveals that men lost 9,500 jobs due to shifts in employment from agricultural to nonagricultural sectors.[5] There is therefore no support at this level of analysis for an explanation that the female share may have risen so weakly because of changes in the sectoral composition of the Irish economy that were adverse for the employment of women.

The second conclusion is that the increase in the female share was constrained not by sectoral shifts but rather by the large negative impact of changes in sex ratios in the subsectors. The total effect of the varying changes in sectoral sex ratios was a *loss* of 24,000 female jobs, 1961–1981. (Correspondingly, males gained 24,000 jobs.) This quantifies the impact of the decreases in many sectoral shares of women shown in Chapter 2 (Tables 2.10 and 2.11) and reveals their severity. In Table 2.10 we saw that sex ratios, rather than rising to levels comparable to those in other EEC countries, fell in four of the eight manufacturing categories, in three of the seven service sectors, and in agriculture. Reexamining Table 2.11, which tabulated the changes in the female share in sectors employing

Table 3.1

Decomposition of the Change in Female Employment, Ireland, 1961–1981

	ACTUAL CHANGE IN EMPLOYMENT	EFFECT OF CHANGE IN TOTAL EMPLOYMENT	EFFECT OF CHANGE IN DISTRIBUTION	EFFECT OF CHANGE IN SEX RATIO	EFFECT OF INTERACTIONS
Agriculture, Forestry, Fishing	−30.30	3.88	−22.84	−18.52	7.19
Industry	8.48	5.72	.21	−1.58	4.13
Mining, Quarrying, Turf Production	−.21	.02	*	−.21	−.02
Manufacturing	5.19	5.54	−.42	−3.05	3.13
Food, beverage, tobacco	−.54	1.19	.95	−2.32	−.36
Textiles, clothing, footwear, leather	−11.42	2.97	−11.68	−2.32	−.39
Wood and wood products	.62	.05	.21	.21	.15
Paper, paper products, printing and publishing	.03	.49	.32	−.74	−.04
Chemical, rubber, and plastic products	1.90	.28	2.63	−.63	−.39
Glass, pottery and cement	1.20	.05	.84	.11	.20
Metal, metal products and machinery	11.14	.32	5.79	1.58	3.45
Other mfg. (incl. transport equipment)	2.26	.19	.53	1.05	.49
Electricity, gas, water supply	.86	.06	.11	.53	.17
Building and construction	2.63	.10	.53	1.16	.85

Table 3.1 (con't)

	ACTUAL CHANGE IN EMPLOYMENT	EFFECT OF CHANGE IN TOTAL EMPLOYMENT	EFFECT OF CHANGE IN DISTRIBUTION	EFFECT OF CHANGE IN SEX RATIO	EFFECT OF INTERACTIONS
Services	78.30	16.27	50.41	-3.89	15.50
Commerce	5.22	4.53	1.79	-1.16	.06
Insurance, finance, business services	16.66	.43	8.10	2.42	5.70
Transport, communication and storage	4.78	.64	1.05	2.42	.67
Public administration and defence	15.24	.74	6.31	3.89	4.29
Professional services	51.59	4.75	41.68	.63	4.52
Personal Services	-18.40	4.62	-12.95	-10.95	.88
Other industry or industry not stated	3.22	.57	4.42	-1.16	-.62
Total	57.00	25.87	27.79	-24.00	26.82

Sources: Calculated from data in *Census of Population of Ireland,* 1961 and 1981.

*< .01

the largest numbers of women, in light of this decomposition analysis reveals that the change in the sex ratio in the seven sectors in which the female share declined cost Irish women 37,000 jobs. The net effect of changes in the female shares including all ten of these sectors was a loss of 30,000 jobs. The increases in the female share in a few sectors were not able to counteract the substantial negative impact in these key sectors.

This result is surprising because, as revealed in Tables 2.12 and 2.13, the percent female in most Irish subsectors was well under the EEC average and because, as Jones (1984a) had found, the share of Asian women in manufacturing rose to levels above those in industrialized countries during development in five export-led countries. It could therefore have been expected that, in the absence of structural impediments, women's shares would have risen substantially in Ireland. It would have been likely that the opening of the economy (accompanied as it was by an influx of foreign direct investment and implementation of EEC equal opportunity legislation) would have resulted in a substantial positive "change in sex ratio" effect on female employment during these years rather than the strikingly negative effect that occurred.

Furthermore, rather than supporting the adverse "sectoral-change" explanation for the weak rise in the female share, the decomposition does just the opposite. It shows that the female share rose to the level it did in Ireland largely because of favorable shifts of employment from agriculture to services. Without this favorable "change in distribution" effect (i.e., if total employment had increased and sex ratios had changed as they did, but distribution of employment between sectors had remained at the 1961 levels), the female share of the labor force would have fallen 2.2 percentage points to 24.2%.[6]

This analysis has provided more information regarding trends on the employment side. Women were clearly not equally incorporated into employment in Ireland. This condition not only continued but the decomposition technique shows that it became more serious as many sex ratios fell, having a large negative impact on women's employment. Why did this happen, especially given dimensions of the development process thought likely to increase sex ratios? Were there constraints which precluded these increases?

The answers to these questions are important not only for our analysis of women's unchanging labor force participation but also because the results of this analysis have potentially serious implications for trends in the female share of total employment in Ireland in subsequent decades. It is likely that the positive distributional effects for Irish women cannot be sustained; the movement out of agriculture is self-limiting, and the government has been limiting the growth of public sector service employment due to fiscal pressures (Mahon, 1987). Therefore, the relatively low levels of female shares of sectors in Ireland and the decreases in many of them take on added importance. If the trends in sex ratios continue, and positive distributional impacts are diminished, increases in the female share of total employment will be restricted further.

Relative Wage Hypothesis

Another potential explanation for the unresponsive female labor force participation in Ireland during these first two decades of export-led development involves wages. Women have widely been considered desirable as employees because it has been possible to pay them less than men. Nevertheless, under the assumptions of neoclassical economic theory, if other things remain constant, a rise in women's wages relative to men's can result in an adverse effect on employment.

The literature has numerous references to the attractiveness of female workers because of their low-wage status. This factor has been cited in many circumstances: in the industrialization of advanced economies, in relation to employment in the service sectors, and in discussions of factors influencing the location decisions of multinational assembly plants worldwide (OECD, *Ireland*, 1974; Elson and Pearson, 1981; Fernandez-Kelly, 1983; Nash and Fernandez-Kelly, 1983).

This was certainly the case with respect to Irish women. They were lower wage workers than Irish men and, on this basis, would be desirable employees for Irish and incoming multinational employers. For most of this period it was legal to pay women lower wages than men and there are numerous documented examples of wage scales that differed by sex.[7]

However, with respect to wage differentials by sex, traditional neoclassical theory would argue that in a competitive economy any increases in women's wages relative to men's would impact adversely on the demand for female labor; this, in turn, could restrain increases in measures of women's participation in the labor force. This neoclassical relative wage hypothesis is a variant of the neoclassical factor-substitution model which discusses how, other things equal, firms alter the proportions of factors of production used (such as capital and labor) as the prices of the factors change relative to each other.[8] The analysis is usually done in terms of ratios or percentage change in them: female–male wages or earnings and how it relates to male–female employment for a firm, industry, or specifically defined unit. Neoclassical economists argue that these two ratios are positively related; that is, as women's wages rise relative to men's wages, men's employment will rise relatively.

The validity of this line of argument (relative wage hypothesis) for understanding the lack of change in measures of women's participation in the labor force in Ireland, 1961–1981, can be investigated by two types of disaggregated analysis in the Irish economy: (1) observation of the relationship between changes in relative employment and shifts in relative earnings in major manufacturing subsectors, and (2) comparison of the size of change in relative earnings and the size of the response of relative employment. (See note 4, Appendix B for discussion of the use of earnings versus wage data.)

First, the neoclassical relative wage argument is a microeconomic analysis applicable at the firm level; the nearest approximation to this for which data are available in the Irish economy is the subsector level. Therefore, if the hypothesis is able to explain changes in the employment of women, it is at this level that we should expect to find the predicted positive relationship between male – female employment ratios and female – male earnings ratios.

Sectoral comparisons in Ireland are complicated by the fact that data on earnings and employment were compiled for different levels of aggregation of the economy. Employment data by sex were compiled for sectors such as "textiles" or "clothing" whereas relative earnings information was tabulated for a more detailed categorization, subsectors of "textiles" such as "woolens and worsted," "linen and cotton spinning," etc. Nevertheless, in some cases, these either correspond directly (as in "paper and paper products, printing and publishing") or trends in relative earnings within all subsectors are the same so that comparison can be made to changes in relative employment (as in "textiles" and "clothing" for 1971–1975).

Table 3.2 illustrates a few of the diverse relationships that existed in Ireland during this period between changes in relative employment ratios (male – female) and changes in relative earnings ratios (female – male). It reveals the lack of consistency between trends at this level and the predictions of neoclassical analysis. For example, in both "textiles" and "clothing" subsectors, relative earnings rose, 1971–1975. However, these increases were accompanied by an increase in the male – female employment ratio in "textiles" and a fall in this ratio in "clothing." The trend in "textile" employment corresponds to the assertions of neoclassical theory; the change in the clothing subsector is in direct opposition. Further, the traditional argument is contradicted by changes in the subsectors of the paper industry, 1971–1975, where increases in relative earnings were accompanied by declines in the male – female employment ratios.

Table 3.2

Analysis of Trends in Male–Female Employment Ratios and in Female–Male Earnings Ratios Selected Subsectors, Ireland 1966–1977

	1966	1971	1975	1977
TEXTILES AND CLOTHING				
Textiles				
(N_m/N_f)	.936	1.075	1.197	1.169
(E_f/E_m)				
woolens and worsted	.68	.63	.68	.66
linen and cotton spinning	.59	.62	.73	.77
jute, canvas	.64	.60	.61	.64
hosiery	.55	.53	.57	.57
made-up textiles	.58	.59	.70	.70
Clothing				
(N_m/N_f)	.518	.336	.328	.40
(E_f/E_m)				
men's and boys' clothing	.60	.53	.66	.68
shirt making	.57	.64	.71	.71
women's and girls' clothing	.59	.62	.66	.66
misc. clothing	.59	.54	.67	.77
PAPER, PAPER PRODUCTS, PRINTING AND PUBLISHING				
Paper and Paper Products				
(N_m/N_f)		2.155	1.692	2.066
(E_f/E_m)		.57	.64	.67
Printing and Publishing				
(N_m/N_f)		2.465	1.937	2.203
(E_f/E_m)		.49	.53	.52

Sources: Employment data: Special tabulation of Census and Labor Force Sample Survey data (Department of Labour, Dublin); earnings data: John Blackwell, "Digest of Statistics on Women in the Labour Force" (Dublin: 1982), Table 6.1.
N_m and N_f are male and female employment in manufacturing; E_f and E_m are female and male earnings in manufacturing.

Table 3.3

Percentage Changes in Ratio of Male–Female Employment and in Ratio of Female–Male Earnings in Manufacturing, Ireland, 1966–1981

	$\%\Delta \left(\dfrac{N_{m,mfg}}{N_{f,mfg}}\right)^{1,2}$	$\%\Delta \left(\dfrac{E_{f,mfg}}{E_{m,mfg}}\right)^{2}$
1966–1971	1.2455	−.3534
1971–1975	.7863	2.1611
1975–1977	5.6785	.8163
1977–1979	.2849	3.1754
1979–1981	.5508	1.5038

Sources: Employment data: *Census of Population of Ireland,* various years; Earnings data: John Blackwell, "Digest of Statistics on Women in the Labour Force" (Dublin: 1982), Table 6.3.

$N_{m,mfg}$ and $N_{f,mfg}$ are male and female employment in manufacturing; $E_{f,mfg}$ and $E_{m,mfg}$ are female and male earnings in manufacturing.

[1]The percentage changes were calculated using census data (which was only available for the years 1966, 1971, 1975, 1977, 1979, 1981).

[2]Percent change on a per-year basis, compounded annually.

These examples illustrate only a portion of the inconsistencies that can be found in the data at the subsectoral level. Although regression analysis of this disaggregated data is not feasible due to the different levels of aggregation of the earnings and employment data, these examples suggest that the relative wage explanation cannot hold up at the level on which it should be most relevant, a more microeconomic level.

It would appear that factors other than relative earnings must be involved in the process. For example, in the textiles and clothing sectors, relative wages were comparable but dramatically different proportions of women were hired. Opposite changes in relative employment accompanied similar changes in relative earnings.

Second, Table 3.3 allows a comparison of the size of change in relative earnings and the size of response of relative employment in Ireland, 1966–1981. If the neoclassical argument is valid, it could be expected not only that increases in relative earnings of women would be accompanied by increases in the relative male–female employment ratio but that the larger increases in relative earnings would have elicited the larger increases in relative employment ratios (and vice versa).

However, the opposite was the case, casting further doubt on the explanatory power of the neoclassical argument. The largest annual change in relative earnings, 3.18 percent per year from 1975 to 1977, was accompanied by the smallest annual increment in the male–female employment ratio (.28 percent a year). Conversely, the largest annual increases in the male – female employment ratio occurred during 1966 – 1971 and 1975 – 1977. These were periods when the relative earnings ratio was either *falling* (1966 – 1971) or experiencing its smallest increase of the fifteen year period (1975 – 1977).

Neither of these types of disaggregated data for the Irish economy support the neoclassical relative wage argument. In addition, this hypothesis can also be explored at the national and regional level. Readers interested in a regression analysis of the relation between male – female employment ratios in manufacturing and female – male relative wages in Ireland and the EEC during this period should review Appendix B. Although a more technical approach, it provides additional insight into male – female relations and women's position in the economy.

In light of these results, the validity of the neoclassical relative wage argument cannot be established. Therefore, we cannot attribute the lack of responsiveness of measures of women's participation in the labor force, 1961 – 1981, to an increase in women's wages relative to men's. What was occurring in the workplace then? Sex ratios had a net negative impact. If they weren't related to changes in relative wages, what might have influenced them?

The last two explanations take a broader view of the social determinants of female labor force activity and consider more than technical explanations. They explore the possibility that either cultural conventions regarding the importance of providing males employment may dampen increases in female labor force activity or unequal relations in the household may constrain labor force activity of married women.

Job Scarcity Argument

Social scientists from a variety of disciplines could suggest that, given cultural norms and a sexual division of labor where the appropriate roles for men and women are generally considered to be, respectively, wage-earner and home duties (including child care), it is the men who get the jobs in an economy where jobs are scarce. To assess the relevance of this explanation for relatively low and unresponsive measures of female labor force activity in Ireland, 1961 – 1981, it is necessary to investigate (1) whether Ireland could be considered a job-scarce economy during that period, (2) if Irish society particularly emphasized the provision of male employment, and (3) whether there was any evidence that men were given priority in employment.

However, for this to be a possible explanation for the failure of female labor force participation to rise, it must be shown that there were supplies of women willing to work (i.e., that the female share was not constrained by the lack of availability of female workers). Once this is established, the applicability of this explanation can be evaluated by examining the three factors listed above.

To begin, evidence exists that supplies of both male and female workers were available throughout this period. The virtually unchanging female labor force participation rates therefore cannot be attributed to a shortage of female workers. To begin, it must be noted that demographically, there was no change in the sex composition of the population of working age; the proportion of women in the population of working age (15 and over) remained constant at 50.1 percent. Therefore, a change of this type could not have affected the supply of female labor.

Research by Walsh and O'Toole (1973) indicates that there was no generalized shortage of female labor near the middle of these two decades and suggests that there was a pool of potential female laborers, which, although not registered as unemployed, could be easily tapped. They examined Live Register Statistics on unemployed women and the returns for the quarterly industrial survey to assess possible shortages of individual categories of female workers and concluded that there was no generalized scarcity of female labor in Ireland in the years just before 1971. From December 1969 to December 1972 the only industry whose expansion was constrained by the unavailability of female labor was "clothing and footwear" between IV 1969 and IV 1970 (31).

Walsh and O'Toole also attempted to determine the existence of excess labor supply via the use of sample survey data.[9] Of the married women interviewed, 28 percent said their main reason for not working was "no jobs available" and 23 percent said they would go back to work immediately if jobs were available. Given reservations regarding this type of data, Walsh and O'Toole (1973) nevertheless concluded that "inadequacy of aggregate demand for women workers is a serious aspect of the present labour market situation in Ireland" (31). These results are buttressed by studies by Fine-Davis (1983a), Manpower Surveys (Department of Labour, various years) and an Industrial Development Authority survey (1983).

Given the availability of women workers, examination of this broader type of explanation (whether Ireland was a job-scarce economy, whether the society emphasized the importance of providing males with jobs and whether there is evidence that men were given priority) can now proceed. To begin, as indicated by high unemployment rates and the extensive out-migration in search of employment in the 1950s, Ireland was plagued by a lack of job opportunities when the export-led growth strategy was initiated (Kennedy, 1975, 1980; Walsh, 1978:33 and Walsh, 1974).[10] The data suggest that it remained a job-scarce economy throughout this period. During the period 1961–1981, the population of working age increased by 281,000 persons (14,000 per year on average). Since 60 percent of the population of working age was employed in 1961, an average of 8400 jobs a year would have had to be provided to maintain the status quo. However, the labor force increased by 98,000 (just under 5000 a year). Another way of providing a perspective on job scarcity is to observe that the population of working age in Ireland increased by 10 percent 1960–1975, substantially exceeding the 2 percent growth in the labor force (OECD, 1979:16, 33).[11]

The increase in the population of working age was fueled by substantial changes during this period in the total population growth rate. [The total population growth rate = the rate of natural increase (birth rate minus the death rate) + the rate of net migration (gross immigration minus gross emigration)]. There was a dramatic turnaround in the rate of growth of the Irish population, with successively larger increases replacing the population declines that had occurred through most of this century. As shown in Appendix C, the growth of total population in Ireland was based on a high and unchanging birth rate and the reversal of patterns of net migration, two particularly dramatic demographic features that occurred in conjunction with typical declines in the death rate.[12] The problem this presented for provision of adequate levels of employment was compounded by the fact that population growth was based in the younger age groups (Walsh, 1974:70).[13]

Because of these demographic trends, the problems Ireland faced in providing a rate of growth of employment appropriate for the rate of growth of population of working age became increasingly difficult, 1961 – 1981, and contrasted starkly with the demographic challenge to full employment other European countries were facing. Seen in the context of the Western European OECD countries (Table 3.4), Ireland's annual growth rate of total population had become the highest by 1977 (1.2 percent).[14]

Although provision of employment was a major goal of the export-led development strategy, substantially increased attention in the 1970s was placed on finding solutions to the "unemployment" problem (Kennedy, 1975; Walsh, 1974, 1978, 1979; Geary and Dempsey, 1977; Whelan and Walsh, 1977; *National Development, 1977 – 1980*; Ross and Walsh, 1979; *Development for Full Employment, 1978*). It was recognized that a long-term problem remained regarding the provision of adequate numbers of jobs (Walsh, 1978).[15]

A number of projections were made (based on different assumptions regarding the extent of emigration) of the growth in the population of working age (or the potential labor force), and estimates were formed regarding the number of jobs that would be required per year either to maintain the current levels of unemployment or to provide full employment. In all cases, there were wide gaps between the increase in

Table 3.4

Total Population Growth Rate,[1] Western European OECD Countries, 1950–1977

	1950–1960	1960–1970	1970–1977
(unweighted) average	0.7	0.8	0.6
Austria	0.2	0.5	0.2
Belgium	0.6	0.5	0.2
Denmark	0.7	0.7	0.5
Finland	1.0	0.4	0.4
France	0.9	1.1	0.7
Germany	1.0	0.9	0.2
Greece	1.0	0.5	0.7
Ireland	**−0.5**	**0.4**	**1.2**
Italy	0.7	0.7	0.7
Luxembourg	0.6	0.8	0.7
Netherlands	1.3	1.3	0.9
Norway	0.9	0.8	0.7
Portugal	0.7	NA	0.8
Spain	0.8	1.1	1.0
Sweden	0.6	0.7	0.4
Switzerland	1.3	1.6	0.1
United Kingdom	0.4	0.5	0.1

Source: World Tables 1980, Social Indicators, Tables 1 and 2.
NA = not available
[1]Compound annual rates of growth based on mid-year population.

the potential labor supply and the increases being achieved in employment (Blackwell and McGregor, 1982; Kennedy, 1975; Sexton, 1981 and 1982; Sexton and Walsh, 1982; Walsh, 1974; Walsh, 1978; Walsh, 1979). According to Walsh (1974), "The results of this exercise are somewhat daunting because of the very high rate of growth of job-creation shown to be necessary to attain full employment" (70).[16]

In light of these results, it can be concluded that Ireland was a job-scarce economy throughout this period. This can have adverse implications for the employment of women in a country where it is considered appropriate to allocate scarce jobs to males. Ireland was such a country. There are numerous indications that it has long been considered appropriate that males obtain paid employment while women are based in the home. For example, according to the Irish Constitution, the proper place for mothers was in the home and they should not be obliged by economic necessity to neglect these duties.

This point of view has persisted throughout this period. Fine-Davis' (1983b) analysis of 1978 survey data shows that 78 percent of those interviewed believed being a wife and mother are the most fulfilling role any woman could want; 70 percent thought that it is bad for young children if their mothers work; and 71 percent believed that in high unemployment married women should be discouraged from working. Further, a Catholic bishop publicly questioned the right of married couples to have two jobs in "these days of unemployment" (*Irish Independent,* May 30, 1983:5), implicitly reiterating the notion that when jobs are tight a family should have one job—the male's.

There is also support for the last aspect of this potential explanation. There is compelling evidence, based on detailed examination of emigration data and information regarding the economic status of female emigrants, that employment opportunities were not equally available for men and women in Ireland.

Changes in migration were one of the most striking demographic changes in Ireland during the last few decades.[17] The net in-migration in the 1970s reversed a net outflow that had occurred almost without interruption since the Great Hunger of the 1840s.[18] However, the aggregate migration statistics obscure considerable diversity in migration patterns by sex and age. The disaggregation of the estimated net migration statistics in Table 3.5 shows an increasingly skewed sex distribution of emigrants during these years. Although absolute numbers emigrating declined in the 1960s, the female proportion of net emigration rose substantially, from 48 percent for the 1956–1961 period to 54 percent for 1966–1971.

Table 3.5

Average Annual Net Migration, Ireland, 1951–1981

INTERCENSAL PERIOD	ESTIMATED AVERAGE ANNUAL NET MIGRATION (INWARD–OUTWARD)		FEMALES AS PERCENT OF TOTAL*
	MALES	FEMALES	
1951–1956	−21,657	−17,696	[45]
1956–1961	−21,915	−20,486	[48]
1961–1966	−7,523	−8,598	[53]
1966–1971	−4,950	−5,831	[54]
1971–1981	5,703	4,435	44

Source: Census of Population of Ireland 1981 Preliminary Report.
*Bracketed items in this column represent net out-migration; the unbracketed item is net in-migration.

Table 3.6

Net Migration by Age and Gender, Ireland, 1961–1979

Age groups	1961–1966	1966–1971	1971–1979
	MALES (000s)		
0–14	4.8	5.6	24.7
15–29	−44.7	−37.7	−9.5
15–19			3.8
20–24			−10.1
25–29			−3.2
30–44	4.3	5.3	31.3
45–64	−2.7	−2.0	7.2
65+	1.3	4.0	7.5
Total males	−37.2	−24.8	38.3
	FEMALES (000s)		
0–14	5.0	6.1	24.6
15–29	−39.9	−34.3	−9.5
15–19			2.8
20–24			−10.4
25–29			−1.9
30–44	−1.0	0.7	23.3
45–64	−6.6	−4.8	1.4
65+	0.5	3.3	7.8
Total females	−41.9	−28.9	47.7

Source: Census of Population of Ireland, 1979, Vol. II: xi, xii.
net migration = [in-migration − out-migration].

Moreover, when net emigration was reversed in the 1970s, women's share of the net in-migration was substantially lower (44 percent) than their recent past share of out-migration (54 percent). In the 1960s women were an increasing proportion of those leaving Ireland; in the 1970s they were a much lower proportion of those returning.

Even more revealing, examination of this data by sex and age in Table 3.6 shows that, although the period 1971–1979 exhibited overall net in-migration, there was still substantial net out-migration for both males and females aged 20–29. This was especially prominent in the 20–24-year-old age group. Out-migration for this group was 20,000, over half of whom were women. Given that more than one-fourth of the Irish female labor force was aged 20–24, this indicates that there was still substantial out-migration of females in the primary working age groups.[19]

This investigation of migration data raises several questions. Why, during the years when the export-led development program was attempting to provide employment opportunities in Ireland, did women become an increasing proportion of those leaving in the 1960s and a smaller proportion of those returning in the 1970s? Why were women in the 20–24-year-old age bracket (which had the highest labor force participation rate for women, 66 percent in 1975) still leaving the country in large numbers in the 1970s?

Analysis of the economic activity status of these female emigrants at their destination indicates possible reasons for emigration. It appears that the primary reason Irish women emigrated was to find gainful employment.[20] Hughes and Walsh (1976) have assembled data for male and female emigrants to Great Britain, 1961–1966, and 1966–1971.[21] (The majority of Irish emigrants went to Great Britain during these years: 86 percent in 1970–1971.)

According to estimates by Hughes and Walsh, the majority of emigrants were not working or were working in unskilled jobs just prior to their departure for Britain. In 1966, however, 64 percent of the 45,000 Irish women in Great Britain classified as five-year migrants were economically active (Walsh, 1970). Similarly, 57 percent of the 29,000 five-year migrant Irish women were at work in 1971 (Hughes and Walsh, 1976). In both years, the labor force participation rate of migrant Irish women was twice that of Irish women in Ireland (28 percent) and substantially higher than the participation rate of British women (33 percent in 1971).

Putting these two types of information together — (1) the examination of the gender composition of in- and out-migration, which revealed that women were an increasing proportion of emigrants in the 1960s, a smaller proportion of net immigrants in the 1970s, and that women in the 20–24-year-old age group were still out-migrating in the 1970s and, (2) the analysis of the economic activity status of female emigrants in Great Britain which implies Irish women emigrated for employment—suggests that the net new employment opportunities being provided in Ireland were not equally available for males and females.

To summarize, this line of argument is clearly relevant to the situation in Ireland, 1961–1981. Ireland was a job-scarce economy (with reserves of both male and female workers available); it was considered especially important in Irish society that males obtain employment; and evidence from emigration data supports the contention that jobs were disproportionately available for men.

However, although compelling, this does not constitute a sufficient explanation for why measures of women's participation in the labor force were relatively unresponsive during this 20-year period of the export-led development program. This analysis takes the sexual division of labor as given and unchanging. It cannot explain why or how, in an open economy experiencing dramatic social and economic changes that appeared favorable for women, the traditional sexual division of labor was maintained. It could have been expected, that given the changes accompanying export-led growth, the traditional sexual division of labor would have been altered. How was the advantage men had in obtaining employment maintained?

Feminist Approach

Feminists could argue that measures of women's labor force participation were relatively unresponsive in Ireland during the export-led development program because Ireland was a male-dominated or patriarchal society. The body of feminist theory that locates the subordination of women in the household[22] would assert that male domination can be maintained systematically via social relations in the household, where males effectively control material resources, decision-making, and female labor time as well as by fertility levels and the delegation of child care responsibilities to women.[23]

The relevance of this explanation for Ireland can be explored by examining two issues: whether the Irish family was patriarchal and how male domination in the household could affect female labor supply. First, that the Irish family was patriarchal for most of this century has been well documented. Irish economist-historian Daly (1981b) reviews the literature regarding rural life in Ireland in the 1930s and urban life in the 1940s, which depicted the marked subordination of women to men (including marriages arranged for women by men, women eating after the men, separate socializing). Schmitt's (1973) study of authoritarianism in Irish democracy in the late 1960s and early 1970s mentions the continuation of male dominance: "within the home the major decisions are traditionally made by the male head-of-family, whose word—especially in economic matters—is absolute" (46). His review of the literature in the 1960s regarding male dominance reveals its multiple dimensions (in addition to the position accorded the husband-father, sons were deferred to by both mothers and sisters).

The extensive analysis of Hannan and Katsiaouni (1977) in the 1970s traces the changes in the economic, cultural, and social environments of interspousal relationships in rural farm families since the

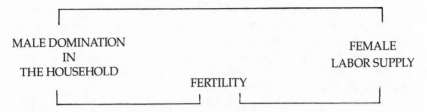

Figure 3.2 The Effect of Male Domination in the Household on Female Labor Supply

1930s and 1950s. However, although they found that changes had occurred that allowed some wives more input into particular aspects of family decision-making, one-half of the families still conformed to the model of the traditional, strictly defined, patriarchal family (5, 113, 116). Although the extremely male-dominated organization of household relations of the 1930s and 1940s had been somewhat loosened (for example, marriages were no longer arranged), it is clear that social relations in the Irish family throughout the two decades, 1961 – 1981, could only be described as fundamentally patriarchal.

Secondly, male domination of social relations in the household is linked to female labor supply decisions in two interrelated ways as indicated by Figure 3.2: by the general importance of the male in household decision-making (which includes the woman's labor supply decision) and via the indirect impact of fertility levels. The first can be documented by regression analyses revealing the importance of husbands' preferences in the labor supply decisions of married women, the second by using demographic data regarding the level and change in Irish fertility rates.

With respect to the direct effect of the importance of the male in household decision-making on female labor supply, analysis of survey data has shown that husbands' opinions regarding their wives participation in the labor force have been of major importance in the labor supply decision of Irish women. The regression analysis of factors affecting the labor supply behavior of nonfarm married women run by Walsh and Whelan (1973 – 1974) revealed that the husband's approval of married women working had a significant influence on participation of married nonfarm women in the labor force.[24] "The increase in labour force participation associated with the "husband approves" response is the largest coefficient obtained for any variable (in the transformed equation), and its contribution to R^2 is also the greatest" (23). Correspondingly the disapproval of the husband would have a negative impact on labor force participation.[25]

The neoclassical analysis of Walsh and Whelan (1973–1974) unintentionally raises a fundamental issue. Whose preferences are being measured: those of a woman exercising her free choice in making a labor supply decision or those of a woman whose options may be constrained by her subordinate position in the household, by the existence of unequal power relations?

Fine-Davis' (1983a) analysis of 1978 survey data indicates the importance of the husband's viewpoint persisted throughout the period. Perceived approval of the husband was the second most important correlate between characteristics of housewives and potential labor force participation.

As already stated, male domination in the household can affect female labor supply indirectly, via its impact on fertility levels. It can be argued that male domination increases fertility and, in turn, fertility and labor force participation are negatively correlated. The theoretical relationship between patriarchy and fertility levels has been explored by Folbre (1983) who argues that unequal gender relations in the household govern reproductive decisions by affecting the costs of children. Her argument suggests that to the extent men have patriarchal control over women, they can shift the costs of raising children onto women and disproportionately reap the benefits of children. This applies to more narrowly described cases where males have patriarchal control over adult children and to the broader situations where children are eventually the supporters of social security from which men disproportionately benefit whether they have children or not (Folbre, 1985).

The correlation between the power of the fathers/husbands and fertility has been shown empirically to exist in Ireland by the Hannan and Katsouiani (1977) study. It revealed that larger numbers of children were linked with greater male power in the home and that, the younger the children, the greater the dependence of women (116).

Examination of total fertility data shows that fertility in Ireland has been the highest of the Western European OECD countries by a very wide margin.[26] Table 3.7 shows that fertility rates for most countries fell below 2.0 in the seventies whereas Ireland's remained well above 3.0. Irish fertility changes also contrast dramatically to trends in Singapore during these same years where the average number of births per woman fell from more than six to just under two (Fawcett and Khoo, 1980).

Total fertility rates have been found to have an inverse relation with labor force participation rates of women in industrializing countries. In his review of the literature on the relationship between fertility and labor force participation rates, Guy Standing (1981) concludes that statistically significant results consistently arise when fertility variables

Table 3.7

Total Fertility Rates, Western European OECD Countries, 1960–1980

	1960	1980	Change
(unweighted) average	2.64	1.89	−0.75
Austria	2.7	1.6	−1.1
Belgium	2.5	1.7	−0.8
Denmark	2.5	1.7	−0.8
Finland	2.7	1.6	−1.1
France	2.7	1.9	−0.8
Germany	2.3	1.4	−0.9
Greece	2.2	2.3	0.1
Ireland	**3.8**	**3.3**	**−0.5**
Italy	2.3	1.8	−0.5
Luxembourg	2.3	1.5	−0.8
Netherlands	3.1	1.6	−1.5
Norway	2.8	1.8	−1.0
Portugal	3.0	2.4	−0.6
Spain	2.8	2.5	−0.3
Sweden	2.2	1.7	−0.5
Switzerland	2.3	1.5	−0.8
United Kingdom	2.7	1.8	−0.9

Source: World Tables, Third Edition, Vol. II, Social Data, 1983.

such as the presence of a child under the age of six and the number of children under the age of eighteen in the household are used as independent variables in cross-section or time-series multiple regression analyses for industrialized countries.[27]

According to his analysis, it is most likely that fertility will depress labor force participation rates of women under the following conditions: where the structure of the labor market does not offer work alternatives such as flexible hours or homework; in societies where the time-intensity and quality of child care is high; where alternative forms of child care are not available; where the motivation of mothers to work, as shaped by past experience and the nature of work available, is low; or where child labor is prevalent.

During the period of time under study, Irish society exhibited most of these characteristics (i.e., a labor market structure not offering flexible hours, high expectations for quality of child-rearing, and a lack of alternative forms of child care).[28] Therefore, it could be assumed that the high fertility rate in Ireland had a major constraining effect on the labor force participation of married women. This is indicated by the

Walsh and Whelan (1973–1974) regression analyses (22). Their results revealed that the presence of children under fourteen years of age had a significant negative impact on the labor force participation of married women.

This line of argument is promising. A feminist explanation appears relevant; that is, that measures of female participation in the labor force remained low and unchanging, 1961–1981, because Ireland was patriarchal. In Ireland the appropriate role for women was considered to be in the home, where unequal power relations prevailed, with males dominating. The evidence suggests that this translated into low labor force participation of married women because of the importance of the husband's opinion in the wife's labor supply decision and by high levels of fertility, which are associated in countries such as Ireland with low participation rates.

But, as with the job-scarcity argument, this explanation is not sufficient. It does not explain how male domination in the household is reproduced in an open economy. In pursuing export-led growth Ireland opened itself to influences which would be likely to reduce the dependence and subordination of women vis-à-vis men. The arrival of foreign firms, many in industries seeking female labor; the enactment of EEC compatible social legislation, which extended female rights in the workplace; and the exposure to cultural changes elsewhere (different lifestyles for women, dramatically lower fertility rates elsewhere in Western Europe) would all tend to undermine male domination.

If this feminist approach is the explanation, how was male domination maintained? An explanation that rests on male domination in the household (or in the household and firm) alone is insufficient. What social structure could have reinforced these unequal gender relations in the household (and in the workplace) during the period of economic change which had tendencies to erode it? Upon reflection, two further questions arise. Why did fertility rates remain so high? Given this explanation, why did the labor force participation rate of married women increase suddenly in the 1971–1975 period (as shown in Table 2.6)?

Conclusions

Examination of these four types of potential explanations has increased our understanding of the social processes involved with women's economic roles in Ireland during this period. Although we do not have an explanation for why measures of women's labor force participation remained relatively low and unchanging during an economic development process considered likely to increase them, we have developed insight into social relations in the household, firm, and society. We have learned that the falling sectoral sex ratios had a substantially negative impact on female employment. These decreases in sex ratio were directly the reverse of the trend expected given Ireland's export-led development strategy and trends in female shares in other export-led nations. Since these could not be attributed to an increase in women's wages relative to men's, we are left wondering what social constraints may have been present at the workplace preventing the increases.

In examining the latter two explanations of job scarcity and the feminist approach, we have found much relevance to the Irish case. Ireland was a job-scarce economy in which it was considered appropriate by society that men obtain jobs, and evidence is available that men were indeed given preference. In addition, the feminist explanation also provides much insight: Ireland was a patriarchal society in which the labor force participation of married women was constrained by unequal relations in the household.

However, although there is much in these latter two explanations that corresponds closely to the situation in Ireland, their explanatory power is limited by the fact that they cannot explain how the given sexual division of labor remains constant and how male domination continues to be reproduced in the household or firm during this period of export-led economic growth. What is missing in this analysis is an explanation of the structures by which female employment was constrained. It is to this issue that we now turn.

Chapter Four

The Role of the State

Introduction

Through a survey of Irish social and industrial policy, we may come to an understanding of why female labor force activity did not increase and of the way in which a male-bias regarding paid employment and male domination in the household were maintained during a development process likely to erode them. This further research reveals that the experience of women in the labor market in Ireland 1961 – 1981 is inexplicable without analyzing the overall impact of a broad range of state policy on economic outcomes for women.

It soon becomes evident in reviewing social policy that Irish state personnel had two primary goals: to promote economic growth and development *and* to reproduce traditional familial relations (i.e., male dominance). It was because of the manner in which state personnel designed policy to meet these dual goals that economic outcomes for women in Ireland differed both from those predicted by traditional economic theory or from the changes in female labor force activity occurring in other countries experiencing these types of structural economic change.

However, the analysis is made more complex by the fact that these two goals of state policy can be contradictory. The promotion of the economic growth process can undermine traditional relations between the sexes by providing paid employment for women. Patriarchal restraints on employment of women can dampen the export-led development process, which has depended heavily on the use of female labor.

The position of women in the labor market in Ireland during this period of economic change therefore reflected the impact of policies designed to attain both the growth of employment via economic development and the maintenance of traditional relations between the sexes, and the manner in which contradictions between these objectives were resolved. Because of this, the relatively unchanging labor force participation of Irish women can only be understood by a theoretical approach that incorporates the role of state personnel, their major purposes, and the impact of a wide range of policies (family and reproductive rights policies as well as employment policies) on women into the analysis. The approach must integrate the contradictions or trade-offs that exist between the goals and the way in which policies are designed to attain these objectives in light of the trade-offs involved between them.

The dual and contradictory objectives of Irish state personnel during this period and the framework of this alternative approach are discussed in the next section in more concrete terms. In constructing this approach I have drawn insights from three literatures — neoclassical, Marxian, and feminist — although my analysis differs from each of them. From the neoclassicists I borrow the concept that elected state personnel are informed decision-makers, interested in perpetuating their tenure in office. From Marxist theory I have taken the realization that the economy and the state have an interactive relationship that involves inequalities among groups regarding access to resources and have adapted it by drawing from feminist theory the fundamental insight that social actors may consider the reproduction of patriarchy a goal. In addition, I develop a simple graphic model that can be used to simplify our understanding of this alternative theoretical approach and the trade-offs involved.

Following that, the next two major sections examine first, employment policies and, second, family and reproductive rights policies to assess their impact on female labor market outcomes. In analyzing the effect of these policies on decision-making and gender inequality in the workplace or in the household, we see that the employment opportunities of Irish women, 1961 – 1981, were not simply shaped by the process of export-led development operating in a competitive market environment. The impact of economic development on women was mediated by the structure of state policy, which had besides the objective of economic growth that of preserving familial relations.

This analysis provides answers to the puzzling questions raised near the end of Chapters 2 and 3, regarding the lackluster measures of female labor force activity: the relatively low female shares in many sectors and the low participation of married women. It answers the recurring question regarding what may have precluded the likely increases in the demand for female labor or the supply during this period of dramatic economic and social change. The main lesson from the Irish case emerges: the importance of incorporating the state (and the effect of a broad range of its policies, family, and reproductive rights policies as well as employment policies, on decision-making or equality of gender relations in the firm and household) into an analysis of women's roles in the labor market or economy.

The Contradictory Goals of the State

Elected officials and state personnel are interested in perpetuating their tenure in office and design state policy with this goal in mind.[1] A survey of Irish social and industrial policy in the early years of this newly independent country reveals that state personnel saw two primary ways of designing economic and social policy to further their own tenure: promotion of economic development via an import substitution strategy and maintenance of traditional familial relationships. Traditional relations between the sexes were not simply a division of labor between equals, but involved the subordination of women.

It is commonly accepted that economic issues (employment, taxes, inflation, and deficits) are objects of interest for state personnel concerned with perpetuating their tenure and that, in fact, political business cycles are caused by the manner in which state officials address such problems, given their interest in reelection. However, it has not been similarly recognized that state personnel may also be developing a variety of policies (employment, family, and reproductive rights) with a vision of appropriate relations between the sexes and a particular view of "the family" in mind. In addition, the extent to which a broad range of state policies and the manner in which they interact affect women's economic roles is only slowly being recognized.

That maintenance of traditional relations between the sexes has been a major goal of Irish policy since the early days of the Republic can be discovered by referring to the Irish Constitution and surveying a range of social legislation. The Constitution of 1937 provides some background regarding the social context within which state policies have been formulated over the years. In its specification of fundamental rights, the Constitution addressed the importance of the family and the role of women in society. According to Article 41, "The Family":

> 41. 1. 1. The State recognizes the Family as the natural, primary and fundamental unit group of Society, and as a moral institution possessing inalienable and imprescriptible rights antecedent and superior to all positive law.
>
> 2. The State, therefore, guarantees to protect the Family in its constitution and authority, as the necessary basis of social order and as indispensible to the welfare of the Nation and the State.

> 41. 2. 1. In particular, the State recognizes that by her life within the home, woman gives to the State a support without which the common good cannot be achieved.
>
> 2. The State shall, therefore, endeavour to ensure that mothers shall not be obliged by economic necessity to engage in labour to the neglect of their duties in the home.

In other words, the traditional family was the core institution of the society; women belonged at home and mothers should not work.

A number of policies were implemented during these years with this Constitutional viewpoint in mind: the Constitutional prohibition of divorce; the establishment of the marriage bar in 1932 when the government barred employment of married women as Civil Service employees;[2] and the prohibition of the sale, advertising, or importation of contraceptives.[3] In addition, until 1957, women could not own property or make contracts (Commission on the Status of Women, 1972:173). During these years, women's roles were subordinate to those of men. Political roles for women were virtually nonexistent, the employment opportunities that were available were low-paid and dead-end, and in Mary Daly's words, the "social structures . . . subordinated their existence to a male dominated family" (1981b:78). Marriage was considered the most important career for women and it was thought undesirable for married women to work.[4]

However, these goals of providing growth in employment and maintaining traditional gender relations became increasingly contradictory in the late 1950s when policymakers came under increasing pressure to pursue economic growth more aggressively with an open economy approach. State personnel adopted a new economic development strategy because economic growth rates were relatively low in Ireland in comparison to the rest of Europe, and emigration rates had soared.[5] A dramatic turnaround in economic and industrial policy was formalized: The import substitution approach was formally scrapped with the official adoption of an export-led development strategy in 1958.[6]

Contradictions between the objectives of economic growth and reproduction of traditional gender relations were more likely to arise under export-led development than under import substitution because the Irish export-led growth strategy depended on attracting foreign firms, many in industries that tended to hire larger proportions of women than the average for Irish industries. In addition, membership in the EEC (necessary to provide foreign firms with tariff-free access to markets) required that Ireland adjust its social policies to correspond with equal opportunity legislation of the Community.[7]

The way in which the ensuing contradictions were resolved (first when export-led growth began to erode patriarchy and then when the strengthened form of male domination was found to constrain the export-led development process) will be detailed in the rest of this chapter. As a way to address the contradictions between these two goals, state personnel did alter the way some employment policies affected labor market outcomes by sex. Family law and reproductive rights legislation, however, which served to maintain traditional relations between the sexes, was essentially not changed during this period. The policies enacted in the 1930s were enforced until the mid-1970s (and in many cases are still operative). Moreover, a number of government policies were added to strengthen them.[8]

Over time, the discriminatory aspects of these policies and the manner in which they increased women's subordination was recognized. This resulted in some pressure for social change that would improve the status of women. The impetus for changing discriminatory state employment policies was generated by forces initially external to Ireland and later lobbied for in Ireland. Pressure to change inequities in family law and reproductive rights legislation, however, came primarily from within the country.[9]

Although state personnel were forced to remove some discriminatory employment policies in the mid- to late 1970s by the imperatives of the export-led development process, there is evidence that employment discrimination persisted. This, in combination with virtually no substantive change in family law, meant that the freedom of women to enter the labor market remained constrained.

To summarize, state personnel interested in reelection seek to garner voter support via their performance to ensure this outcome. In the Irish case this performance primarily involved policies that increase the growth of employment or that maintain the traditional relations between the sexes of male domination (which for simplicity I will term "patriarchy," recognizing the baggage and problems this terminology brings with it). Complications arise, however, because these policies can be contradictory and involve trade-offs. For example, in the absence of structural constraints, augmentation of the economic growth or accumulation process undermines traditional relations between the sexes. Therefore, state personnel seek to promote a feasible combination of these two general types of policies that will result in the greatest voter support.

These points can be represented in a graphic model that assists in highlighting the role of state and its perpetuation of male dominance. The basic graphic model is represented in Figure 4.1, part 3; the underlying components from which it is developed, in parts 1 and 2. The re-

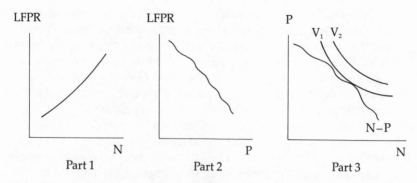

Figure 4.1   Relationships Underlying the Patriarchy-Growth of Employment Trade-off   (LFPR is the labor force participation rate of women; N is the growth of employment; P represents patriarchal relations; V curves are levels of voter support)

lationship between employment and patriarchy (the *N-P* curve of part 3) is derived as follows. First, in the absence of structural constraints, increases in the rate of growth of employment (*N*) are accompanied by increases in the labor force participation rate of women (LFPR). This is shown in part 1 of Figure 4.1 by the positive relation between the two variables (movement away from the origin signifies higher values of each variable). However, as the female participation rate increases there is a weakening of male domination in the household. As McCrate (1985, 1987) argues, women become less dependent economically on men as female employment increases. If they are not able to negotiate a more favorable position in the household the increased economic independence may allow them to terminate a marriage. This is shown in part 2 of Figure 4.1 by the inverse relationship between the labor force participation rate of women (*LFPR*) and patriarchy (*P*). (Movement away from the origin on the horizontal axis signifies stronger forms of male domination.)

Finally, the transformation curve (*N-P*), representing trade-offs between employment and patriarchy as shown in part 3 of Figure 4.1, is derived from part 1 and part 2, by graphing the sets of *N* and *P* which correspond to the same LFPR. The basic objective of state personnel, implementation of that feasible combination of employment and family policies that will generate the greatest amount of voter support, is represented as follows: Any of the combinations of employment policies (*N*) and patriarchal policies (*P*) which lie along the trade-off curve (*N-P*) or within it are feasible. If resources are being fully used efficiently and other variables such as state policies remain constant, the society is operating on the *N-P* curve. It is called a trade-off curve because, once functioning on it, the rate of employment growth cannot be increased without giving up some degree of patriarchal power.[10]

Given levels of voter support are depicted by the V curves. Each curve represents a particular level of voter support, with higher curves (farther away from the origin) indicating greater support. Because each curve represents one level of voter support, it shows that there are various combinations of growth of employment and patriarchal policies that result in the same level of voter support. (See Appendix D for a mathematical representation of the V curves.) Graphically, state personnel reach the highest V curve, given resource constraints and the trade-offs involved, if they establish the set of policies where the N-P curve is just tangent to (just touches) a V curve.[11] All else constant, policies that generate this rate of growth of employment (N) and this degree of male domination (P) are both feasible and result in the greatest voter support possible.

Therefore, the graphic model presented in Figure 4.1, part 3 illustrates in a straightforward visual fashion the points developed regarding Irish state personnel: that state personnel have two primary goals; that these goals are contradictory and state personnel can face difficult trade-offs in facilitating employment growth while still trying to maintain traditional relations between the genders; and that they must either make difficult choices given these constraints or they must attempt to alter the terms of the trade-off.

In addition, as Robinson (1988) argues, the fact that elected officials are predominantly male has substantial impact on policy formation. (It should be noted that even though women constitute approximately half of the electorate, policies that maintain the family but also gender domination may still be sustained because to alter them may raise fears of damaging the institution of the family, which has some value for a substantial number of voters.)

In this new formulation, state policy can be a constraint that precludes the predictions of the main variants of economic theory regarding the incorporation of women into the labor force as economic growth or development occurs. State policies can alter the terms of the trade-off between economic growth and the reproduction of unequal relations between the sexes. For example, state employment policies can change the relationship between the rate of growth of employment and the female labor force participation rate (part 1 of Figure 4.1). Any policy that could restrict the access of women to employment would shift this curve to the right, meaning that a given LFPR would then be associated with a faster rate of employment growth. Correspondingly, the employment-patriarchy (N-P) transformation curve in part 3, Figure 4.1 would shift to the right. This would allow greater growth of employment at given

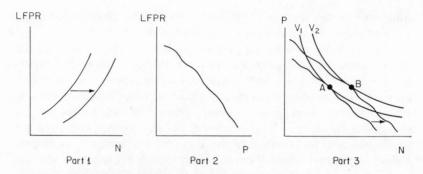

Figure 4.2   State-Induced Changes in the Relationships Underlying the Patriarchy-Growth of Employment Trade-Off, Ireland   (LFPR is the labor force participation rate of women; *N* is the growth of employment; *P* represents patriarchal relations; *V* curves are levels of voter support)

levels of patriarchal domination and would generate greater voter support.[12] (These types of shifts will be illustrated in Figure 4.2.)

This model can be used in the following surveys of employment, family, and reproductive rights policies in Ireland, indicating how they influenced the location of the trade-off possibilities. It can also be utilized to suggest how these trade-offs in Ireland compare to those in other countries.

Employment Policy

The first step in analyzing the impact of employment policies on women's roles in the Irish economy is to assess the attention given to provision of jobs to men or women in the general discussions of the problem of employment in Ireland. Once this overall perspective is presented, we can shift the focus to a range of policies that directly impact on women's employment. Particularly detailed attention is given to policies designed to promote the export-led development strategy. The contradictions arising between the dual goals of export-led growth and maintenance of traditional relations between the sexes and how they were handled are carefully examined. In addition, a brief survey of a variety of other discriminatory employment policies such as the marriage bar, training and apprenticeship programs, and protective legislation is presented.[13]

Women are only rarely mentioned in discussions of the unemployment problem in Ireland and are not referred to at all in the major government pronouncements establishing the development strategy.[14] These sources indicate interest in the provision of increased employment opportunities and the use of human capital, but there is no discussion of this by sex. It is only when more detailed publications of specific government agencies (such as the Industrial Development Authority [IDA]) are examined that employment issues are addressed by sex.

To the extent women are mentioned in the literature discussing unemployment and equality of opportunity, excerpts from Geary and Ó Muircheartaigh's *Equalization of Opportunity in Ireland: Statistical Aspects* (1974) published by the Economic and Social Research Council and Walsh's *The Unemployment Problem in Ireland* (1978) are representative of attitudes regarding women's relative qualifications and what labor market choices the authors think women are likely to make. In addition, they consider what might be best for society in terms of women's employment if unemployment is a problem and what solutions would then exist for women.[15]

On the one hand, *Equalization of Opportunity* focuses primarily on the issue of equalizing access to jobs and incomes in terms of socioeconomic status. Little attention is given to equal access by sex.[16] The authors acknowledge that "on average men have by far the better jobs, whether 'better' be adjudged by pay or by skill required to practice, or both" (19) even though women are better educated. However, they say "It remains to be seen if the situation is unfair to women. Fully free, they might opt for domesticity; i.e., regard the unpaid married state as the most desirable of all" (20). However, as we have seen in Chapter 3, there is evidence that this is not the case, that there were married women wanting to work.

Although this publication states:

> It is a positive good that married women should be free to take outside jobs should they wish to do so, good from the view point of society (i.e. efficiency), good for the woman herself,

they add

> Of course there are other considerations ... for instance, in an unemployment situation it may be judged expedient to sacrifice efficiency in the interest of what is judged a more equitable distribution of paid jobs. (22)

They acknowledge that it could be advantageous for married women and for society (in terms of efficiency) if they were free to take jobs in the paid labor force, but go on to say that in an unemployment situation, such efficiency should perhaps be sacrificed to obtain a more equitable distribution of jobs (i.e., that males get the jobs).

More revealing, the authors say

> The most heartening feature of Irish demography has been the in-
> crease in the marriage rate in recent years, after decades of stag-
> nation when this rate was notoriously by far the lowest in Europe
> and almost the lowest in the world. (15)

> The dramatic increase in the marriage rate over the past few years
> is . . . to be welcomed as opening up a great swathe of opportunity
> for many more women than formerly." (110)

In other words, in spite of the dramatic inequality they acknowledge
women face in access to jobs and income, the solution the authors of this
publication embrace for women is marriage (which has been associated
with their departure from paid employment) rather than efforts to alleviate job segregation and extend equal pay. They recognize that economic efficiency requires the incorporation of women in the labor force,
but ironically, their definition of equity is that males are given jobs.

On the other hand, Walsh (1978) briefly mentions the labor force
participation of married women in his discussion of policy options for
alleviating Ireland's unemployment problem.[17] He acknowledges that
certain policies, such as the income tax code and social welfare codes,
discriminate against the participation of married women. He continues,

> However appropriate it may appear in light of the unemployment
> problem among the young, it is obviously pointless from a social
> and political point of view to advocate imposing any further dis-
> incentives on married women's labour force participation. More-
> over, the point must be taken that what might be desirable is a re-
> duction in the number of multiple-earner households, not
> specifically in the number of working wives. (56)

Given the framework of family and employment policy, it is highly
unlikely that anyone but wives would be under pressure to remove
themselves from the labor force in the process of attaining fewer multi-
ple-earner households. Enactment of Walsh's policy suggestion would
have resulted in fewer married women in the labor force because of the
implicit social assumption that the employment of married women was
of less importance than employment of male breadwinners.[18]

Although it is acknowledged that women are more qualified and
that they are discriminated against, there is no more than the hope that
multiearner families will make choices appropriate to alleviating the unemployment problem. This literature reflects the prevailing notion that
marriage and the home are a very viable solution for occupying women.

Export-Led Development Strategy

Moving from the general discussion of employment/unemployment in Ireland to a more specific set of policies, we see that the strategies of the IDA did involve considerable emphasis on whether the employment it generated was for men or women. They wanted to provide male employment, even though an export-led development process typically used large percentages of female workers. As will be shown, the IDA developed and adapted its policies because of the contradictions that existed between the generation of employment growth and the maintenance of traditional relations between the sexes.

The way this developed began in the 1960s as the export-led development strategy started to undermine traditional gender relations by providing women employment. Foreign firms entering Ireland in the 1960s were said to prefer female workers (Donaldson, 1965; Stanton, 1978/1981:58, 60 – 63; Wickham, 1982:149). The first wave of foreign direct investment consisted largely of firms in the textiles and metals sectors. It was argued that women were preferred largely because of their lower wages. It was legal to pay female workers less than males until the end of 1975. Donaldson (1965) reports in the early 1960s that "wage rates normally run $29.50 to $36.50 per week for skilled adult men, and $23.60 to $29.50 for unskilled and semiskilled; skilled women receive $15 – $20 and unskilled $12 – $17. There is a 40 – 45 hour work week" (114).[19]

This preference of foreign firms for female employees is confirmed by two different databases compiled in the 1960s that indicate foreign firms hired greater proportions of women workers than domestic firms. Richard Stanton (1978) studied the export-processing zone at Shannon, Ireland, which consisted almost totally of small foreign-owned enterprises engaged in assembly or simple fabrication (12 – 20). Established in the late 1940s, it was the first export-processing zone in the world. Table 4.1 shows that the percentage of the workforce on the Shannon Industrial Estate that was female in the 1960s exceeded the percent female in the total Irish manufacturing workforce.

This was also the case on a countrywide basis for manufacturing. According to census data, women's share of manufacturing employment in 1966 was 31.8 percent. By contrast, information collected for the *Survey of Grant-Aided Industry* (1967) reveal that the percent female in grant-aided manufacturing industries was 40 percent (43). These grant-aided industries were largely foreign; in the 1960s, foreign firms received three-quarters of the funds dispersed under the IDA New Industries Program.

Further, as shown in Table 4.2, grant-aided firms hired larger percentages of women in every major manufacturing subsector than the

Table 4.1

Percent Female, Shannon Export-Processing Zone and Irish
Manufacturing, 1960–1971

	PERCENT FEMALE SHANNON INDUSTRIAL ESTATE	PERCENT FEMALE IRISH MANUFACTURING
1960	37	
1961	37	33.4
1962	38	
1963	47	
1964	43	
1965	46	
1966	45	31.8
1967	40	
1968	41	
1969	38	
1970	35	
1971	34	30.5

Source: Stanton, 1978: 13; *Census of Population of Ireland,* various years.

Table 4.2

Sex Composition of Grant-Aided and All Manufacturing Industries,
Ireland, 1966

SECTOR	FEMALE SHARE OF GRANT-AIDED INDUSTRIES	FEMALE SHARE OF ALL MANUFACTURING INDUSTRIES
Food	47.7	27.8
Drink and Tobacco	38.5	20.8
Textiles	59.1	51.6
Clothing and Footwear	82.6	71.2
Wood, Wood Products, Furniture	10.6	8.3
Paper and Printing	48.6	33.8
Chemicals	31.9	27.8
Clay, Cement	28.3	11.9
Metals, Engineering	27.8	15.5
Other Manufacturing	33.1	31.6

Source: Farley, 1972:19. (Based on data in *Census of Population of Ireland, 1966* and *Survey of Grant-Aided Industry,* 1967.)

average for the sector as a whole (Farley, 1972:19). The probability that this could occur (i.e., that the percent female in foreign firms would exceed the percent female in domestic firms) if for any individual sector it was equally probable that the percent female in domestic firms could be above or below the percent female in foreign firms, is .00098. There was a significant difference in the hiring preferences of foreign and domestic firms.[20]

In terms of the trade-off between growth of employment and male domination, the events of the 1960s suggest that the increase in the growth of employment accompanying export-led development would result in a weakening of male domination as women gained employment opportunities.

However, in 1969 a major reorganization of the Industrial Development Authority resulted in a more sophisticated promotional strategy to attract foreign investment and generate economic growth that could potentially circumvent such an adverse movement. The IDA formulated a set of economic and social criteria according to which proposed industrial projects would be evaluated and financial incentives awarded at the discretion of the IDA.[21] Included in these objectives was an explicit position regarding the sex composition of the new employment. The *IDA Annual Report 1971/72* stated:

> We are currently selecting industrial development candidates which will produce goods employing predominantly *men*, have low capital intensity, use local raw materials, have rapid growth potential, and a low probability of technological obsolescence (emphasis mine) (27).[22]

The IDA continued to exhibit an explicit interest in the proportions of male jobs created via their New Industry grants in annual reports through the first half of the 1970s. They also defined "predominantly men." Their *Annual Report 1970/71* specified: "In economic terms, the needs are for 11,000 direct jobs to be taken up each year in manufacturing industry, of which over 75 percent should be for men" (15). The *IDA Annual Report 1972/73* stated that they approved new industry grants during the previous year with a job potential of 10,303, 75 percent of which were male jobs (12). They expressed satisfaction: "The male/female balance was in line with our target."[23] This preference for males was widely announced. The IDA placed a 20-page advertisement in the March 1975 *Fortune*. Near the beginning, in discussing "Ireland — Incentives for Industry in a Changing Land," it states, "The prime criterion is to provide stable jobs for Irish-men."

O'Neill (1972), who at the time was an executive director of the IDA, explains how these economic and social objectives are attained. IDA policy was to locate

> industrial projects which yield a high national economic benefit in relation to the investment involved. A ranking of projects on this basis does not necessarily correspond to a ranking on the basis of commercial profitability. New industrial projects are rated on the ... major indicators of economic benefit (42).[24]

He explains the process of ranking projects:

> Quantified versions of these indicators provide the framework through which the IDA's project selection process is conducted in its initial stages. A project having a high rating on all of these criteria does not necessarily have higher commercial profitability than one with low ratings on all of the criteria. However, the project with high ratings would obviously attract larger incentives per unit of investment since it would deliver higher national economic benefit (42).

Provision of male employment is deemed an industrial objective which may override the imperatives of commercial profitability (IDA, *Annual Report*, 1973–1977). O'Neill (1972) provides an example of this evaluation process and illustrates how funds for economic development are utilized to further broaden social goals such as provision of male employment:

> For example, an export-based project involving a product which is at the growth stage of a long life cycle, employs 80 percent *male* workers of medium skill, and uses Irish raw materials, would attract a higher level of incentive than a *female*-employing, export-based project with a low skill content and using imported materials—even though both projects have the same prospective rate of return on capital employed (42).

He acknowledges that this process is discriminatory.

> It follows from this discrimination on grounds of economic benefit that it is incorrect to regard the IDA's financial incentives solely as a means of generating projects in which to utilize national resources of capital and labour. Incentives are also the vehicle for the promotion of a product policy for industrial growth. Variations in

the rate of incentives to new industrial projects are a key method by which the overall pattern of new industrial expansion is made to conform with national development needs, such as a high *male* content in new job creation, stability and permanence of employment, and use of local raw materials (emphasis mine) (42–43).[25]

Evidence that selectivity was exercised appears in another *Annual Report* (1974):

> The process of selectivity in relation to new industries which we sought to attract to Ireland was further refined during the year. For example, in the textile sector, one in four of the inquiries generated from overseas firms were not pursued by IDA because they did not meet the criteria which IDA employs in screening new industrial proposals (3–4).

Since the "textiles" sector was a major employer of women, this lack of IDA effort would impact negatively on female employment.

The majority of the growth accompanying the export-led development strategy occurred in a social and economic framework designed to provide largely male employment (the 1970s were the decade in which there was growth in total employment and which experienced the largest inflow of foreign firms). The effectiveness of the IDA in achieving the goal of providing largely male employment (and therefore its impact on women's employment opportunities) can be examined in three ways: by an analysis of the percent female in the projects approved in the 1970s, by examination of data from a 1974 profile of grant-aided industry, and by surveying unpublished data from the IDA describing the workforces of foreign grant-aided and domestic grant-aided, 1973–1981.

An analysis of data in IDA *Annual Reports* for the five-year period 1970 through 1974, presented in Table 4.3, indicates that the IDA kept to its guidelines.[26] Males constituted 74 percent of the projected full employment labor force of all projects approved during this period. The female share of new employment (26 percent) was well under the female share of all manufacturing (30.5 percent in 1971 and 29.5 percent in 1975). This was a distinct reversal of the pattern of IDA approvals during both the 1952–1970 period[27] (also shown in Table 4.3), and the 1960s [when the female share in grant-aided firms (40 percent) had exceeded the female share of manufacturing (31.8 percent)].

Information collected in 1974 for an IDA analysis of grant-aided industry indicates that the tendency observed in the 1960s (for grant-aided industries to hire a larger percentage of women than the national

Table 4.3

Sex Composition of IDA-Approved Industrial Projects, Ireland, 1952–1970 and 1970–1974

| YEAR[1] | PROJECTED NEW JOBS AT FULL EMPLOYMENT[2] | ACTUAL NEW JOBS | | |
		TOTAL	OF WHICH FEMALE	% FEMALE
1970–71	12,487	12,800	2,600	20.3
1971–72	8,734	6,500	1,900	29.2
1972–73	14,139	11,742	2,933	25.0
1973–74	23,316	20,640[3]	5,676	27.5
to Dec. 1974	19,818	17,877[3]	5,080	28.4
Total 1970–74	78,494	69,559	18,189	26.1
Total 1952–70	68,208	70,400	25,800	36.6

Source: Compiled from data in IDA *Annual Report,* various years.
[1]Financial years, April 1 to March 31.
[2]According to the *Annual Report, 1974—Review of 1970–74,* Section 4, p. 4.
[3]The number accounted for by sex is below the total because of the omission of data for the MidWest region from the *Annual Report.*

Table 4.4

Sex Composition of New Industry and All Manufacturing Industries, Ireland, 1973

SECTOR	FEMALE SHARE OF NEW INDUSTRY	FEMALE SHARE OF ALL MANUFACTURING INDUSTRIES
Food	22.4	26.8
Drink and Tobacco	16.3	22.1
Textiles	46.5	47.4
Clothing and Footwear	67.7	66.7
Wood, Wood Products, Furniture	11.1	11.2
Paper and Printing	32.5	30.2
Chemicals	22.7	24.2
Clay, Cement	12.8	12.7
Metals, Engineering	23.2	21.3
Other Manufacturing	23.8	27.1

Source: Calculated from unpublished data provided by McAleese, 1977b.

average in every sector) had been eliminated (McAleese, 1977b).

As shown in Table 4.4, there was no longer a clear difference between the sex composition of the labor forces in new industry and all industry. There were only three sectors in which the percent female in new industry exceeded the percent female in the national average for each sector.[28] Although the categories are defined differently (grant-aided in 1967 in comparison to new industry in 1974), they are comparable.[29]

The low proportion of female employment in the projects approved, 1970–1974, and the elimination of the distinct differences in the percent female employed by foreign industry vis-à-vis the Irish average suggest that during this period, IDA policy was effective in fulfilling its commitment to providing "predominantly male" employment. The overall female share of new industry was reduced to 29 percent from its level of 40 percent (percent female in grant-aided) in 1967, placing it in line with the overall proportion of women in Irish manufacturing (29.5 percent in 1975).

The effect of IDA policy specifying the provision of male employment on the trade-off between the growth of employment and maintenance of traditional familial relations (the N-P curve) can be depicted in Figure 4.2. As shown in part 1, IDA policy altered the relationship between the female labor force participation rate and the growth of employment in a manner adverse for women because, although it promoted increases in employment, the jobs were largely for males. This resulted in shifting the curve in part 1 to the right, because now a given rate of growth of employment is associated with a lower female labor force participation. This in turn shifted the N-P trade-off curve to the right, allowing a greater growth in employment for a given level of patriarchy. Because of this type of policy, state personnel were able to increase the growth of employment for a period of time without undermining male domination, as normally would have happened.

However, data from the unpublished IDA Employment Survey suggest that the control of the IDA over the sex composition of the employment provided by foreign firms weakened in the latter half of the 1970s.[30] Figure 4.3 shows that the female share of the foreign grant-aided work force exceeded that of the domestic grant-aided in all years and that since 1975, the gap between these has widened, from 3.6 percentage points to more than ten. The percent female in the foreign grant-aided rose to 36 percent in 1981 and the percent female in domestic grant-aided fell to under 26 percent. (It also reveals the growing importance of foreign firms in providing manufacturing employment, rising from 22 percent of manufacturing employment in 1973 to over 30 percent in 1981.)

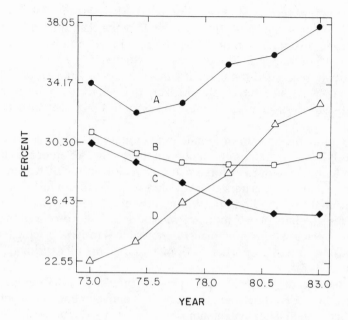

A   % of the foreign grant-aided work force which is female
B   % of all industrial work force which is female
C   % of the domestic grant-aided work force which is female
D   % of industrial employment which is in foreign grant-
    aided firms

Figure 4.3   Percent Female in the Foreign Grant-Aided Work force, Domestic Grant-Aided Work force, and All Industry, Ireland, 1973–1981   (Source: IDA Employment Survey, 1983)

Further detailed investigation of subsectors is presented in Table 4.5. It lists the top 20 foreign grant-aided industries in descending order of the total number of women employed.[31] A comparison of the percent female in the foreign grant-aided with the percent female in domestic grant-aided for the entire period shows that in three-quarters of the sectors the percent female in foreign grant-aided exceeded that of domestic grant-aided for all of the years involved.[32]

This erosion of IDA control over the sex composition of new employment can be explained as follows. By the latter part of the 1970s, there is evidence that the IDA recognized the contradictions arising between their employment-generation efforts and other state policies regarding women (and within their efforts to engineer male employment growth). They generated a difficult trade-off the Irish government had

Table 4.5

Female Share of Foreign Grant-Aided and Domestic Grant-Aided
Industry, Ireland, 1973–1981

NACE SECTORS	% FOREIGN	1973		1981	
	1981	PPFGA	PFDGA	PFFGA	PFDGA
Electrical Engineering	63.8	43.8	38.8	50.8	29.6
Computer/Office Machinery	80.4	62.7	58.7	49.7	36.1
Healthcare Products	92.0	35.3	0.0	54.7	18.2
Metal Products	23.3	20.8	13.5	20.7	9.9
Textiles	45.5	35.5	38.3	20.0	37.7
Pharmaceutical Chemicals	76.2	39.6	22.9	26.9	37.6
Clothing	22.6	83.6	78.1	84.5	78.9
Alcoholic Beverages	54.8	18.9	13.6	17.1	13.2
Chocolate and Sugar Confection	46.7	50.8	22.8	42.2	22.3
Rubber Products	76.1	17.6	12.1	16.8	12.9
Mechanical Engineering	48.6	11.7	9.0	10.3	10.7
Motor Vehicles and Parts	41.2	10.8	8.5	17.8	8.4
Plastic Products	48.5	22.2	29.9	27.9	20.9
Chemical, Oil, Tar	34.4	9.1	11.8	11.9	10.6
Man-made Fibers	97.2	14.7	9.1	19.3	3.1
Toys, Sports, and Instruments	49.9	60.0	31.3	53.6	38.8
Other Means of Transport	56.8	7.1	4.3	5.4	5.4
Other Food	43.4	44.8	28.4	39.9	38.5
Footwear	34.4	55.8	50.8	58.3	52.1
Instrument Engineering	71.4	36.2	29.5	57.4	29.0

Source: Compiled from information in the IDA Employment Survey, 1973–1983
(unpublished).
% Foreign = the percent of employment in the sector in foreign firms; PFFGA =
percent (of the workplace which is) female in foreign grant-aided firms; PFDGA =
percent female in domestic grant-aided firms.

to face. Foreign firms likely to locate in Ireland were in industries that
hired substantial numbers of female workers. To the extent the IDA
specified provision of male employment, the influx of foreign capital
would likely be dampened and the growth of employment would be restricted. But to abandon the specification of male employment could enhance the growth of female employment, undermining traditional relations between the sexes.

The trade-offs were difficult since the legitimacy of the government depended on generation of employment and preserving the male-
dominated structure of society. IDA personnel were aware of the critical

importance of generating large yearly tallies of new employment. Provision of employment opportunities was a major political issue in this labor surplus economy, with its increasing population of working age. In addition, there was substantial expense involved in the extensive financial incentives program to attract foreign investment. The IDA had to present detailed annual reports and was increasingly held accountable for funds spent and employment generated.

It became evident that to attract foreign capital, the engine of employment generation, more was needed than the handsome financial incentives packages offered by the IDA. Foreign firms needed freedom to hire the type of workers they preferred. The IDA recognized that certain state policies designed to preserve traditional roles between the sexes were hindering its efforts to stimulate the growth of employment and the accumulation process. The choice was clear. In order to prevent a stalling of the export-led development process and engender employment growth, IDA personnel were forced to reverse their explicit position regarding women.

For example, in 1978, it lobbied for the repeal of protective legislation prohibiting night work for women, arguing that it had "proved to be a serious problem for us in our promotional work abroad in relation to female employing industries such as electronics and textiles" (Employment Equality Agency, 1978:29). It realized that its bargaining position in an increasingly competitive international environment was being impaired by the restrictions placed on the employment of women.

In addition, beginning with the *Annual Report* for 1975 the IDA dropped the provision of predominantly male employment from its list of objectives and no longer reported the number of jobs at full employment in approved projects by sex.[33] In 1979, even housewives were acknowledged as a source of employees for foreign firms by the IDA. An IDA survey of the recruitment pattern and age structure of the work force in new industry indicated that housewives were about 8 percent of the labor force for new industries (IDA, *Annual Report*, 1979:2).

However, in spite of the recognition by the IDA in the later 1970s that explicit policies limiting the availability of the female labor force were to their disadvantage in generating new employment, it continued to pursue the goal of provision of male employment on an *ad hoc* and informal manner as the individual situation allowed. For example, Stanton (1978/1981) cites an IDA executive who in 1977 described "resolute bargaining by the Authority to persuade a new investor, proposing a 90 percent female workforce, to cut this percentage" (66).

Even in the early 1980s, the head of an IDA office in the United States stated in an interview that the financial incentives structures at that time were flexible, and more benefits would be offered a prospective investor if the project fit certain criteria, one of which was the proposed sex of the workforce. According to this official, all other things equal, a company proposing to hire more males would be offered more than one seeking largely female employees (1982 interview with the author). The procedure outlined by O'Neill in 1972 was still utilized in the early 1980s.

The overall effect of such *ad hoc* procedures can be best gauged by comparisons of the percent female in foreign grant-aided firms in the key sectors in Ireland to the percent female in foreign firms in these same sectors in other export-led countries. Unfortunately, the information available along these lines internationally is limited; data exists in comparable form only for the electronics labor force.[34]

Results of a 1981 survey by Wickham and Murray (1983) indicate that 72 percent of non-craft production workers in the Irish electronics industry are women, while 51 percent of the total work force in this sector is female. Evidence from other countries indicates this is low. For example, Grunwald and Flamm (1985) have shown that 82 percent of electronics production workers in Mexico in 1980 were female. The proportion is even higher in Malaysia. Grossman (1980) indicates that 90 percent of assembly workers in electronics plants in Penang are women.[35] (In all cases, the production units referred to were largely foreign owned.)

This suggests that the IDA desire to provide largely male employment, although weakened somewhat in the late 1970s by the imperatives of promoting the development process, were relatively effective. It is likely that informal IDA pressures dampened the tendencies of foreign firms in many of these industries to hire large proportions of females.

In conclusion, the demand for female workers was not simply the outcome of the process of export-led development in a competitive economy. It was shaped by structural constraints placed on the development process by state policy rather than by market forces. The experience of the 1960s indicated that export-led growth would enhance female employment opportunities and weaken male domination. However, the political economy of Ireland was more complex than a competitive economy; state personnel interested in perpetuating their tenure needed to promote job opportunities while maintaining traditional familial relations and designed policies to these ends. In the 1970s, the decade of major employment growth, they were able to alter the trade-off possibilities between the growth rate of employment and patriarchal domination (the *N-P* curve) by developing policies that specified provision of male employment. This was designed to ensure that the export-led development strategy would not undermine male domination.

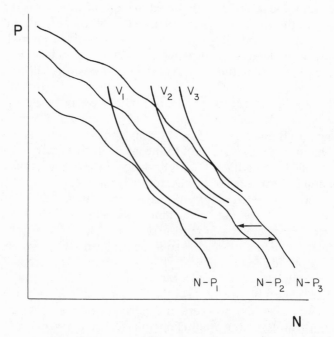

Figure 4.4   Shifts in the Patriarchy-Growth of Employment Trade-off, Ireland in the 1970s   (LFPR is the labor force participation rate of women; N is the growth of employment; P represents patriarchal relations; V curves are levels of voter support)

As shown in Figure 4.4, from the point of view of state personnel, this improved the terms of the trade-off by shifting the N-P curve to the right (for example, N-P_1 to N-P_3). This permitted greater employment growth without eroding male domination.

By the late 1970s, the contradictions between the two major policies had intensified. IDA personnel realized their efforts to increase employment growth were hampered by constraints on the availability of female workers. However, although they had to defer to the fundamental need for net new employment and eliminate some explicitly discriminatory policy, they were still able to influence the sex composition of the labor force in foreign firms via *ad hoc* bargaining and discretionary use of funds. The fact that they had to alter some policies may have allowed more female labor force participation at given levels of employment growth. The N-P curve would correspondingly shift slightly to the left, although not back to its original position (i.e., as from N-P_3 to N-P_2). This would mean that, compared to the first part of the 1970s, a given level of employment growth could now be attained only by reducing the level of male domination slightly.

Marriage Bar/Training and Apprenticeships/Protective Legislation

In addition to the development strategy, other Irish employment policies, such as the marriage bar, training and apprenticeship programs, and protective legislation, sharply curtailed women's access to employment during most of this period. These ensured a better trade-off between the growth of employment and maintenance of traditional relations between the sexes than would exist in the absence of these policies (i.e., they allowed a greater growth of employment without sacrificing traditional familial relations).

Marriage Bar/Maternity Leave. The marriage bar meant that "in general, females employed in clerical jobs in service industries, banks, local authorities and semi-state bodies are required to resign from their employment on marriage" (*Commission on the Status of Women*, 1972: para. 252). This practice was mimicked by some private sector employers.[36]

Since the service sector was the major source of employment for women in Ireland (62 percent of females employed in 1961 and 75 percent in 1981 were in the service sector, with one-third and two-fifths of these in the public sector in these respective years), the marriage bar limited a broad arena of opportunities to a certain type of worker: single women or males. (A married woman could only be reinstated in cases of hardship, meaning where she could prove desertion).

Estimation of the impact of the marriage bar is difficult because its removal occurred over a period of four years, 1973–1977. In 1973 it was rescinded for the Civil Service and it was later removed by the Local Authorities and Health Authorities. In 1977 the Employment Equality Act (effective July 1977) made it unlawful to discriminate on the grounds of sex or marital status in recruitment for employment, conditions of employment, in training, or in work experience, or in opportunities for promotion (*Progress Report*, 1976:8–9). However, any sudden changes in the labor force participation rate of married women during these years which were unattributable to other sources could indicate its adverse influence in former years. As shown in Table 2.6, the participation rate of married women doubled from 1971 to 1975, jumping from 7.5 percent to 14.5 percent. Since this sharp response was not the result of demographic changes, it is likely that it reflected the termination of this constraint on the labor force participation of married women.

In addition, in situations where the marriage bar was not operative, married women's access to employment was controlled by the "baby bar." Female employees who remained at work after marriage were terminated when requiring maternity leave. There were no economywide legal provisions that would ensure women the right to adequate leave of absence for maternity and guaranteed right to reinstatement in the original employment. Very little progress was made in this area during this period. It was only in 1977 that a provision was enacted whereby a women dismissed for pregnancy could sue for redress. The plea by the Commission to extend even the very small maternity benefits for women under compulsory insurance (which apply to only a limited number of workers) to twelve weeks did not get past discussion during these years.

It has been pointed out that equal employment opportunity legislation that has been enacted (such as the Employment Equality Act and the Unfair Dismissals Act) will mean little to women without provisions to ensure maternity leave and reinstatement (*Second Progress Report*, 1978:10). This suggests that the absence of state policy in specific cases can have as negative an impact on women's employment as the existence of other items of legislation. In this case the lack of legislation regarding maternity leave impeded the supply of labor decision in much the same way as the presence of the marriage bar did. Women's labor force participation decisions were influenced by the absence of a legal guarantee that they could bear a child and return to the same job within a reasonable time without loss of job, seniority, and benefits.

Training and Apprenticeships.   Job training was needed to promote economic growth by increasing worker productivity, providing workers equipped with skills needed to attract foreign firms, and to cope with displacement of workers from traditional industry (Wickham, 1982). Women were being displaced from employment with the decline of the agricultural sector and the textile industry in addition to displacement occurring because of adverse changes in sex ratios in many sectors. However, although both men and women were affected by economic restructuring, it was chiefly male workers who were trained/retooled during most of this 20-year period.

The establishment of training programs for women dragged even under pressure from the Commission on the Status of Women. In 1973 less than 1 percent of AnCO trainees were women (Wickham, 1982). Although the percent female in training programs finally rose to 32 percent in 1979 (29 percent in 1980), the largest proportion of women were enrolled in traditional female occupations such as clerical work, hairdressing, and office procedures (*Equality for Women*, 1980). In 1980 the female share in traditionally male courses was only 10 percent (AnCO, 1980).

Throughout most of this period it was virtually impossible for women to become apprentices. Under pressure from the Commission on the Status of Women, access to apprenticeships was finally opened; but in 1980 only 50 of the 13,680 trainees were female apprentices.[37]

Protective Legislation. The two major types of protective legislation that restricted women's access to industrial positions were the ban on night work for women and the weight-lifting provision. The latter affected women in the clothing sector. Women were prohibited from lifting weights exceeding 16 kilos while employment regulations for "general workers" specified the ability to lift such amounts. The former became an issue in the textiles and electronics sectors as shift work became important (Employment Equality Agency, 1978). Evidence that night work legislation had a negative impact on the demand for female labor came from the IDA. Their testimony in hearings to rescind this policy indicated that, without this ban, their ability to attract foreign investment would be enhanced, suggesting that greater female employment opportunities could have been provided.

For example, the ban's negative impact on female employment in textiles has been documented by case studies. The decline in the textile industry had been countered by rationalization. Foreign firms imported technologically advanced processes that necessitated substantial investment and which for cost-efficiency were run on shifts. In 1981 McCarthy studied two large new firms in the textile industry. In the first, a cotton texturing and weaving plant, women constituted 3 percent of the work force and were employed only in clerical functions. She found that the rotation for production work included seven units of night work per 28-day cycle, effectively excluding women. In the second, a synthetic fiber firm, women were one-quarter of the work force. They were restricted from night shift and from jobs in the fiber plant, and were employed solely in the spinning operation and in administration (European Foundation, 1982).

Research by Harris documents the movement of men into what have been considered "women's jobs" in textile firms in County Mayo. She contends that this occurred because there were few jobs for men in these areas and due to the restriction on night work (1983).

To summarize, the marriage bar and protective legislation are examples of how a policy can constrain labor market choices of both firms and individuals/households. With respect to the marriage bar, for almost two-thirds of the period under study, the labor supply decision of many women was curtailed. Married women, whether with children under 18 or not, could not freely choose to supply themselves to this type of employer. Similarly, employers in the public sector and an unknown number of private sector enterprises were not able either to retain women after marriage or employ older women desiring to reenter the labor force.[38]

In like fashion, by precluding women from jobs that operate around-the-clock and from particular job categories, protective legislation clearly reduced the demand for female labor and restricted women's employment opportunities. In making their decision to enter the labor market (particularly in rural areas where many of these firms located and where alternative employment opportunities were limited) women knew that these types of job openings could not be attained and did not offer themselves. Evidence exists that in many such areas women were seeking employment.

Also, it appears that the bias toward providing largely male jobs, expressed by the IDA, permeated AnCO during most of these years. Rather than reshaping the supply of labor (both males and females) with the skills necessary to fulfill the needs for labor in new and restructured industries, the training facility continued to reinforce the traditional roles for women.[39]

Family Law and Reproductive Rights Legislation

Similarly, a broad range of family law and reproductive rights legislation reinforced and reproduced male domination in the Irish household, sustaining it against forces generated by the export-led development process that could seriously erode it. These unequal gender relations in turn limited women's freedom to choose to enter the labor force. In addition, this was reinforced or supplemented by at least two other types of state policy, the income tax code and child-care policy. Only minor modifications, rather than any substantive changes, were made in these policies during this period in Ireland. Persistence of these types of state policies precluded the alteration in the growth of employment-patriarchy trade-off that was occurring in other countries as such legislation was eroded. In these other nations the *N-P* curve shifted left, indicating that a given rate of growth of employment was now associated with a weaker form of male domination.

The structure of the Irish legal system during this period placed married women in positions of subordination to their husbands.[40] Marriage curtailed the rights of women and their range of choice regarding their lives. It was considered appropriate that a husband had primacy in household decision-making, deciding where and how his family might live. Exit from marriage was extremely difficult. Divorce was illegal throughout this period; state financial support in the cases of desertion was not easily obtained; laws regarding abuse in marriage, particularly sexual abuse, gave women little to no protection. Further, all women faced few options in exercising control over biological reproduction. Abortion was illegal and access to contraceptives was limited throughout this period.

This, in conjunction with the aspects of economic subordination of women just reviewed (the limited employment opportunities resulting from the marriage bar, the desire of the IDA to provide male employment, and the paucity of training opportunities) and further economic constraints to be discussed (income tax code and lack of child care) ensured that Irish married women remained in an unequal position in the household. They were legally subordinate and economically dependent. For those few married women working, both the low remuneration (resulting from lower pay for equal work which was legal until 1976 and occupational segregation), and the provisions of the income tax code (taxing married women's income at a higher marginal rate) ensured their economic inequality.

The ultimately powerful position of the husband in household decision-making has been described as follows by the Commission on the Status of Women (1972):

> There is a presumption in law that where a husband and wife are living together, the wife has authority to contract on his behalf in all matters concerning the supply of necessaries for the husband, herself and the household. The goods and services so contracted for must be suitable in kind, sufficient in quantity and necessary in fact according to the conditions in which *the husband chooses his wife and family shall live*. In deciding what are necessaries of life, the criterion is not primarily the husband's means but the standard at which *he decides* his family shall live. Where the husband supplies the wife with necessaries or with the money to buy them he has the power to cancel the authority of his wife to contract on his behalf or to pledge his credit.

The Commission describes the economic roles of the husband and wife and the distribution of benefits among family members from them under common law during this period:

> The day's work of a housewife looking after children at home is fully committed to the purposes of the family and the Constitution recognises this. The day's work of the husband in earning an income is on the other hand, in the eyes of the law, committed to the purposes of the family only to the limited extent outlined

above. He has the right to profit fully from his wife's work at home. She, in the eyes of the law, can claim from the profits of his work only necessaries plus such further addition to the family's standard of living as *he — not she — may decide.* (emphasis mine) (174)

In addition, although the Constitution specified the desirability of a woman working in the home, the legal system has not guaranteed her equal input into decisions regarding its disposition nor any claim to a portion of its value. The Married Women's Status Act of 1957 established the right of women to own property and enter contractual agreements, but the family residence continued to be owned typically by the male, who could dispose of it and its contents without the consent of his wife. The issue was not addressed until, under pressure from the Commission on the Status of Women, the Family Home Protection Act was enacted in 1976. It prevented the sale of the family home without the consent of the wife, but still guaranteed her no portion of its value unless it could be shown that she had contributed toward home payments.

Compounding this lack of power in household decision-making, Irish wives had few options legally or economically in the event of marital breakdown. For example, if the husband became abusive, it wasn't until the late 1970s that the wife had even limited legal recourse. (He could be barred from the home for up to three months if she or the children were in danger, but the police did not have the power to arrest a husband violating this order.) There was no relief for marital sexual abuse. Marriage presumes the right of the husband to sexual relations; therefore he could not be prosecuted for raping his wife.[41]

If the husband deserted the wife and children, she had to prove desertion to obtain social benefits, which was often difficult. Before 1971 a deserted wife could receive only £4 per week support if she could obtain a maintenance order against her husband in the District Court. The Social Welfare Act, 1970, made public funds available after six months to deserted wives who fulfilled certain conditions: passage of a means test and demonstration that she had made "reasonable efforts within the means available to her to trace her husband and to secure support and maintenance from him" (Commission on the Status of Women, 1972:181–182). The amount available through the maintenance order was increased in 1971 to £15 per week for the wife and up to £5 per week for a child. The restrictiveness of the conditions was somewhat eased in 1974 (*Second Progress Report*, 1978:25). See also O'Higgins

'he problem of desertion was often compounded by the issue of
 '. "Wives, minors and lunatics are given the domicile of depen-
 Martin, 1977:91). The domicile of a married women is that of

her husband, even if he has deserted and moved abroad. This has adverse implications for married women in terms of nullity, divorce, illegitimacy, succession, and inheritance. For example, the Irish courts have upheld an English divorce awarded to an Irishman residing in England while his wife was in Ireland. The second wife was considered the legal wife, eliminating any claim of the first to his property. However, a similar case involving an Irish women obtaining a divorce in England was not upheld by Irish courts. Her children from the second marriage were considered illegitimate (*Progress Report on the Implementation of the Recommendations in the Report of the Commission on the Status of Women*, 1976:70).

Divorce is illegal in Ireland according to the Constitution.[42] The only legal recourse available in Ireland is to obtain an annulment, a divorce granted by the High Court based on adultery or cruelty or a separation deed. The first two are expensive and time-consuming and, under the terms of the latter, neither party can remarry during the lifetime of the other. English divorces may be recognized under certain conditions but acceptance of them in Ireland can be arbitrary and discriminatory. (Divorce was a controversial issue in the 1980s. A referendum to amend the Constitution to allow a slow-paced form of divorce was held in June, 1986. It was rejected by 63 percent of the voters [Mahon, 1987; Prendiville, 1988].)

In short, women and their dependents were particularly vulnerable economically in cases of marital breakdown, much more so than men. The problems women experienced through most of this period in obtaining financial support (public assistance or maintenance from the husband) were intensified by discriminatory employment policies.

Compounding this network of legal inequalities that maintained male domination in the household, all women, married or not, encountered government legislation that limited their control over biological reproduction and/or curtailed their sexual freedom. Access to contraceptives was limited. Even in the late 1970s it was illegal to advertise or import contraceptives for sale; they could be imported for personal use only. There were only six family planning clinics in the Republic, three of which were in Dublin (Martin, 1977:125). Although the Family Planning Act of 1979 allowed contraceptives to be sold, it was only by a physician's prescription and only to married couples for bona fide family planning purposes (Mahon, 1987).

Abortions are illegal in Ireland. (It is now prohibited by a 1983 Constitutional amendment that was approved by the electorate after a year of bitter debate [Barry, 1988; Mahon, 1987].) However, they were available in England for those able to make the trip. The range of legal and reproductive options varied by the woman's class position. The more advantaged had much better access to travel to England for divorce, abortions, or contraceptives. Between 1967 and 1976, 11,132 abortions in the United Kingdom were performed on women from both parts of Ireland, 6159 of whom said they were from the Republic.[43]

Unmarried women had even more limited access to contraception than married, as marriage was the prerequisite condition before the physician could prescribe or the druggist could provide contraceptives. Any children unmarried women bore faced the legal status of illegitimacy.[44] Their welfare benefits were limited and many were forced to obtain any available employment. Income had to be concealed to prevent reduction of social benefits. The problem of obtaining housing was reportedly acute and they faced the lack of child-care facilities (*Singled Out*, 1983 passim). The implicit message was that sexual relations were only for the married. Any woman operating outside of these mores would face potentially severe social stigmatization. The inconsistency between the low Social Welfare allowance and the constitutional pledge to secure the place of the mother in the home indicated that the constitution was "protecting" a certain type of mother: a married mother (Robinson, 1988).

This survey of family and reproductive rights legislation provides insight into two of the issues raised near the end of Chapter 3. It reveals why fertility rates remained so high in Ireland during this period of social change and, more broadly, why the compelling feminist explanation for the low female participation rates is a key component of our understanding of the failure of women's labor force activity to rise.

With respect to fertility rates, in light of the legal structure regarding reproductive rights and male perogatives in the household in Ireland, it would be logical to conclude that the Irish fertility rate was the highest among Western European OECD countries largely because of state policy. Fertility was high because of the limited options for controlling reproduction (based on state policies that constrain access to reproductive options) and the overall dominance of the male in the household (which was reinforced by state policy). Given the right of the husband to sexual relations and the limited birth control options, male domination translates into high fertility rates. In turn, these high rates augment inequality in the household by increasing the wife's workload in home duties and child care.

This is also the case with respect to the very different profiles of fertility change in Ireland versus in Singapore during these years. In Ireland fertility fell very little (3.8 to 3.3), while in Singapore births per woman fell from six to under two. Quite in contrast to this overview of state policy regarding reproductive options in Ireland, the Singapore state had established family planning programs which were found to be instrumental in substantially reducing fertility (Fawcett and Khoo, 1980; Salaff, 1985).[45]

At a broader level, it was argued in Chapter 3 that the patriarchal household impacted adversely on the labor force participation of married women directly via the powerful overall position of the male in household decision making and indirectly via high fertility rates. (See Figure 3.2.) This was shown to be the case in Ireland but the explanation was critiqued for its inability to explain the persistence of male domination during economic and social changes generated by export-led growth. This section has revealed that the persistence of male domination in the household (and therefore both of these impacts) during this period of economic and social change likely to erode it can be attributed to state policy—family law and reproductive rights legislation.

The direct importance of the husband's preferences in the labor force participation decision of the wife has been shown to be based on legal and economic inequality in the household, which has placed the female in a materially disadvantaged position. Further, it can be argued that most Irish males have directly opposed rather than supported the employment of married women on a number of grounds. First, as stated in the Constitution, women are believed to contribute to social welfare by their role in the home, performing housekeeping and child-care duties. For them to do otherwise implied neglect of these critical duties. Secondly, married women in the labor force would compete with males for the relatively scarce employment opportunities. There are two further unstated dimensions to male opposition to female employment. It has been argued that the employment of women/wives lessens their economic dependence on men and weakens male domination by providing women options in addition to entering or continuing a marriage. Lastly, because of sexual mores, a husband could be reluctant to have his wife working for another male.

With respect to the indirect impact of the patriarchal household on the labor force activity of married women illustrated in Figure 3.2, the results in this section suggest it was perpetuated by the combination of this state-reinforced male domination in the household and the restricted legal access to contraception.

However, there are at least two more types of state policy (or lack thereof) that must be examined for their impact on female labor supply — the income tax code and child-care policies. Particular formulations of these policies can either reinforce male domination in the household and therefore impact negatively on female labor supply in this indirect manner or directly constrain female labor supply even if male domination in a particular household is weaker and the male does not oppose his wife's employment.

The income tax code, until its revision in 1980, discriminated against the participation of married women in wage work. According to the Finance Acts, the income of a married woman was considered for tax purposes as the income of her husband (Commission on the Status of Women, 1978:55), therefore added to his income and taxed according to the schedule for marrieds, which moved them more rapidly into higher tax brackets. Any two-worker couple whose income exceeded 2,000 Irish pounds a year would have been taxed more than if they were single and living together in the same household (Commission of the European Community, 1974:42).

Therefore, for all but the last year of the period under study, a married woman making a labor force participation decision looked at a net return that was substantially reduced by being taxed at the couple's higher marginal tax rate. This, in combination with the evidence that women's earnings are substantially less than men's, resulted in a small relative return to the woman's employment. (This can be diminished further by the cost of child care and lack of tax allowance for such services.) Since the remuneration involved in paid employment is a critical factor in a labor force participation decision, it also acts to depress female labor supply.

In addition, provision for child care was lacking. Throughout this period the Health Board provided a small number of centers with partial funding only for those children in serious need. Even in 1981 only 3 percent of preschool children of working parents were cared for in day-care centers or preschools. The rest were cared for in their homes or other homes, possibly by relatives, with very few experiencing any educational or developmental program.

Studies based on random sample interviews during these years revealed that child care was one of the critical limitations faced by nonworking mothers expressing a desire to return to work. In a survey conducted in 1971 by Walsh and O'Toole (1973) for the Economic and Social Research Institute, 5000 Irish women respondents were asked what they considered the most helpful policy government or employers could enact to assist married women interested in working. The three most commonly mentioned items were establishment of flexible hours, provision of day-care centers (most favored state-run facilities) and changes in the tax laws. Over one-quarter of the nonworking nonfarm women responding mentioned child-care provision as being most helpful.

Advances in state provision of child care have not been made and a study in the early 1980s by Fine-Davis shows that this was still very much an issue (1983a). Her survey of 1021 women nationwide in 1981 included 440 nonworking women. Sixty percent of them expressed a desire to return to work. Queried about their reasons for not working, most responded that they wanted to be with their young children, followed closely by structural barriers such as a shortage of part-time jobs and a lack of child care.

The lack of provision by state personnel of this social service was as constraining to women's options as protective legislation or the marriage bar. The absence of child-care facilities coordinated well with the general tenor of state policy, which was still rooted in the belief that mothers belonged in the home and which reinforced traditional gender roles. The lack of such policy also contrasts sharply with the fact that governments have often provided child-care facilities when it has been considered acceptable and economically (or militarily) necessary for women to be in the labor force (for example, World War II in the United States).

Almost all of this discriminatory and restrictive family law and reproductive rights legislation remained in place in Ireland from 1961 to 1981. The growth of employment–male domination trade-off curve can be used to examine the effect of state family and reproductive rights policies. The fact that these policies remained in force in Ireland meant the N-P curve was not altered because of them. This indicates that the N-P curve was more adverse for women in Ireland (i.e., it was farther to the right) than in most other Western European countries where this type of restrictive family law and reproductive rights legislation was being eroded. In the latter, as such policies were made more equitable for women, the N-P curves shifted to the left, indicating that a given level of growth in employment was associated with weaker male domination.[46] Therefore, because of these state policies in Ireland, a given level of growth in employment was associated with greater male domination than in many other countries.

Conclusions

State personnel in Ireland perceived two types of economic and social policies that would enhance their tenure: promotion of economic growth and reproduction of traditional familial relations. Although these two objectives of state policy can be contradictory (i.e., the economic development process tends to undermine male domination in a competitive market economy by drawing women into the labor force and providing them increased economic independence), this tendency was prevented in Ireland by state policies that reinforced gender inequalities.

Although the Irish government was forced by the exigencies of the export-led development strategy to alter some discriminatory employment policy in the latter part of the 1970s, the evidence indicates these discriminatory practices continued on an *ad hoc* basis. Further, family and reproductive rights policies that subordinated women in the household were scarcely altered throughout this period. The overall result was to reproduce gender inequalities in the household and firms, influencing the labor market decisions of both.

This assessment of the effects of this broad range of state policy on women provides answers for the questions raised in Chapter 2 and explored in Chapter 3: the main issue (why measures of women's labor force activity remained low and relatively unchanging during economic and social changes considered highly likely to increase them) and for its two underlying subquestions (why female shares in sectors of the Irish economy remained low or fell during this period and why the labor force participation of married women was so relatively low even though there was a sudden rise in it, 1971–1975). It reveals the structural constraints preventing the likely increases in the demand for female labor or in the supply of female labor.

First, to begin with the underlying subquestions, the relatively low proportions of women in the manufacturing sectors in Ireland vis-à-vis EEC countries was caused by a variety of employment policies designed to provide male employment. Secondly, the low participation rate of married women has been shown to be the result of male domination in the household and male opposition to female employment as well as to high fertility, both of which were buttressed by state family and reproductive rights policies. In addition, the lack of child-care facilities and discriminatory income tax provisions dampened female labor supply. The one-time sharp increase in the participation rate of married women that occurred in the 1971–1975 period can be attributed to the elimination of the marriage bar.

The effect of export-led development on Irish women's labor force activity was therefore mediated by this full range of state policy. The main lesson of the Irish case is that, to understand economic outcomes for women, it is necessary to use an approach that incorporates the role of the state and the effect of family and reproductive rights policies as well as employment policies on gender inequality and labor market decision-making in the firm and household and society in general. These policies reinforced a male-bias regarding the sex composition of paid employment and gender inequality in the household and society in general. They were the structural constraint that kept female labor force participation rates and the female share of the labor force relatively low and unchanging throughout this period.

The usefulness of this lesson for the labor market and economic development literatures as well as its insights for feminist theory and the theory of the state were suggested in Chapter 1 and will be explored further in Chapters 5 and 6. However, a few specific comments can be made here. First, this assessment of the effect of family policies raises a critical point. Although substantial attention has been given to the effect of equal employment legislation in the literature, there has been little analysis of how state policies affect structural inequalities in the household and, in turn, impact on the female labor supply. This chapter has shown the importance of family and reproductive rights legislation in maintaining unequal gender relations in the household. Changes in employment policies are necessary to achieve gender equality; however, their impact can be circumscribed or prevented by the continued existence of discriminatory family policies or by the absence of policies such as child care, which would alleviate some of the household responsibilities which typically fall unequally on women.

Secondly, this examination of family and reproductive rights policies also contributes to the analysis of the relationship between male domination and fertility by stressing that state policy can directly augment male power in the household and can curtail women's options regarding biological reproduction, both of which affect fertility levels. This enhances the argument that fertility decisions are substantially influenced by unequal gender relations.

Lastly, this type of analysis can be extended to other types of policies that cannot be so clearly categorized as either employment policy or family policy. For example, there are at least two other state policies that can impact on women's labor force activity—the pension and social insurance systems. In Ireland, they were both implicitly based on the presumption that women are dependent on men who support them and therefore need fewer benefits or provisions than males. Such discriminatory legislation also altered the growth of employment-patriarchy trade-off (shifted N-P to the right) and had an adverse impact on women's labor supply function. (See Appendix E for more detailed information on each of these.)

In short, the political economy in Ireland ensured that Irish women were not facing the labor market with the same options as Irish men (or women in many other Western European OECD countries). The effect of these policies and changes in them can be illustrated in terms of the graphic model and compared to trends which were occurring in other Western European countries at the same time. Even if we assume Ireland and the other countries began the period at the same growth of employment-patriarchy curve (for example, N-P_2 in Figure 4.5), we find Ireland at the end of this period in a relatively worse situation. (Ireland probably began on one more adverse for women, i.e., farther to the right.)

With respect to Ireland, it was shown that the adverse impact of discriminatory employment policies on women's participation in the labor force intensified in the early 1970s as the state actively sought to pro-

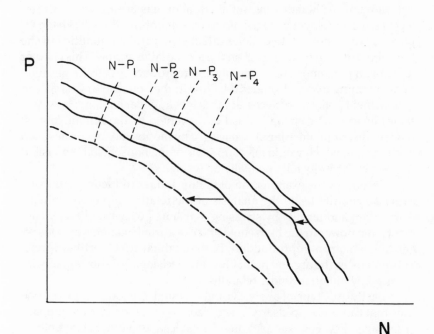

Figure 4.5   Shifts in the Patriarchy-Growth of Employment Trade-off, Ireland, and An Average for Other Western European OECD Countries during the 1970s   (LFPR is the labor force participation rate of women; N is the growth of employment; P represents patriarchal relations)

vide male employment. The effect of this IDA policy was to alter the N-P trade-off by shifting the curve to the right (e.g., N-P$_2$ to N-P$_4$). From the point of view of state personnel, this enhanced the trade-off by allowing greater growth of employment for a given level of male domination. However, as it became clear that these policies in turn were constraining the export-led development process, state personnel were forced by the necessity to promote employment to modify explicit discriminatory policies. As they eliminated some discriminatory policies, the trade-off became more favorable for women, as the N-P curve shifted left, meaning a given level of growth in employment was associated with less male domination. However, given that employment discrimination continued to operate on an informal, case-by-case bargaining basis and given the problems of enforcement of equal opportunity employment legislation (Employment Equality Agency, *Annual Reports,* 1978 to 1981), this gain was not totally eroded by the elimination of biased employment policies. (The N-P curve may have shifted only from N-P$_4$ to N-P$_3$.)

On the other hand, family and reproductive rights policies were scarcely modified during this 20-year period in Ireland in contrast to substantial changes in other Western European OECD countries. (As shown earlier, average shifts in other OECD countries could be thought to shift their N-P curves from an initial position of N-P_2 to N-P_1 in Figure 4.5.) The net result is that the N-P curve at the end of this period remained farther from the origin in Ireland (N-P_3) than the average for other Western European countries (N-P_1). This meant that a given rate of growth of employment in Ireland was associated with a greater level of male domination than elsewhere.

Chapter Five

The Main Lesson of the Irish Case Examined at the Regional Level

Introduction: The Lesson of the Irish Case

It is now appropriate to recap the main insight of the Irish case study and examine its implications in a broader context. The experience of women in Ireland during the export-led development strategy, 1961 – 1981, differed from the expectations of traditional economic theory that women will be brought into the labor force as economic development occurs. Measures of female labor force participation remained relatively low and unchanging, contrasting sharply to the experience of women in the labor market in other Western European OECD countries and Singapore, another small, export-led economy.[1]

In addition, explanations that could be advanced by traditional economic theory for why expected labor market outcomes did not occur were shown to be inapplicable. These surprising results could not be explained by changes in the distribution of employment among sectors in the economy that were adverse for women. Nor could they be attributed to increases in relative earnings of women vis-à-vis men which, according to neoclassical economic theory, would lead to an adverse movement in the male – female employment ratio. Although offering a more promising line of argument, they could not be attributed to the argument that in a job-scarce economy, given the traditional division of labor, men get the jobs. This latter analysis could not explain how, in light of forces generated by the export-led development process, the sexual division of labor would not be altered to include more women.[2]

The feminist argument that patriarchal domination as reproduced in the household can constrain women's options added an important dimension to the analysis: the relevance of examining unequal gender relations as they exist in social institutions.[3] However, it could not explain

103

how male dominance was maintained in the household through the economic and social changes occurring in Ireland. The employment opportunities generated for women by export-led development would increase women's economic independence, and in the absence of structural constraints, reduce inequality in the household, undermining male domination.

Another line of feminist argument suggests that male dominance is fundamentally reproduced in the firm. According to Heidi Hartmann (1976), "Job segregation by sex . . . is the primary mechanism in capitalist society that maintains the superiority of men over women, because it enforces lower wages for women in the labor market. Low wages keep women dependent on men" (139). Because the labor force participation of women was low in Ireland and most women were not in the workplace, this line of argument regarding the structure of patriarchy in Ireland has much less applicability. It was for this reason that the feminist argument investigated in Chapter 3 was the variant positing the reproduction of male domination in the household. Nevertheless, the role of the firm in maintaining male domination can be investigated for that portion of women who were employed.

For reasons similar to those delineating the inadequacy of the male domination in the household explanation, this argument based on gender inequality as reproduced in the firm is also not sufficient. One might argue that domestic firms could remain discriminatory; however, in the absence of structural constraints, there is no reason why foreign firms in industries that hired larger proportions of women than the average for Ireland would abide by this cultural convention. Export-led growth would undermine each of these ways in which feminists have argued patriarchy is reproduced.

A survey of social and industrial policy in Ireland revealed the legal foundations of the systematic inequality between men and women that existed in Ireland. Discriminatory state employment and family policies reinforced gender inequalities in the household and firm in the presence of economic changes that would erode them. This adversely affected the labor market decisions of each regarding women's participation and prevented the expected increase in female participation in the labor force. The way state policy affects gender inequalities is central to understanding the integration of women into the labor force.

In examining the manner in which state policies have reinforced gender inequality (male dominance) in the firm and household and in turn constrained women's opportunities in the labor force, this explanation builds on the feminist approach. It broadens the original argument regarding patriarchy as fundamentally based in household relations by extending it to the workplace and to the way state policy can reinforce gender inequality in both of these institutions.

Here then is the main insight of the Irish case: We cannot understand the role of women in the labor force or in the economy without
utilizing an approach that focuses on gender inequality in social institutions, that is, a feminist approach. More specifically, such an approach must include the role of the state and the manner in which the
full range of its policies affects gender inequalities in the workplace, the
household, and society in general. This type of view of the factors influencing women's economic roles can be potentially insightful in analyzing the position of women in industrialized countries as well as wom-
en's roles in developing nations.

In this chapter, the validity of the traditional approaches and the
possible usefulness of a theory of gender inequality are explored in two
further ways: first, by econometric work on a regional level and, second, by comparing the changes in Ireland to the average trends in the
region obtained in these regressions and by reassessing how the approach developed thus far explains the differences between Ireland and
the region. Critiques of the traditional approaches have largely come
from studies undertaken in individual countries and the observed de-
viation of experiences of women in the labor forces of these countries
from that expected by these paradigms. This chapter uses regression
analysis to explore whether there is evidence at a regional level that increased labor force activity for women occurred in accordance with the
factors emphasized by modernization, neoclassical or Marxian approaches, or whether an alternative focusing on gender inequality
might be more applicable. These results are used to evaluate the relevance of the explanation developed for the failure of labor force participation to rise in Ireland during this period.

Testing of the Traditional Approaches

Because of inavailability of comparable data for a group of export-led
economies, 1961–1981, the study examines 17 Western European OECD
countries during this period.[4] Although in 1961 these countries were
well past the initial industrialization period, this 20 year time frame (following the disruption of World War II and the postwar recovery) provides a valid opportunity to study the usefulness of modernization, and
neoclassical, or Marxian approaches. This was a period exhibiting the
types of economic and social changes these conventional approaches
examine—rapid economic growth, increases in educational levels, urbanization, and extension of wage labor. At the beginning of these two
decades women's share of the labor force was low relative to their share
of the population and increased almost one-third during the period. It
averaged 28.9 percent in 1961 and rose to 37.3 percent in 1981. In addi-

tion, although having economic, political, and cultural diversity, the region nevertheless offers a group of countries with many similarities. This allows needed diversity in the data without exposing the analysis to the disruptive impact of analyzing extremely heterogeneous situations.

What were the reasons for this increase in the average female share of the labor force? It would seem likely that empirical support could be found for either an argument that the change occurred because of social enlightenment (as modernization theory argues) or because of increases in wage labor as capitalism spread (as both neoclassical and orthodox Marxian approaches imply).

The explanatory power of the traditional approaches can be examined econometrically. Regression analyses of the change in the female share of the total workforce in the 17 Western European OECD countries can be executed on two different types of variables: 1) independent variables chosen to represent the process of modernization and economic development and 2) an independent variable constructed to focus on the fundamental structural change in these economies as capitalist production relations and competition were extended through them—the change in the proportion of the total labor force engaged in wage labor.

Except for the work of Ward and Pampel (1985), this econometric work analyzing women's participation in the labor force differs from that of other researchers in two ways. First, the regressions are based on changes over time in these countries in contrast to most labor force participation studies, which are static multiple regressions of cross-sectional data (Standing, 1981: vi; Standing and Sheehan, 1978). The project is to determine what factors have influenced changes in women's relative position in the workforce, 1961–1981. Such relationships cannot be adequately approximated by cross-section analyses for a given year. Additionally, in both of these sets of equations the change in the female share of the workforce (SHARE-C) is used as the dependent variable rather than the more commonly used female labor force participation rate. SHARE-C focuses on women's position in the work force over time relative to men, rather than on the intragender information presented by the latter. This type of information has been used descriptively but not to analyze the relative effects of the development process on women.

Using pooled cross-section data, Ward and Pampel (1985) examined determinants of the level of the female share of the labor force in 16 OECD countries throughout the world at five different points during the period from 1955 to 1975. Although their analytical technique examines effects over time, my analysis differs from theirs by analyzing the determinants of the *change* in the female share over a period of 20 years and by utilizing changes in all variables rather than levels. Other differences include the countries examined (these new regressions focus solely on Western European OECD countries), the independent variables selected, and the time period.

This examination of the relevance of the traditional theories in explaining the change in the female share of the labor force in this region can begin with the modernization/integrationist point of view. As the integrationist variant of modernization theory has been applied to chiefly developing countries and as this regional analysis is based on the Western European region because of data availability, it is the modernization version that is more applicable and that will be explored econometrically here.

Modernization theory argues that during the economic development process traditional particularistic values and cultural practices are eroded and more universalistic values are adopted. It has been thought that with economic development and the spread of liberal ideas of equality, it would be considered fair that all people regardless of sex, race or ethnic group be included in political and economic processes. This process of enlightenment would result in a fuller participation of women in social activities and practices.

The equations developed to examine the relevance of the modernization approach include combinations of the following independent variables (or their logarithmic transformation): GNP-C (the change in per capita gross national product, 1961–1981); EDUC-C (the change in total secondary school enrollment ratio); URBAN-C (the change in the percent of the population living in urban areas, 1961–1981). These variables were chosen as representative of the processes of economic and social change that typically accompany economic development and are generally considered proxies of modernization.

The results in Table 5.1 show that, taken in any combination (or transformation), none of these traditional variables had any explanatory power for the change in the female share of the labor force during this period for the Western European OECD countries taken as a whole or for Ireland. (The variables are defined in Table 5.2.) These regressions produced negligible adjusted R^2s and large sum of squares of residuals. The error terms for Ireland were large. The sign on the educational variables was unexpectedly negative. Not only did the predictions of modernization theory not hold for Ireland, these results suggest that the approach did not capture the dynamic of social change in any of these countries. The argument that change (i.e., "progress") occurred for women by a process of enlightenment cannot be validated.

Two other sets of regressions, one substituting the change in the labor force participation rate of women for SHARE-C as the dependent variable, the other replacing the GNP-C variable with the change in the

Table 5.1

Regression Results: Change in Female Share on Modernization Variables, Western European OECD Countries, 1961–1981

Independent Variables	(1)	(2)	(3)	(4)	(5)	(6)	(7)	(8)	(9)	(10)	(11)
						t in ( )					
GNP-C	.001 (.42)					.000 (.19)		.000 (.94)		.000 (−.06)	
LNGNP-C		5.61 (.54)					6.197 (0.59)		5.641 (.50)		4.968 (.44)
EDUC-C			−0.124 (−1.03)			−0.118 (−0.92)		−0.141 (−1.02)	−.146 (−1.11)		
LNEDUC-C				−5.920 (−1.08)			−6.092 (−1.09)			−6.914 (−1.05)	−6.690 (−1.12)
URBAN-C					.066 (.26)			.144 (.526)	.112 (.40)	.147 (.54)	.109 (.397)
Constant	6.481	4.901	12.510	11.827	7.675	11.410	8.022	11.016	8.421	11.052	7.887
$\bar{R}^2$	.012	.019	.066	.072	.005	.068	.095	.088	.105	.093	.106
Residual S.S.*	737.41	732.07	696.77	692.06	742.62	694.98	675.02	680.51	667.83	676.84	666.94
Error (Ireland)	−4.92	−5.68	−2.84	−3.54	−5.97	−2.50	−3.19	−2.26	−2.08	−3.39	−3.06

*Total sum of squares = 746.08
See Table 5.2 for definition of variables and sources of data.

Table 5.2

Definition of Regression Variables

EDUC-C	is the change in the total secondary school enrollment ratio, 1960–1980. The secondary school enrollment ratio is the enrollment of males and females of all ages in secondary schools as a percentage of the male and female population of secondary school age, 12–17.
FERTHAT-C	is the estimated change in total fertility, 1960–1980, calculated from GNP-C and the percent change in real GNP per capita, 1961–1979.
GNP-C	is the change in the gross national product (GNP) per capita (in U.S. dollars at the exchange rates and price levels of 1975) between 1960 and 1980.
LNEDUC-C	is the ln (EDUC 1980)–ln (EDUC 1960), where ln (EDUC 1980) is the ln of the secondary school enrollment ratio for 1980 and ln (EDUC 1960) is similarly defined.
LNGNP-C	is LN (GNP 1980)–LN (GNP 1960), where LN (GNP 1980) is the ln of GNP in 1980 and LN (GNP 1960) is similarly defined.
FERT-C	is the change in the total fertility rate between 1960 and 1980.
SHARE-C	is the change in the proportion of total labor force which was female between 1960 and 1980.
URBAN-C	is the change in the proportion of the population living in urban areas between 1960 and 1980.
WAGE-C	is the change in the proportion of the total labor force which was engaged in wage labor between 1960 and 1980.

Sources: EDUC-C, LNEDUC-C, FERT-C and URBAN-C are from World Bank, *World Tables*, Vol. II, *Social Data*, 3rd ed., 1983; SHARE-C and WAGE-C are from ILO, *Yearbook of Labour Statistics*, various years; GNP-C and LNGNP-C are from OECD, *National Accounts of OECD Countries*, 1950–1979.

proportion of the labor force in agriculture, also produced no significant results that could support the modernization approach.[5]

Surprisingly, the neoclassical and Marxist arguments regarding the incorporation of women into the labor force can be examined together: They both suggest that, as capitalist relations of production permeate an economy, women will increasingly participate in the labor force. Capitalism is fundamentally characterized by the use of wage labor; as it develops there is a decline of small independent producers and a corresponding rise in the proportion of the work force that is engaged in wage labor. Therefore, the spread of capitalist relations of production can be approximated by the change in the proportion of the total labor force that is engaged in wage labor. Then, to examine the neoclassical and Marxian arguments regarding the impact of the spread of capitalism on women's labor force activity, SHARE-C can be regressed on WAGE-C, the change in the proportion of the labor force engaged in wage labor.

Both approaches imply that WAGE-C would have a positive coefficient. For Marxists this follows from the argument that as capitalism develops and many activities formerly performed by women in the home are provided in the larger economy, women would be incorporated into the wage labor force. With respect to neoclassical theory, if there are proportionately fewer women in the work force of a society that has gender equality and no other structural constraints on participating in the labor force, decisions on both the demand and supply sides of the labor market would reduce this imbalance and increase the female share as the proportion of the total labor force that performs wage labor increases. Firms would seek to hire male and female workers interchangeably because those that did not would draw from a smaller labor pool and be at a competitive disadvantage. Similarly, labor supply decisions made in households where social relations of equality prevailed and women faced the same set of choices as men would be likely to increase the supply of women workers to the labor market.

In addition, it is likely that the female share would increase as wage labor became more predominant because of the historical problem in the specification of "economically active." Women's economic activities as unpaid family laborers (on farms or in family businesses) are normally undercounted (Abel, 1987; Ciancanelli, 1983). It could be expected that, as the proportion of wage labor increased and as own-enterprises decreased (where the male owner or worker tended to be counted but female workers, if any, were unpaid workers and not as likely to be listed as economically active), more women would be reported as labor force participants.

Regression of the change in the female share of the labor force on the change in the proportion of the labor force in wage labor for the 17 Western European OECD countries is shown in Table 5.3. The result is significant but surprising: Rather than the positive relationship expected by the neoclassical and Marxist approaches, this regression reveals a highly significant inverse relationship between WAGE-C and SHARE-C.

This directly refutes the expectations of traditional formulations of neoclassical and Marxian theory regarding the effect of economic development on women's position in the labor market. The increase in the female share of the labor force in these countries cannot be explained by the relative increase in wage labor accompanying the spread of capitalist relations of production.

Table 5.3

Regression Results: Change in Female Share on the Change in Proportion of Labor Force Engaged in Wage Labor, Western European OECD Countries, 1961–1981

Independent Variables[2]	SHARE-C[1] on	
	(a)	(b)
WAGE-C	−.604	−.575
	(−2.722*)	
Constant	12.193	
$\bar{R}^2$	.29	
Residual S.S.	499.39	

*t statistic significant at the .99 level
[1]Column (a) reports regular regression coefficients; Column (b) reports standardized coefficients.
[2]See Table 5.2 for definitions of the variables and sources of the data.

If there is not empirical support for the implications of the modernization, neoclassical, or Marxist approaches, what theoretical perspective could provide insight into the processes at work? Furthermore, why would we encounter a statistically significant negative relationship between the increase in wage labor and the change in the female share of the labor force? It is here that theorists examining the existence of barriers to equality based on gender may offer a potentially insightful explanation and an agenda for future research.

Examination of the Alternative Approach

Many scholars analyzing the role of women have developed fundamentally different approaches by which the subordinate position of women can be understood, calling for an understanding of social life as differentiated along lines of gender (or gender/class, or gender/class/race). They consider the theories just reviewed inadequate formulations of the systematic subordination of women.[6] The Irish case suggests some dimensions for an alternative econometric approach that not only widens the perspective on the structural changes occurring in society as economic growth or development proceeds but also considers the role of gender inequality and how it mediates the impact of these structural changes on the female share of the labor force.

The major changes occurring in society during economic development are in the organization of work, in the structure of the household, and in the rural–urban patterns of social organization. This model uses the following independent variables to represent them respectively: WAGE-C, the change in the proportion of the labor force engaged in wage labor; FERT-C, the change in the total fertility rate; and URBAN-C, the change in the proportion of the population living in urban areas.[7]

WAGE-C, which measures the spread of capitalist production relations, represents the change in the organization of economic activity as capitalist growth occurs. FERT-C captures changes in family structure. A transition to lower fertility rates (i.e., a smaller average completed family size) has generally accompanied the development of capitalism (Folbre, 1983). URBAN-C is a proxy for the change in the form of social organization as people moved off the land into urban areas where employment in an industrializing economy was concentrated.[8]

These variables clearly represent key dimensions of structural change in society as growth or development proceeds. However, gender inequality and the way it can mediate the impact of these changes on the female share of the labor force (SHARE-C) are also involved because WAGE-C and FERT-C are variables that can be directly affected by unequal gender relations. With respect to WAGE-C, although this approach appears to build on the simple regression used to examine the neoclassical and Marxian arguments by using WAGE-C, its use of this variable differs conceptually. In the absence of gender inequality, it is logical to reason as the traditional approaches have, that increases in wage labor (WAGE-C) would have a positive impact on women's share of the labor force. However, with the recognition of the existence of unequal relations of power between men and women and the incorporation of gender inequality as a fundamental dimension of analysis, a very different relationship between WAGE-C and SHARE-C is predicted than that expected by the neoclassical and Marxian analyses.

For example, feminists who locate the reproduction of male domination in the firm or household could argue that the relationship between these two variables could be inverse. If there were structural constraints to hiring women in the firms then, as the importance of wage labor increased, it could result in a lower share of employment for women. Similarly, if the household was an arena of gender-based domination and conflict, there are very compelling reasons the spread of wage labor could result in a falling female share. Males dominant in the household could resist the tendency of economic development to incorporate women on any or all of these grounds: that there would be a decrease in household services provided by women (Fernandez-Kelly and Garcia, 1989); that women would compete for jobs and economic resources with men (Gallin, Whittier, and Graham, 1985; Hartmann,

1976); that increased economic independence of women could weaken the relative power of males in the household (McCrate, 1985); and that "their" women could come under the control of other men in the workplace (Fernandez-Kelly and Garcia, 1989).

The Irish case study has shown that another social institution, the state, can also affect the relationship between WAGE-C and SHARE-C, with an adverse impact on the female share. State family and reproductive rights policies and employment policies can reinforce gender inequality in both the household and the firm, also constraining women's labor force activity as wage labor increases. Changes in one type of policy alone (for example, employment policies), unaccompanied by changes in other policies (e.g., policies that subordinate women in the household and/or constrain their reproductive choices), may be insufficient to alleviate this negative impact on women's labor force participation.

The change in fertility, FERT-C, is an empirical variable that represents changes in family structure as economic growth proceeds. It is related to women's labor force activity and reflects gender inequality. It is widely acknowledged that reductions in fertility are correlated with increases in women's labor force participation.[9] This variable can reflect unequal gender inequality in a number of ways. It can be affected by male domination in the household and/or by state policies. The lower portion of Figure 3.2 illustrates the argument that male domination could affect fertility rates and in turn female labor supply. For example, if males dominant in the household determine that it is to their advantage to have more children, fertility rates rise, having a negative impact on female labor supply. However, if males dominant in the household decide it is in their economic interest to have fewer children, the fertility rate may decrease, which is expected to impact positively on female labor supply. Note that in this latter case, Figure 3.2 suggests that, although this may erode part of the adverse impact of male domination in the household on female labor supply, it does not eliminate it all. The direct effect of male domination on female labor supply, represented at the top of the figure, can remain intact.

The Irish case has contributed insights regarding the manner in which state policies affect fertility both directly (limited access to contraception or abortion) and indirectly via reinforcing the power of the male in the family (lack of divorce, inadequate provision in cases of desertion, and male rights of property ownership and sexual access). Therefore, state policies can also affect unequal relations between the sexes in ways that alter fertility rates and impact on female labor supply.

The result of the regression of the change in the female share of the labor force on these variables for the 17 Western European OECD coun-

Table 5.4

Regression Results: Change in Female Share on Structural Changes in the Workplace, Household, and Society, Western European OECD Countries, 1961–1981

	Eq. 1[1] SHARE-C on		Eq. 2 SHARE-C on	
	(a)	(b)	(a)	(b)
Independent Variables[2]				
WAGE-C	−.899	−.856	−.920	−.877
	(−4.004***)		(−4.199***)	
FERT-C	−7.361	−.387		
	(−1.789)			
URBAN-C	.594	.609	.568	.582
	(2.545**)		(2.645**)	
FERTHAT-C			−9.965	−.410
			(−2.044*)	
Constant	1.688		.158	
$\bar{R}^2$	.43		.489	
Residual S.S.	328.59		309.75	

*t statistic significant at the .90 level
**t statistic significant at the .95 level
***t statistic significant at the .99 level

[1]Column (a) reports regular regression coefficients;
Column (b) reports standardized coefficients.

[2]See Table 5.2 for definitions of the variables and sources of the data.

tries is shown in equation 1 in Table 5.4. All variables are significant and WAGE-C and FERT-C exhibit the signs expected by this approach incorporating structural change and gender inequality. Standardized coefficients are included in column (b) to provide a clearer perspective on the magnitude of the effect of each variable.

WAGE-C (the change in the proportion of the labor force engaged in wage labor) exhibits a highly significant negative relationship. The incorporation of gender inequality into the analysis offers an explanation for this inverse relationship: the presence of unequal gender relations in the household and/or workplace (possibly reinforced by state policies) that constrain female labor force activity.

Changes in fertility (FERT-C) have the expected inverse impact on the female share of the labor force. Decreases in fertility in most of these countries have accompanied the upward trend in the female share of the labor force. This suggests that there have been at least some changes in the internal structure of the family or household (i.e., reduced number of children) that have facilitated women's labor force participation. The change in urbanization (URBAN-C) has a plausible positive impact. Its direct effect may be due to the fact that as women move from rural areas where their labor is often not counted in the official statistics to urban areas and the type of employment that tends to be counted, there is a positive effect on SHARE-C.

Further work with fertility was done to ensure that there was not bias in these coefficients. Since fertility changes are also influenced by economic change and development, a two-equation system using an instrumental variables approach was established (to avoid having fertility correlated with the error term). Fertility changes were regressed on changes in gross national product (GNP).[10] This equation was in turn used to estimate the change in fertility (FERTHAT-C) for each of the countries. Equation 2 of Table 5.4 is the regression of SHARE-C on this estimate of fertility change (FERTHAT-C), WAGE-C, and URBAN-C. This process produced significant results similar to Equation 1 but with an improved adjusted R^2.

In addition, other regressions were designed to investigate the effect on the regional level of another social institution, the Catholic Church. As noted in Chapter 4, much state policy in Ireland corresponded to the precepts of the Catholic Church (for example, with respect to divorce, contraception, and abortion) (Mahon, 1987). However, although the Church in Ireland has been a very strong social force, it was the presence of the broad range of family and reproductive rights policies as well as employment policies in Ireland, rather than the Church, that constrained women's labor force participation during export-led development. The low level of female participation in Ireland vis-à-vis the experience of women in the other OECD countries cannot be explained by Catholicism. Tables 2.3 and 2.5 show that in other predominantly Catholic countries (such as Italy, Spain, Portugal) measures of women's participation increased from 1961 to 1981. However, to further explore this relationship between the Church and women's labor force activity, two different variables for Catholicism were subsequently included in the regressions. Neither the percent of the population that was Catholic nor a dummy variable (1 if the country was over 90 percent Catholic, 0 if not) produced a coefficient significantly different from zero.

To summarize, the results of regressions using this alternative approach (shown in equations 1 and 2 of Table 5.4) contrast sharply with both the lack of significance of the regressions on modernization variables and the results of the examination of the neoclassical and Marxian approaches, which, although significant, had the opposite sign from that expected. In this new formulation, all variables are significant with the expected signs and the adjusted R^2s are higher. This provides empirical support at the regional level for the relevance of this alternative approach: that the change in the female share of the labor force is influenced by structural changes in society as mediated by relations of gender inequality.

Putting this all together, what does it mean regarding the trend in the female share of the labor force in these Western European OECD countries, 1961–1981, the factors contributing to it, and the underlying explanation regarding their impact? In Table 5.5, sections 1 and 3, the average change in each of the independent variables was inserted into the regression equations 1 and 2 of Table 5.4, respectively. The resulting calculations show that the average increase in the female share of the labor force in these seventeen countries was composed of

1. the negative impact of the average increase in proportion of the labor force in wage labor (the increase in WAGE-C × its negative coefficient in equations (a) of Table 5.4),

2. the positive impact from the average decline in fertility (the decline in FERT-C or FERTHAT-C × its negative coefficient in the Table 5.4 equations), and

3. the positive impact of the average increase in urbanization (the increase in URBAN-C × its positive coefficient).

With respect to the effect of the change in proportion of wage labor (WAGE-C) on the change in the female share of the labor force (SHARE-C), this alternative feminist approach suggests that, although WAGE-C was on average rising in these countries, it had a dampening effect on SHARE-C because of the existence of unequal gender relations in the firm or household (or because of state policies that reinforced male domination in either of these sites). The positive impact of changes in fertility (i.e., its decline × its negative coefficient) suggests that the overall effect of male domination in the household on female labor supply as it operates through fertility was somewhat ameliorated by the reduction in fertility, as the process illustrated in the lower portion of Figure 3.2 shows.

However, in looking at the effect of the change in the percentage of the labor force in wage labor (WAGE-C) and the change in fertility (FERT-C) together, it would appear that although this one dimension of gender inequality (male domination as it affects fertility and female labor supply) was lessened, nevertheless the direct effect of male domination in the household on female labor supply (the process shown in

Table 5.5

Comparison of Components of Change in Female Share in Ireland to Average Changes in Western European OECD Countries, 1961–1981

COMPARISONS BASED ON EQUATION 1 FROM TABLE 5.4

For the seventeen countries:

SHARE-C	= constant	− .899 WAGE-C	− 7.361 FERT-C	+ .594 URBAN-C	
8.44	= 1.688	− .899 (6.223)	− 7.361 (−.753)	+ .594 (11.45)	
(1)	= 1.688	− 5.595	+ 5.521	+ 6.801	

For Ireland:

(2) 2.50	= 1.688	− .899 (11.6)	− 7.361 (−.50)	+ .594 (12.00)	+ R
	= 1.688	− 10.428	+ 3.6805	+ 7.128	+ .43

COMPARISONS BASED ON EQUATION 2 FROM TABLE 5.4

For the seventeen countries:

SHARE-C	= constant	− .920 WAGE-C	− 9.965 FERTHAT-C	+ .568 URBAN-C	
8.44	= .158	− .920 (6.223)	− 9.965 (−.753)	+ .568 (11.45)	
(3)	= .158	− 5.725	+ 7.503	+ 6.504	

For Ireland:

(4) 2.50	= .158	− .920 (11.6)	− 9.965 (−.62)	+ .568 (12.00)	+ R
	= .158	− 10.672	+ 6.178	+ 6.816	+ .02

The variables with bars over them are the (unweighted) mean changes in the respective variables for the seventeen countries; R = error term for Ireland.

the upper portion of Figure 3.2) could have remained during this period. This, in combination with gender inequality in the firm and any state policies that maintained gender inequality in either social institution, would result in the negative impact of WAGE-C on the change in the female share of the labor force, SHARE-C. Although one of the several dimensions of male domination was diminished, evidence is strong that other aspects remained and dampened the increase in the female share of the labor force in these countries. From sections 1 and 3 of Table 5.5, it is clear that if the impact of WAGE-C had not been negative, the average increase in the female share of the labor force would have been even larger in these countries.

Reexamination of the Irish Explanation in Light of the Regional Analysis

What further information can these econometric results at the regional level provide regarding the situation of women in Ireland during this period? This question can be answered by using the estimated model, which this regression provides in two variants, equations 1 and 2 of Table 5.4. Average changes in the group as a whole can be inserted into each of these and compared to the changes in women's share of the labor force in Ireland as is done in Table 5.5. The explanation developed for the failure of Irish women's participation to rise can be evaluated further in terms of these empirical results.

As indicated in Table 5.5, both of these regressions of the change in the female share of the labor force on these independent or explanatory variables explain the Irish situation well. The error terms for Ireland are respectively .43 and .02, meaning that most of the variation has been explained by the independent variables (WAGE-C, FERT-C or FERTHAT-C, and URBAN-C). Table 5.5 permits comparison of the average change in each variable for the Western European OECD countries as a whole and its impact on SHARE-C with the effect of the change in each variable in Ireland on its female share for each of the two equations modeling the alternative approach. For example, sections 1 and 2 in Table 5.5 allow comparison between the change in the female share in the 17 countries and in Ireland and reveal the different ways the independent variables (WAGE-C, FERT-C or FERTHAT-C, and URBAN-C) affect SHARE-C.

Both equations show Irish women were disadvantaged in two ways, by the change in Irish fertility rates relative to the other countries and by the change in wage labor as a percentage of total labor. The average change in fertility had a larger positive impact for the 17 countries as a group than in Ireland. If the change in fertility in Ireland had been equal to the average for the 17 countries, then the change in the female share of the labor force (SHARE-C) would have been two percentage points higher. Additionally, the average change in the proportion of the workforce engaged in wage labor had a larger negative impact for Ireland than the group average.

The results of the regressions in Table 5.4 and the comparisons between changes in Ireland and average changes for the Western European countries in Table 5.5 support the explanation that the virtual lack of change in women's participation in the Irish labor force, 1961–1981, was due to discriminatory state policy. First, the fertility variable (FERT-C), shown to be significant in its effect on the female share of the labor force, was directly influenced by Irish state family policies. Fertility did not decrease so much in Ireland as it did in the other countries (Table 3.7) because of the continuation of family and reproductive rights policies during this period, which maintained unequal gender relations in the household and constrained access to control over biological reproduction.

Secondly, WAGE-C can be affected by both state employment and family policies. Employment policies can facilitate or hinder women's entry into the labor force. In addition, this variable can also be affected by state family policies which, by reinforcing male domination in the household, restricted the supply of female labor as wage labor became increasingly prevalent.

The negative sign is only explicable using a feminist argument that there are systemic structural constraints on women's participation in the work force; that is, a form of unequal gender relations. In Ireland, both state employment and family policies constrained women's gains in wage labor. Part of the negative effect of WAGE-C can be explained by the presence of employment policies—the direct IDA policies to attract foreign firms that hire predominantly males, the marriage bar, protective legislation, and access to training and apprenticeship programs— which restricted the demand for female labor. In addition, family and reproductive policies, perpetuated in Ireland by state personnel, maintained male dominance in the household and kept the high fertility rate from falling. The joint effect of unequal social relations in the household, male opposition to female entry into the labor market, and greater child-care duties in Ireland curtailed women's options in making labor supply decisions.

Conclusions

The regional analysis provides two results. First, it suggests that change in the female share of the labor forces in these countries did not occur because of social enlightenment (as modernization theory implies), because of increased competition (as the neoclassical approach suggests), or because of the increase in social production (as indicated by the orthodox Marxian approach). Results at this wider level support the alternative approach: that change for women is affected by structural change in social institutions such as the household or workplace and the manner in which gender inequality persists within them.

Secondly, when the results of the data analysis at the regional level are applied specifically to the changes occurring in Ireland during this period of time, they explain the surprisingly small change in the female share of the Irish labor force very well. Female participation in the labor force is not the simple result of the operation of a competitive market economy. The political economy is much more complex, characterized by unequal social relations by gender and by structural constraints. Economic outcomes for women are fundamentally affected by these factors. The type of approach that best explains the change in the female labor force activity during economic growth is one that focuses on gender inequality in major social institutions—the firm, the household, the state and the manner in which state policy reinforces (or, alternatively, alleviates) male domination in both of them.

Chapter Six

Lessons for the Women in the Economy Literatures and Implications for the Theory of the State and Feminist Theory

Introduction

This book began by describing a specific puzzling situation regarding women in the labor force and raising two questions. The concrete issue was the failure of measures of female labor force participation in Ireland to rise during export-led development and shifts of economic activity from agriculture to industry and services, two types of structural change likely to substantially increase women's participation. The first question posed was: Why did this happen, quite in contrast to empirical trends elsewhere and to the expectations of several major theoretical perspectives? The second and broader question was: Why is the case study of importance *now* to a wide range of social scientists interested in understanding the subordinate role of women in the economy and/or feminist theorists interested in understanding the foundations of male domination?

This chapter is concerned with the latter question. In finding an explanation for why women's labor force activity in Ireland did not rise during this period, we have uncovered insights useful for two more general levels of analysis: the labor market and economic development literatures examining the role of women in the economy and, at a more theoretical level, the theory of the state and feminist theory. As found in Chapters 2 through 5, the answer to the first question regarding why this occurred in Ireland was because state policies reinforced unequal gender relations in the firm and household and constrained their labor market decisions regarding women.

Because sex discrimination was so explicit in Ireland and the way in which it operated so easy to understand, an alternative approach to understanding male domination and its impact on female economic activity emerged clearly from the analysis. This was the main insight of the Irish case, and the reason it is important to a wide range of social scientists and feminists—that to understand the role of women in the economy it is necessary to use a feminist approach to gender inequality that incorporates the role of the state and the manner in which its policies (family and reproductive rights policies as well as employment) influence unequal gender relations in the firm and household, affecting the decisions of both regarding the economic roles of women. It provides a substantially broader view of the underlying causes of women's subordinate position in the economy and in society. It puts into sharp relief how the state, in addition to and interactively with the firm and household, can be involved in reinforcing (or, alternatively, alleviating) male domination.

With respect to the second question then, this case study is important in two major ways. First, this approach to understanding women's roles in the economy can be useful in addressing critical issues in the labor market and economic development literatures. Secondly, the case study is of value because of the insights it provides for the theory of the state and feminist theory. This analysis provides a new and broader perspective on how gender inequality is maintained, which can be the basis for an alternative feminist approach to male domination.

In this chapter I outline the relevance of the insights and the importance of the approach developed in explaining the Irish case for current controversial issues in the labor market and economic development literatures. These literatures are seeking to understand factors influencing women's economic roles and to develop strategies for change. This approach can be used to understand other dimensions of women's economic roles than simply labor force participation and can be applicable in a range of other countries. I then suggest the broader implications that arise from insights provided in the Irish case for the theory of the state and feminist theory. Its relevance for possible revisions of the theory of the state are simply suggested; however, implications for feminist theory are outlined more specifically. I present an alternative approach to understanding male domination which I call the social structure of patriarchy. This approach emerged in reflecting on the process of male domination in Ireland within the wider theoretical context of feminist endeavors to understand male domination and its relation to class domination. I close by outlining the dimensions of this reformulation and suggest the ways in which it can be useful.

Relevance for Labor Market and Development Literatures

The lessons that can be drawn from this study contribute to both labor market and economic development literatures in two ways: by adding to our understanding of women's subordinate position and via its implications regarding what may be necessary to redress it. The Irish case has provided an alternative perspective for understanding the role of women in the economy. It shows that economic outcomes for women are shaped by gender inequality in the household and firm, including the way state policy affects unequal gender relations in each of these social institutions and influences their economic decision-making regarding women.

This type of approach can be helpful in understanding other dimensions of women's subordinate position in the labor force (for example, lower relative earnings, occupational segregation, unequal access to resources, and lower positions in the employment hierarchy) in industrialized countries and can provide useful input into the controversies surrounding their causes and potential solutions. In addition, the approach to understanding women's economic roles that has emerged from the study can be adapted to provide insights regarding women's disadvantaged roles in many developing countries.

The Irish case provides further insight regarding each of the three current trends in labor market literature mentioned in Chapter 1: the increasing use of approaches that recognize discrimination and structural barriers to women's labor force activity, the increasing recognition of the adverse impact of women's disproportionate household duties on their positions in the paid labor force, and the policy reevaluations and debates occurring in environments that have become increasingly conservative in the 1980s.

First, the Irish case substantiates the need for a theory of gender inequality that examines discrimination and structural barriers to women's economic activity on both the demand and supply sides of the labor market. Discrimination was clearly prevalent in Irish firms and structural barriers to women's labor force activity existed both in the household and at the workplace, reinforced by a range of state policies. With respect to the second issue, the Irish case clearly shows how social relations in the household and women's disproportionate responsibilities restrain their labor force activity and roles.

Just as elsewhere, Irish women are not equal in the formal workplace nor are they equal at home. However, the overall approach developed provides more than simply further verification of these two points. It offers a new and broader perspective on the causes of women's subordinate status and what is necessary to alleviate it: It involves a feminist point-of-view that incorporates the state in conjunction with the household and firm. Since conditions in both the workplace and home impact on women's labor force participation decision and can affect the way in which women are incorporated into the paid labor force, both institutions need to be brought into the analysis. In addition, as shown so clearly in Ireland, gender domination, which would have been likely to erode in both sites during the development process, was reinforced by a wide range of state policies, reproductive rights and family policies as well as employment policies. Therefore, not just in addition to but interactively with the firm and household, the state in Ireland shaped labor market outcomes.

Moreover, the explanation developed with respect to Ireland is a feminist explanation because it has shown that the failure of Irish women's labor force participation to increase was due to unequal power between men and women in both the firm and household and the way the predominant power of men was sustained by state policies even when forces of the development process would have otherwise eroded it. Correspondingly the alternative approach to understanding women's economic roles this study suggests for the wider literatures is also fundamentally feminist.

The validity of this type of feminist approach has been established by (1) exploring a number of potential arguments regarding labor force activity of women in Ireland and showing that it is only when we utilize a feminist theory of gender inequality that an explanation is found; and (2) by empirical work at the level of Western European OECD countries that not only validates the usefulness of this type of approach for the Irish case but underscores its wider applicability. As shown in Chapter 5, the results of regression analyses using data from these 17 countries for this same period suggest that change in the female share of the labor force did not occur because of social enlightenment (as modernization theory implies), because of increased competition (as the neoclassical approach suggests), or because of the increase in social production (as indicated by the orthodox Marxian approach). Results at this wider level support the alternative approach: that women's participation is fundamentally influenced by the way gender inequality mediates the effect of structural change in the major social institutions in the economy.

This brings us to the third trend mentioned in recent labor market literature, that of increasing reassessments and debates regarding the appropriate role of policy, given women's subordinate economic position. This case study indicates that, clearly, state policy does matter. In analyzing the Irish case, a number of insights regarding state personnel, their goals, and the effect of a broad range of policy were developed. As will be shown, they are important not only for the labor market and development literatures but also for the theory of the state and feminist theory.

To review briefly, we found that state personnel in Ireland had two primary goals, economic development with generation of employment and maintenance of traditional relations between the sexes. This revealed that the motivation of state personnel can be more complicated than otherwise thought, that state personnel may also have a view of appropriate gender and familial relations that underlies their policy-making. In addition, we saw how these goals can be contradictory. For example, support for the export-led development strategy would, in the absence of structural constraints, erode male deomination. In Ireland, we saw how this conflict was at least temporarily resolved by use of state policy to avoid the adverse trade-off between growth of employment and patriarchal relations by changing the terms of the trade-off (shifting the N-P curve to the right).

Lastly, it became clear that to understand the constraints on Irish women's labor force participation, we needed to examine the impact of a broad range of state policy, rather than assessing policies on a one-by-one basis. When some explicitly discriminatory employment policies were altered in the later 1970s, Irish women were still relatively constrained in their labor market choices, now by the remaining adverse impact of family and reproductive rights legislation. We concluded that it is because state policy can have these two major objectives which can be contradictory that labor market outcomes for women can differ from those expected by traditional approaches.

What does this contribute in terms of present policy debates? To begin with, it shows us how the broad range of state policy can affect labor market outcomes for women. The Irish case has been a clear demonstration of the manner in which this wide range of state employment policies as well as family and reproductive rights policies subordinated women and precluded the increase in labor force participation. The explicitness of sex discrimination in Ireland and the way in which it works alerts us to the ways in which state policy can constrain women elsewhere and with respect to different dimensions of their economic lives (such as occupational segregation or relative earnings).

In addition, because it provides a broad picture of how state policies subordinate women, it suggests how they must be altered in a coordinated manner to move to a more equitable society. This case shows how changes in one type of policy (such as discriminatory employment policies) can have little effect if other policies (such as family and reproductive rights policies) keep women in subordinated positions. Although substantial attention has been given to the effect of equal employment legislation in the literature, there has been much less analysis of how state policies affect structural inequalities in the household and, in turn, impact on the female labor supply. This case illustrates that such analysis is needed. Because women's economic activity depends on unequal social relations in the household as well as the firm, it is the full spectrum of policies, rather than one particular policy, that shapes women's economic roles. What is needed to facilitate gender equality is a coordination of appropriate employment policies and family and reproductive rights policies that provide women in the home with the same range of choices men have had.

This approach allows us to understand how gender inequality can remain robust even in light of forces that tend to erode it. One aspect of gender domination may be alleviated (such as explicitly discriminatory employment policies in Ireland in the 1970s), while others remain. The ongoing adverse policies then become a major obstacle to labor market equality (family and reproductive rights policies in Ireland). This makes a coordinated approach to policy formation even more critical.

These points regarding the effect of a broad range of state policies are important. It is widely recognized that women are in subordinate positions because of discrimination, it is increasingly recognized that disproportionate household duties have an impact on this, and the critical question is what the appropriate role of public policy is in addressing these issues. Policy options are being considered in political environments that became more conservative in the 1980s, with shrinking funding and substantial deregulation. In addition, policies are evaluated and considered on a one-by-one basis. From what we've learned in analyzing the Irish case, however, this may put the construction of an appropriate set of policies in jeopardy.

In addition to showing that policies do have a substantial impact on women's economic roles, the Irish case shows their effectiveness cannot be accurately ascertained on a one-to-one basis. As in Ireland, the effect of a particular policy may be somewhat limited in two ways. In can be constrained by the presence of other discriminatory state policies, or by the absence of other state policies that would either remove some discrimination on the demand or supply side of the labor market or that would alleviate some of women's disproportionate responsibilities in the household. The potentially liberating effect of the policy under examination (or reevaluation) may be severely limited. The results of the evaluation may therefore be distinctly misleading. Either to fail to enforce existing policies based upon less than dramatic results or to fail to enact additional policies may be a serious mistake.

This realization that we must consider the overall impact of a broad range of policies on women's economic lives sheds light on why some policy changes thought to be beneficial to women have in fact been detrimental in many cases. For example, no-fault divorce, which made obtaining independence from a male more readily possible, has resulted in relative impoverishment of women vis-à-vis their former spouses. In addition, maternity leave in Brazil, thought to address women's home responsibilities at the time of a birth, has resulted in women not being hired for jobs. This wider view of state policy suggested by the Irish case would remind us that in the absence of other policies supportive of women's equality (for example, legislation to ensure equality in the workplace so that divorced women can support themselves and their families or affirmative action programs requiring hiring of women of childbearing age), such pieces of legislation thought to be helpful would in fact be economically disadvantageous for many women.

The Irish case suggests government policies do have a clear impact on women's economic activity. Conservative political environments notwithstanding, the insights from Ireland indicate appropriate policies are definitely necessary. However, what is missing from the current debates regarding policy is the recognition that the importance of public policy rests with the broad spectrum, rather than the effectiveness of particular policies, which may be modest in isolation. Since the causes of women's disadvantaged status lie in their unequal positions in both the firm and household, a wide range of policies are needed to address the problem, not simply either employment policies or family policies. Together, the impact of these types of policies may be much larger.

The Irish case deals with the negative impact of state policies, and the limited effect of omitting one discriminatory policy in this overall policy context. However, it implies that what is needed to affect positive social change regarding women's economic roles is a broad, coordinated policy effort to remove discriminatory policies (family and reproductive rights as well as employment) and an effort to enact other sets of policies that might facilitate equality in the economy.

In spite of the fact that state policy can make a difference, the caveat noted in Chapter 1 remains. Such coordinated change in state policy is necessary but not sufficient for achieving gender equality, including equality in the economy. Although it can be a major improvement, state policy is not the total answer; also needed are changes in social relations in the household and firm that often lie beyond the scope of legislation and/or enforcement.

With regard to developing countries, there has been growing realization that women have been marginalized or exploited by the economic development process. For example, it has been recognized that the failure of food supply systems and many development projects and plans can be attributed to the lack of incorporation of women. However, in order to integrate women, it is necessary to understand the ways in which they have been disadvantaged by development. The general approach suggested in this analysis of the Irish case can be adapted to many of these countries. In examining gender inequality in the household, community or workplace and, particularly how state policies contribute to and reinforce it, we can make substantial gains in understanding the dimensions of Third World women's subordination. As discussed in Chapter 1, the state has contributed to women's subordination in a myriad of ways. Once we understand this fully, it is possible to begin coordinated policy formation to alleviate the situation. Because the state is so deeply involved in the development process, this could be facilitated or promoted through use of state policy.

The ways in which the lives of women in the industrialized world differ from those of the Third World are legion, and have been explored in the rich literature of the past decade and a half. However, understanding some general ways in which subordination of women via state policy exists in both industrialized and developing nations may establish important bonds between groups of women who have been divided. These literatures—labor market literature examining the role of women in industrialized countries and development literature — have been separated, reflecting and reinforcing different perspectives and perhaps unnecessarily dividing groups of women who live in a world increasingly interconnected by economic and political processes. In ways the literature is now exploring, women in industrialized countries and in Third World countries do share major forms of subordination, particularly with respect to their treatment by multinational corporations. Strategies for change may involve coordinated efforts among these groups of women, including efforts to change state policies. This approach developed in analyzing the Irish case, itself a country spanning both the industrialized world and the export-led nations of the developing world, can be insightful in both.

Implications for the Theory of the State

We have learned much about the operation of the state and its impact on women and economic outcomes from analysis of women in Ireland. Now we can sketch a few implications for the theory of the state. The lessons of the Irish case for this theoretical body of knowledge revolve around the fundamental issue that this literature has not integrated gender as a dimension of social life (Skocpol, 1985). There is need for a theory of the state (i.e., why state personnel formulate the policies they do) that incorporates the importance of gender-based as well as class-based relations and how they affect economic outcomes. Much has been done in terms of a class analysis of the state. However, notwithstanding the numerous studies of the gender impact of particular policies and the political issue of the "gender gap," there has been no fundamental incorporation of gender into the analysis. Because of this critical omission, it has not been recognized that in many cases the state may have dual (or multiple) purposes, the gender structure of outcomes being in many cases an implicit goal. Further, the theory of the state must recognize the possibility of such dual goals and then recognize the conflicts and contradictions that can develop between them as illustrated in the case of Ireland.

In analyzing the mode of operation of the Irish state I have presented the framework of an alternative approach to the theory of the state. I have drawn from a relatively undeveloped neoclassical thread of analysis that argues state personnel are informed agents objectively formulating state policy to perpetuate their tenure, subject to constraints. To this I added the Marxist perceptions that social life is characterized by structural inequalities between groups of individuals and that the state mediates economic conflict between classes. Lastly, I have drawn from feminist theory the insight that gender relations are an axis along which structural inequalities persist; social actors may consider patriarchy a goal.

However, my analysis differs from each. I have altered the neoclassical analysis by adding the view that state personnel mediate conflict between capitalists, capitalists and workers, and men and women. Although I agree with the arguments of Marxists that the state has a legitimate function, I have added another dimension to their insights that the state legitimates capitalists (O'Connor, 1973) and the needs of the working class (Bowles and Gintis, 1982). The state also has to legitimate the desires of males in power. I have modified feminist theory by showing that patriarchy is not just reproduced by social relations in the household (or workplace) but can be systematically perpetuated via state policies at the level of society and as these policies affect social relations within the household and capitalist firm.

This is a more complex view of the state and the motivation of state personnel. The state can be part of the institutional structure that reproduces male domination as well as that which perpetuates capitalist social relations. As shown in the case of Ireland, conflicts can arise in attempting to attain both types of objectives. Economic outcomes, such as labor market outcomes for women, must be understood in light of these factors and can differ sharply from the predictions of traditional economic approaches. Outcomes can depend in a complex fashion on the relative strength of state goals, the contradictions between them, the manner in which they are resolved, and the way policies reinforce inequality in other institutions.

Implications for Feminist Theory

The story that we have uncovered in this case study revealed that employment opportunities of Irish women, 1961 – 1981, were not simply shaped by the process of export-led development operating in a competitive market environment. It indicated that the political economy was much more complex. The impact of the influx of multinational corporations and the shift of employment from agriculture to industry and services on female labor force participation was mediated by the structure of state policy and its impact on gender relations. By reinforcing male domination in the household and workplace in the presence of changes that would normally erode them, state employment and family policies adversely affected the labor force decisions of both with respect to women.

This led to the main lesson of the Irish case: to understand women's roles in the economy, we need a feminist approach that considers the objectives of the state and includes a comprehensive examination of the effect of a broad range of government policies on inequality in gender relations and the sex structure of outcomes in the economy. This conclusion is relevant for feminist theory in four ways.

First, and at the most basic level, this case underscores the importance of a distinctly feminist theory of gender inequality. The unexpected lack of increase in women's labor force participation in Ireland could not be explained by traditional approaches. Further support for a feminist theory of gender inequality came from the regional analyses. They showed that change for women does not occur via the line of reasoning of modernization theory, neoclassical theory, or Marxian theory but rather can be explained via a theory incorporating structural changes in the economy as mediated by gender inequality. A feminist approach is required and can no longer be marginalized by adherents of other mainstream analyses. This is a significant step forward in understanding the roles women take in the political economy.

Secondly, this research contributes the recognition that feminist theory must fundamentally incorporate the role of the state in maintaining gender inequality. Although it has lent support to earlier feminist perspectives that we cannot understand the economic roles of women without focusing on unequal gender relations in the household or workplace, the Irish case has shown that the analysis must be developed further, that explanations based on male domination in either the household or firm were inadequate. The perpetuation of patriarchy in Ireland in the face of forces that could erode it required an understanding of the role of the state in maintaining gender inequality. It has shown that state personnel can design policies to maintain traditional relations between the sexes, policies that reproduce male domination at the level of society and maintain unequal gender relations in the household or workplace.

This case study provides the insight that a wide spectrum of state policies must be examined. It illustrates how failure to assess the impact of all state policy on women may lead to incomplete understanding of women's subordination and inadequate policy formulation for effective change. (As discussed earlier in the chapter, altering only discriminatory employment policies may be relatively ineffective in moving women into the labor force if family and reproductive rights policies which place women in disadvantaged positions are still in place. Changes in both types of policy are necessary to move women into positions of equality.)

This builds upon several lines of analysis in the feminist literature, both the literatures cited earlier, which examined male domination as fundamentally reproduced in either the household or the capitalist firm; and upon the more recent feminist literature regarding the role of the state in unequal gender relations. However, it provides a distinctly new perspective by arguing that male domination is not reproduced primarily in any of these institutions, but rather by all of them and the manner in which they interact. This leads to another implication of the case study for the feminist literature.

Third, this study suggests that we must return to and build upon structuralist analyses of gender inequality that have been virtually ignored in the 1980s as interest shifted to pursuing psychoanalytical approaches and postmodern feminism, including the deconstructionist approach. It is only by change in the structured social practices, which can vary among social institutions, that movement toward gender equality can proceed expeditiously.

To review briefly, feminists analyzing women in industrialized countries have developed a set of approaches to understand the subordinate position of women by recognizing that unequal social relations exist along lines of gender (or gender/class, or gender/class/race). They consider the orthodox theories (modernization, neoclassical, and Marxist) inadequate formulations of the systematic subordination of women.

The term "feminist theory" encompasses a wide range of diverse analyses (Tong, 1989). For example, there is liberal feminism (based on the liberal ideology of autonomy of the individual and the importance of independence and equality of opportunity but recognizing the collective subjugation of women), Marxist feminism (which places primacy on the class structure in determining the subordinate role of women), and radical feminism (gender domination is primary). Socialist feminists argue that women are oppressed by the dual systems of class and gender. Other approaches focus on existential or psychoanalytic reasoning. Lastly, there has been a trend to adapt the deconstructionist approach and question whether we have moved to a postmodern feminism.

During the 1970s and early 1980s analyses of female subordination in industrialized countries focused largely on how women were dominated in various social institutions. Although radical feminists argued that male domination was manifest throughout society and social institutions, the position of women in the economy has been thought by most to depend fundamentally on their subordinate position in the household (or private sphere). Alternatives to this were advanced by those who argued that gender inequality is reproduced in the workplace and others who initiated discussion of "public patriarchy." Somewhat similarly, most feminists examining the experience of Third World women locate the roots of women's oppression in their involvement in the "reproductive sphere" of life (this refers to activities performed in the household).

In the 1980s different types of feminist approaches have been emphasized and developed, either focusing heavily on psychoanalytic processes, or questioning the existence of "difference" between male and female and its implications for equality, or deconstructing the meaning of universal concepts regarding male domination and questioning the existence of boundaries between categories of analysis. Structural approaches to male domination were no longer the focal points of analysis.

I argue that it is necessary now to reformulate and renew analysis of gender inequality in key social institutions. The Irish case explicitly illustrates that gender inequality exists and that it is reproduced not only through the institutions primarily examined by the earlier feminist literature, households, and firms, but also via the state and its interaction with social relations in these two sites. The results of this study show that approaches locating patriarchy in the household or firm are incomplete. This provides a more complex view of the way social relations in specific institutions maintain gender inequality than has been presented before.

To progress toward equality, we must recognize and resume examination of the specific and often very different ways in which gender domination is practiced within various social institutions. This necessitates fundamentally revitalizing and extending the structural analysis of male domination in particular social institutions by drawing on earlier structural feminist work (on gender inequality in the household and firm) yet using it in a different type of analysis, which incorporates other social institutions, such as the state, and examines how these social institutions interact to perpetuate gender inequality. The literature of the 1980s has been insightful in adding dimensions to the analysis and in debating underlying issues; however, I would argue that development of effective strategies for change requires an understanding of the manner gender inequality is maintained within specific social institutions and the way social institutions interact to perpetuate male domination.

Lastly, reflection on the insights of the Irish case regarding the way male domination is perpetuated in changing circumstances provided the framework of an alternative feminist approach, which I call the social structure of patriarchy. In the next section, I present a brief outline of the dimensions of such an approach, the roots from which it is formulated, and suggest some of the ways it may be useful.

The Social Structure of Patriarchy:
An Alternative Feminist Approach

As discussed in the previous section, this case study has shown the need to fundamentally broaden the institutional scope of a feminist approach to understanding economic outcomes for women to include the state in addition to the household and firm. It has demonstrated the importance for feminist theory of formulating a comprehensive analysis of the effect of state policy. Understanding the range of ways in which state policies perpetuate gender inequalities provides a sound basis for constructing alternative strategies for change. However, much more can be done.

First, there is widespread acknowledgment of the need for an enhanced conceptual framework for understanding women's subordination and its interaction with other forms of domination. First of all, existing theories are challenged when attempting to explain either (1) the manner in which patriarchy is reproduced within a country, encompassing situations in which it changes form, or (2) the differences in the structure patriarchy assumes cross-culturally. Ireland is a particular example of the former. The perpetuation of male dominance was threatened in Ireland by the export-led development strategy. However, it was maintained because state policies reinforced gender inequality in the firm and household in the face of economic and social forces that could erode it. Other examples exist: For instance, how can existing feminist theory explain the persistence of male domination in a society such as the United States, where a large population of women work and there is a growing percentage of women living in households without males? Similarly, with respect to cross-cultural differences, how can we characterize or explain the differences in gender inequality among countries such as Italy and Spain, or China, Israel, and Sweden?

Second, there is no theory of the interrelationship between capitalism and patriarchy that can explain the variations in their cross-cultural interaction. For example, how can we explain the sharply different changes in the proportions of women in the labor force in different countries that are employing similar economic development strategies (such as Ireland and Singapore)?

The need for further development of feminist theory is further accentuated by the numerous challenges that have arisen from internal debates and external sources. Divisions among feminist theorists have occurred over issues such as the meaning and usefulness of universal concepts; whether male domination is fundamentally materially based or located in culture/ideology; or the nature of the relationship between gender domination and class domination. With the growth of the conservative movement, the relevance of feminism has been further challenged.

I argue that understanding these wider dimensions of patriarchal domination, its variation cross-culturally and over time and differences in the way it interacts with capitalist economic development requires a new conceptual framework. As a step in this direction, I suggest the use of an approach I call the social structure of patriarchy, to analyze the social mechanisms by which patriarchy is reproduced. The social structure of patriarchy is the configuration of social institutions that maintain gender domination in a society at a particular time. It integrates an analysis of the overall impact of a broad range of state policy (ranging from employment policy to family policy) into a framework where the joint impact of a variety of other social institutions (household, firm, educational, and religious systems, unions and the military) are assessed. It facilitates understanding how gender domination is maintained by political, economic, and ideological practices as shaped or structured in these social institutions.

The results of this study can be expressed in terms of this framework. With respect to Ireland, I have shown that the state is one of the primary components of the social structure of patriarchy, in addition to, and as it interacts with, the household and the firm. More broadly, as I will outline below, this type of theoretical approach can be useful because it has the conceptual framework and flexibility to explain either how gender inequality is reproduced within a country, including situations in which it changes over time without being dissipated, or how and why it differs cross-culturally.

The roots of this theoretical reformulation are dual. It is based upon recent developments in the theory of political economy that examine the role of the institutional environment in perpetuating class domination and upon the rich yet somewhat compartmentalized literature that discusses, on an individual basis, the importance of social institutions in the perpetuation of male dominance.

To begin with some examples of the latter, most analyses have been based on male domination in the household or firm. More recently, substantial interest has been generated in the role of the state. However, prior to this case study of Ireland there has been no comprehensive analysis of the overall impact of a broad range of state policy in maintaining gender inequality. The importance of the Church in perpetuating male dominance has been examined by Caldwell (1978). The assistance provided by the educational system in maintaining traditional social roles by gender has been studied (Hannan and Breen, 1983; O'Donnell, 1984). Enloe has analyzed the importance of the military (1983, 1984). The role of unions has been discussed by Hartmann (1976), Cook, Lorwin, and Daniels (1984), Brenner and Ramas (1984), Lewis (1985), and Maroney (1983).

Specific social institutions such as these have often been studied by scholars in their research on unequal gender relations. However, these results have not been integrated. No one has formulated a systematic analysis of how a number of key institutions interact to produce patriarchal domination in ways which may vary over time and cross-culturally. The fact that such an integrated analysis has not been made presents pitfalls for constructing strategies for change. Plans formulated with the use of incomplete conceptualizations of systems of domination and access to power and resources will be unable to achieve their desired results. For example, strategies developed from analyses based strictly on one of these dimensions (such as the firm) are unlikely to achieve the desired results because of the omission from the analysis of other fundamentally important institutionalized social relations (in the household, state, religious or educational systems, military, etc.) that interact to perpetuate gender domination. This has been illustrated in the case of Ireland: Changes in employment policies (almost always the type of change made by any government to increase women's opportunities in the labor market) were relatively ineffective in providing equality of access for women to employment because family and reproductive rights policies that subordinated women to men remained unchanged and constrained their options.

The other basis of this theoretical reformulation is a relatively recent development in the theory of political economy that comprehensively analyzes the role of the institutional environment in perpetuating class domination. It offers an approach that could be adapted to understanding the perpetuation of patriarchy, that could incorporate and build upon the insights of these feminist studies.

The institutional structure of capitalism has long been of interest to economists. Much recent comparative work on capitalist countries has analyzed the different institutional arrangements that reproduce capitalism in the respective countries (e.g., firms and diverse forms of organization of production, varying patterns of state involvement in the economy, different institutional arrangements between management and labor, various financial systems and their relationship to corporations). However, work along these lines was *ad hoc*. These studies have been conducted in isolation from one another with no theoretical foundation linking them.

The development of the concept of the social structure of accumulation offered the first comprehensive theoretical approach to the importance of social institutions (and the way they change) in maintaining capitalist relations of production (Gordon, 1980; Gordon, Edwards, Reich, 1982; Bowles, Gordon, and Weisskopf, 1983). The social structure of accumulation is the set of institutional arrangements in a capitalist society that reproduces capitalism, at least temporarily. More specifically, capitalist development and growth occurs within concrete structures (firms and households buying and selling in markets) that are surrounded by others that impinge on the accumulation process (money and credit systems, the pattern of state involvement, and the pattern of class conflict) (Gordon, Edwards, and Reich, 1982). According to Bowles, Gordon, and Weisskopf (1983), a capitalist social structure of accumulation is composed of social and economic institutions that assure cooperation of other classes (especially the working class) in productive economic activity, the benefits of which flow disproportionately to the capitalists.

I suggest that a similar analysis can usefully be developed for gender domination, that comparative work on women's social and economic position vis-à-vis men's must be based on a complete assessment of the institutional basis for the reproduction of gender inequality in each society. An analogous conceptual approach can be useful in integrating the lines of feminist research that investigate the importance of a variety of social institutions in the subordination of women. This results in the creation of a new theoretical construct: I have suggested the social structure of patriarchy, the specific configuration of institutions that maintain gender domination in a society at a particular time.

Adaptation of this particular approach in political economy to a study of gender inequality offers two specific benefits. First, the dimensions included in the analysis are appropriate for this project: It analyzes unequal power relations in a framework that is historical and dialectical, focusing on contradictions that arise and the process of change. Second, to the extent the categories of analysis used in class analysis are adaptable in constructing an explanation of gender inequality, then an understanding of how class and gender domination interact is facilitated.

Theory is developed to understand the world and to change it. This alternative approach to the reproduction of male domination can make a contribution to both projects. Gender inequality is perpetuated by individuals and groups whose choice of actions and alternatives are structured by a range of institutionalized social practices. Male domination is mediated on an institutional level and on an individual level, within the institutional context. The social structure of patriarchy approach facilitates understanding how gender domination is maintained by political, economic, and ideological practices as shaped by a variety of social institutions that may include any of the following: social relations in the household, firms, the state, unions, educational and religious systems, the media, *and* the manner in which they interact. As illustrated in the case of Ireland, the analysis must be rooted in an understanding of how gender inequality is maintained by interaction among social institutions, that gender inequality in some may be reinforced by inequalities in others.

This alternative approach provides a framework by which to understand fully the distribution of power and access to resources as it differs by gender, how the range of choices differs by gender, and where social change must occur in order to achieve gender equality. Although it delineates the structured practices by which male domination is reproduced over time, it by no means relegates the subordinated to objects or victims. It provides a clear understanding that, although people's actions are constrained and structured by institutionalized social practices, changes that facilitate equality can be planned and executed. This approach can therefore be used as a basis for policy-making. As it models the reproduction of patriarchy on a broader scale, including the manner in which key social institutions interactively reproduce it, use of such an analysis increases the likelihood of developing strategies that are able to promote gender equality. This alternative approach shows that strategies for change must be broad-based. Transformation is necessary in a number of social institutions, depending on the social structure of patriarchy in the country involved.

This new conceptualization can be used to address the problems of analysis faced by existing feminist theory. It is an analytical device that can capture the varying patterns in which patriarchy occurs over time in a society and how it varies cross-country. To provide examples of the former, as one institutional component of male domination diminishes in a country (e.g., male domination in the household may be reduced as women obtain wage labor), another dimension of gender inequality may be enhanced (gender inequality in the workplace may be augmented); or as gender inequality in the workplace is curtailed, state family policy that subordinates women in the household may continue reinforcing their subordination there. This has happened in the United States. In either case, the net result may be little change in overall gender domination; rather, simply an alteration in the institutions that perpetuate it. Without use of a comprehensive approach such as the social structure of patriarchy, the overall effect would not be observed. Analysis of only one of the trends in either example would be misleading.

In addition, although the social structure of patriarchy is historically specific, as empirical work on women's roles in advanced and/or developing countries is reevaluated in such a framework, it may be possible to specify different general types of patriarchy. This would parallel what has occurred in examining capitalist societies. Each capitalist country has an individual social structure of accumulation according to the institutional arrangements prevailing in it. However, general types of capitalist economies have been specified (e.g., market-based economies, welfare capitalism, etc.). For example, with respect to patriarchy, in some cultures the structure of the religious institutions is the major pillar of patriarchal domination. In others, it may be based primarily on customs and laws regulating inheritance and access to land and resources. Arab countries are an example of the former, many African nations of the latter. Use of the social structure of patriarchy approach would allow the historical specificity necessary for development of successful strategies for change while being integrally linked with general types of male domination.

Similarly, this reconceptualization can be utilized in understanding the interrelationship of patriarchy and capitalism (or other class-based systems of domination) and, in turn, for constructing policies for equitable change. If capitalism is understood to be reproduced by social structures of accumulation and male domination by social structures of patriarchy, the manner in which they interact can be more fully specified by analyzing the institutional components of each. For example, depending on the institutional structure of male domination in two societies, the penetration of the same form of capitalist development may have different effects on women's economic roles. This helps us in understanding the different responses in female labor force participation during export-led development in Ireland and Singapore. The social structures of patriarchy differed sharply in these two countries: In the former, the state was a major component of the social structure of patriarchy; in the latter, at least during the two decades analyzed, it was not.

Because the reconceptualization adapts categories used in analysis of class systems, it locates analysis of class and patriarchal systems of domination in somewhat similar theoretical concepts and enables more systematic and complete examination of their interaction. This contributes to the debate over the relative importance of male domination and capitalist exploitation, the manner in which they interrelate, and how they can be alleviated. This contrasts to some analyses at the general level which have often placed too much importance on one dimension of male domination with the result that the implications of changing this aspect were misrepresented. Marxist analyses of "the woman question" are an example. It had been assumed that capitalist development would eradicate gender differences because equality in the sphere of wage labor would destroy the family and the basis for patriarchy. Yet this did not occur. The basic theoretical error in this analysis was to assume there would be no changes in either the institutional structures of patriarchy or capitalism as the two systems of domination interacted and that patriarchy would therefore be eradicated. It was precisely because of the changes in the institutional structures of each that the latter continued to exist, although in a different form. In the case of Ireland, policies were developed by Irish state personnel to reproduce both capitalism and patriarchy: The state was simultaneously an institution in the Irish social structure of accumulation and its social structure of patriarchy.

This is an outline of an alternative approach to male domination, born of reflection on the insights of how male domination was reproduced in Ireland during a critical period of economic and social change. I would argue that understanding the social structure of patriarchy in a country is necessary for developing successful strategies for change and that such an approach can be developed in a manner useful for understanding male domination in ways that differ over time and cross-culturally.

Conclusions

The Irish case has been rich with insights. What we have learned about the state and about the maintenance of gender domination provides us with an approach to understanding male domination and its impact on economic outcomes for women useful elsewhere. It provides a timely perspective on the importance of public policy in ameliorating gender inequality, proving that policy does have an effect and showing that broad-based changes must be made to facilitate equality. This basic insight is useful in both developing and industrialized countries, where the success of development plans and strategies to maintain growth and international competitiveness may depend on the full integration of women.

Furthermore, this case study, addressing issues of gender and the state, also has insights for the theory of the state and feminist theory. Both could not be explored in the scope of this book. Because of this, I simply mentioned a few further implications for the theory of the state, leaving the development of them for a future work. The implications for feminist theory were outlined in more detail. I closed by presenting the framework of an alternative feminist approach, the social structure of patriarchy, discussing the analytical bases for this type of feminist approach, and suggesting the ways it could be developed and used to examine previously unexplainable changes and variations in male domination and the way it interacts with other forms of domination.

Appendix A: The Decomposition Analysis

The decomposition of the change in female employment can be more formally presented: the change in female employment (ΔN) consists of four major components:

1) the total employment effect (change due to increase/decrease in total employment, holding the sex ratio and distribution constant at 1961 levels)

$$\sum_i (\Delta N_i)(d_i)(f_i)$$

2) the distribution effect (change due to altered distribution of employment between sectors, holding total employment and sex ratios constant at 1961 levels)

$$\sum_i (N_i)(\Delta d_i)(f_i)$$

3) the sex-ratio effect (change due to increase/decrease in sex ratios in individual sectors holding total employment and distribution constant at 1961 levels)

$$\sum_i (N_i)(d_i)(\Delta f_i) \text{ and}$$

4) interactions between these effects

$$\sum_i (N_i)(\Delta d_i)(\Delta f_i) + \sum_i (\Delta N_i)(\Delta d_i)(f_i) + \sum_i (\Delta N_i)(d_i)(\Delta f_i) + \sum_i (\Delta N_i)(\Delta d_i)(\Delta f_i)$$

where

d_i = the proportion of the total labor force in industry i in 1961

Δd_i = the change in the proportion of the total labor force in industry i, 1961–1981

f_i = the proportion of the labor force in industry i that was female in 1961

Δf_i = the change in the proportion of the labor force in industry i that is female, 1961–1981

N_i = total employment (male and female) in 1961 and

ΔN_i = the change in total employment, 1961–1981

Appendix B: Relative Wage Hypothesis

According to the neoclassical relative wage hypothesis, the ratio of female to male wages is negatively related to the male to female employment ratio. *Ceteris paribus*, the size of the change will vary according to the elasticity of substitution.[1]

The validity of this line of argument for understanding the lack of change in measures of women's participation in the labor force in Ireland, 1961–1981, can be investigated by examining its explanatory power for Ireland and for the EEC. Regressions can be run of the natural logarithm (*ln*) of the ratio of male employment in manufacturing to female employment in manufacturing on the *ln* (female hourly earnings in manufacturing ÷ male hourly earnings). Support for the neoclassical relative wage hypothesis would be provided by a positive coefficient significantly different from zero on the dependent variable.

As shown in Table B.1, a regression on Irish data from 1966 to 1981 produces a significant positive coefficient on *ln* relative earnings suggesting that the neoclassical argument may have explanatory power.[2] However, to conclude that this significant positive relation represents a response of relative employment to changes in relative earnings requires that we assume other factors constant during this 15-year period and that we therefore accept a technological interpretation of the elasticity of substitution (i.e., that it represents trade-offs in the production process between two types of labor, male and female).

In contrast to this position, I argue that the elasticity of substitution is not simply an economic variable, but that it has political and social determinants. This analysis is not simply measuring the impact of changes in relative earnings on the employment ratio, because there are many other determinants of the demand for female labor which cannot be assumed to be constant. In particular, I suggest that this relationship could be more plausibly interpreted as measuring the power (or lack thereof) of women rather than the elasticity of substitution in a neoclassical sense.

The relevance of the neoclassical interpretation of the elasticity of substitution and my alternative can be examined for the European Community as a whole by running similar regressions using data for the EEC.[3] As shown in Table B.2, regressions on data for the year 1964 and the year 1980 produced a statistically significant negative coefficient on the *ln* relative earnings.[4] This was true for equations that included Ireland (EEC-9) as well as those which excluded it (EEC-8). In addition, regression of the change in *ln* (male ÷ female employ-

Table B.1

Regression of Male–Female Employment Ratios in Manufacturing on Female–Male Earnings Ratios, Manufacturing, Ireland, 1966–1981

		t in ( )
		$\ln \left(\dfrac{N_{m,mfg}^{1}}{N_{f,mfg}} \right)$ on
constant		1.3697
$\ln \left(\dfrac{E_{f,mfg}}{E_{m,mfg}} \right)$		.9772
		$(8.8139)^*$
R^2		.827

Sources: Employment data: calculated from *Census of Population of Ireland*, various years; earnings data: calculated from information in John Blackwell, "Digest of Statistics on Women in the Labour Force" (Dublin: 1982), Table 6.3.
$N_{m,mfg}$ and $N_{f,mfg}$ are male and female employment in manufacturing;
$E_{f,mfg}$ and $E_{m,mfg}$ are female and male earnings in manufacturing.
[1]Data for the years 1966, 1971, 1975, 1977, 1979 and 1981 are directly from Irish Census data; all other years are extrapolations from these.
*significant at the .99 level

ment) on the change in *ln* (female ÷ male earnings), 1964–1980, produced a negative coefficient that was not statistically significant (see Table B.3). This means there is not sufficient evidence to reject the hypothesis that there was no relation between changes in relative earnings and changes in relative employment.

These results at the Community level indicate that the neoclassical relative wage argument is unable to explain changes in employment of women in manufacturing during this period of time. Further, they suggest that my interpretation of the elasticity of substitution is more nearly correct than the neoclassical. In many countries women have both higher levels of earnings relative to men and higher employment ratios (female ÷ male). This could be attributed to the fact that in such countries women have acquired relatively more power politically and have therefore been able to achieve these dual gains.

Table B.2

Regression of Male–Female Employment Ratios in Manufacturing on Female–Male Earnings Ratios, Manual Manufacturing, EEC Countries, 1964 and 1980

	t in ( )			
	1964		1980	
	Eq. 1 (EEC-8)	Eq. 2 (EEC-9)	Eq. 3 (EEC-8)	Eq. 4 (EEC-9)
	$\ln\left(\dfrac{N_{m,mfg}}{N_{f,mfg}}\right)$	$\ln\left(\dfrac{N_{m,mfg}}{N_{f,mfg}}\right)$	$\ln\left(\dfrac{N_{m,mfg}}{N_{f,mfg}}\right)$	$\ln\left(\dfrac{N_{m,mfg}}{N_{f,mfg}}\right)$
	on	on	on	on
constant	.1998	.3835	.3323	.3690
$\ln\left(\dfrac{E_{f,mm}}{E_{m,mm}}\right)$	−2.210	−1.594	−2.5623	−2.3286
	(−3.208)**	(−1.980)*	(−2.114)*	(−2.028)*
R^2	.632	.359	.359	.370

Sources: Employment data: *ILO Yearbook of Labour Statistics,* various years; earnings data: calculated from data in John Blackwell, "Digest of Statistics on Women in the Labour Force" (Dublin: 1982), Table 6.11.
$N_{m,mfg}$ and $N_{f,mfg}$ are male and female employment in manufacturing and $E_{f,mm}$ and $E_{m,mm}$ are female and male earnings in manual manufacturing.
*significant at the .90 level
**significant at the .99 level

In light of these results at the regional level the validity of the neoclassical interpretation of the elasticity of substitution is suspect in Ireland. According to my alternative formulation, the significant positive relationship exhibited in the data for Ireland suggests that Irish women were in a politically disadvantaged position relative to men during this period. It is logical to conclude that the lack of responsiveness of measures of women's participation in the labor force, 1961–1981, cannot be explained by the neoclassical factor substitution argument.

Table B.3

Regression of Change in *ln* of Male–Female Employment Ratio in Manufacturing on Change in *ln* of Female–Male Earnings Ratios, Manual Manufacturing, EEC Countries, 1964–1980

	t in ( )	
	Eq. 1 (EEC-8)	Eq. 2 (EEC-9)
	$\Delta \ln \left(\dfrac{N_{m,mfg}}{N_{f,mfg}} \right)$	$\Delta \ln \left(\dfrac{N_{m,mfg}}{N_{f,mfg}} \right)$
	on	on
constant	.0010	.0315
$\Delta \ln \left(\dfrac{E_{f,mm}}{E_{m,mm}} \right)$	$-.5321$	$-.0581$
	$(-.908)$	$(-.094)$
R^2	.120	.001
D.W.	1.79	1.95

Sources: Employment data: *ILO Yearbook of Labour Statistics,* various years; earnings data: calculated from data in John Blackwell, "Digest of Statistics on Women in the Labour Force" (Dublin: 1982), Table 6.11.

$N_{m,mfg}$ and $N_{f,mfg}$ are male and female employment in manufacturing and $E_{f,mm}$ and $E_{m,mm}$ are female and male earnings in manual manufacturing.

Appendix C: Components of the Change in Population in Ireland, 1901 – 1981

Table C.1

Demographic Profile, Republic of Ireland

	(Average Annual Rates per 1,000 of Average Population)				
	Change in Population	Natural Increase (B–D)	Estimated Net Migration	Births (B)	Deaths (D)
1901–1911	−2.6	5.6	−8.2	22.4	16.8
1911–1926	−3.7	5.2	−8.8	22.1	16.0
1926–1936	−0.1	5.5	−5.6	19.6	14.2
1936–1946	−0.4	5.9	−6.3	20.3	14.5
1946–1951	0.4	8.6	−8.2	22.2	13.6
1951–1956	−4.3	9.2	−13.4	21.3	12.2
1956–1961	−5.6	9.2	−14.8	21.2	11.9
1961–1966	4.6	10.3	−5.7	21.9	11.7
1966–1971	6.4	10.1	−3.7	21.3	11.2
1971–1979	15.4	11.1	4.3	21.6	10.5
1979–1981	10.6	11.9	−1.3	NA	NA

Sources: Statistical Abstract of Ireland 1978; Census of Population 1981 Preliminary Report.
NA = not available.

Appendix D: Vote Maximization Function

The following is a mathematical representation of the social processes underlying the V curves of part 3 in Figure 4.1.

$$V = f(N, P)$$

where

> V = number of votes
> N = rate of growth of employment
> P = maintenance of traditional relations between the sexes (which I term patriarchy) and
> $f'(N) > 0$
> $f'(P) > 0$

and

$$N = f(A) \qquad f'(A) > 0$$
$$P = f(A, S) \qquad P'_a < 0 \text{ and } P'_s > 0$$

where

> A = accumulation process or economic growth process
> S = propatriarchy state policy

Appendix E: Other State Policies

These two policies are based on the implicit notion that women are dependent, supported by (or will be supported by) a male and therefore not needing equal benefits.

Pensions

Considerable discrimination in occupational pension plans existed between males and females. For example, a woman often encountered eligibility requirements not applied to a male: She might not be eligible for the pension plan until she had a certain number of years service (the idea behind this was that women can become participants when they reach an age where they are unlikely to marry); compulsory retirement ages for women could be lower than for males *and* lower than the age at which social welfare retirement pensions are payable; female benefits might be a fixed amount rather than based on a percentage of salary.

A 1978 survey commissioned by the Irish Transport and General Workers' Union (ITGWU) found that, in over one-half of the plans, women were eligible at a later age or with more years of service than men, that in 40% of the plans women were required to retire five years earlier than men, that many had lower pension pay scales for women, and that one-third had a lower benefit payment in the event of the death of a female member than for a death of a male member. (The rationale given was that they had higher withdrawal rates than males and that they usually don't have dependents who must be provided for upon their death.)

Social Welfare

Social welfare codes throughout this period were based on the notion that a married man had economic responsibility for his dependents, that a married woman was a dependent and therefore did not need the same coverage. According to Martin's *Essential Guide for Women in Ireland* (1977) "a man receives an automatic increase with all benefits when he marries. A woman is not entitled to this increase unless her husband is an invalid. Women workers pay proportionately higher contributions and receive proportionately less benefits as well as having to qualify by fulfilling substantial, additional conditions" (58).

For example, unemployment benefits for women last three weeks less than for men or single women, married women are refused benefits if they have children (on the grounds they are "unavailable" for work, even if they worked for many years before submitting a claim); a married woman cannot claim unemployment insurance unless she is not dependent on her husband and has a dependent herself (Council for the Status of Women, *Newsletter,* July 1982).

Notes

Chapter 1

1. Northern Ireland is the primary site of the internecine strife in the past 20 years.

2. The European Economic Community (EEC) consisted of the following nine member countries by the latter part of the 1970s: Belgium, Denmark, Federal Republic of Germany, France, Ireland, Italy, Luxembourg, Netherlands, and the United Kingdom. They were referred to as the EEC-9. This group has been expanded to 12 with the addition of Greece, Spain, and Portugal in the 1980s. It is now being referred to as the European Community, the EC. Plans are in motion to remove all trade barriers within this group of countries by 1992 as the first step in what may be much fuller economic and social integration. Consistent with what the nine country group was called in these decades under study, they will be referred to throughout this book as the EEC.

3. The terms "export-led growth" and "outward-looking development" strategy will be used interchangeably.

4. There are several perspectives regarding women in development. In addition to the integrationist point of view discussed here, Tiano (1987) also discusses the marginalization thesis (that as capitalist development occurs, women are marginalized and face reduced access to resources and constrained productive roles) and the exploitation thesis (women become a low-wage source of labor for capitalists as development occurs).

It is the integrationist/modernization perspective that is relevant to an analysis of female labor force participation in the Irish case, during export-led growth. In analyzing trends in labor force participation rates, the issue is whether women are incorporated or not, rather than if they are incorporated in an exploitative manner. Further, export-led growth elsewhere incorporates women because they are low-wage workers; therefore, in this type of development strategy it is the integrationist approach, not the marginalist approach that would be applicable.

5. It is assumed that Irish women are as productive as Irish men and therefore that differences in the demand for male and female labor would not, on the average, involve differences in productivity. This assumption can be made by virtue of the educational data presented in the next paragraph.

The other major line of argument of neoclassical economists regarding the position of women in the labor market is human capital theory. This approach focuses chiefly on the supply side, the labor supply decision, whereas the discrimination models (tastes or statistical) are demand-side approaches. A primary measure of the human capital people accumulate, and upon which they calculate their expected returns to paid labor force participation, is education. A variety of statistics on the relative levels of education for men and women reveal Irish women were in an advantageous position. OECD data show that it is only in Ireland where the total years of education received by women exceeds that by men (OECD, *Ireland* 1974). In addition, school enrollment of girls above the minimum leaving age is above that of boys only in Ireland, Finland, and France (OECD, 1980). Therefore, to the extent investment in human capital by virtue of education is a determinant of labor force participation, Irish women were not at a disadvantage.

Because of this and because the export-led development process involved an influx of multinational corporations that elsewhere hired large proportions of women, the neoclassical argument regarding women's disadvantaged labor market position and what should happen to it during economic growth that are most applicable are the demand-side models of discrimination.

6. This point is also made by others. For example, according to comprehensive research by Standing (1981: 19), since 1945 labor force participation rates of women have risen substantially in a number of industrialized countries. Mincer (1984) writes that labor force rates of women rose in most of the industrialized countries, 1960–1980.

This is not to be interpreted as an unqualified success for women as for the most part they have been integrated into low-paying, sex-segregated jobs.

7. The increase in the female share of the labor force for Singapore is documented in more detail by Wong (1981).

8. Multinationals locating in developing countries also seek political and economic stability and security. Such stability was available in these Southeast Asian countries, in large part due to repressive political regimes. It was also present in Ireland.

The motivation for location of multinationals worldwide can also include desire to penetrate market areas. This is particularly the case when multinationals locate in other industrialized areas of the world (a substantial part of foreign direct investment).

With respect to Ireland, multinationals were seeking all three: access to the EEC market area, low wages and other financial incentives, and political stability.

9. Payment of lower wages to women did not reflect an assessment of women's productivity as being lower than that of men. Quite the contrary, women were widely considered to be more productive workers.

10. See Blau and Ferber (1986), Chapter 10, for an overview of indicators of women's economic status.

11. The literatures examining women's roles in the labor market are vast, and this book will make no attempt to review them. However, the reader interested in reading further could begin with books providing an overview of the topic such as those by Bergmann (1986) or Blau and Ferber (1986) and references cited in them. For a more complete compendium of the literature, the reader can consult Ferber (1987), a selected, annotated bibliography regarding women and paid and unpaid work.

12. This is somewhat similar to the "vicious cycle" discussed much earlier by Lloyd and Niemi (1979).

13. Industrialized countries diverge most sharply with respect to formulation of family policies, with some such as Sweden having a broader range of policies favorable for women.

14. The term "feminist" encompasses a wide range of approaches, which in the words of Tong (1989), seek to "describe women's oppression, to explain its causes and consequences, and to prescribe strategies for women's liberation" (1).

The word "feminist" as used in this book means an approach that recognizes that relations between the sexes are fundamentally characterized by unequal power, with males dominant over women. In other words, unequal gender relations occur not because the two sexes, choosing from the same set of options simply make different choices, but rather because males on the average have positions of greater power and authority. More specifically, in analyzing male domination in Ireland and the insights it provides, I use a feminist approach that examines how male domination is reproduced by the interaction of institutions such as the household, the firm, and the state. In Chapter 6, I suggest the outline of an alternate structural way of understanding how male domination is reproduced in society, an approach I term the social structure of patriarchy. See Tong (1989) for an overview of all the prominent lines of feminist thought.

In her carefully documented analysis of the definition of the term "feminism" in different times and places, Offen (1988) says "feminism emerges as a concept that can encompass both an ideology and a movement for sociopolitical change based on a critical analysis of male privilege and women's subordination within any given society" (151). This subordination includes social, economic, and political power inequities.

15. The literature studying women in development has also grown enormously since the topic first was formally brought to the attention of the development literature by Boserup (1970). The reader interested in further information on this topic might peruse books by Sen and Grown (1987) or Charlton (1984) or articles by Tiano (1987) and Ward (1987) regarding the general role of women in development. Other sources cited throughout this section and the text are recommended for somewhat more specific areas or topics.

16. Further discussion of lines of feminist thought locating the reproduction of male domination in the household are discussed in Chapter 3 and note

22 of that chapter. More discussion of patriarchy as maintained by social relations in the firm occurs in Chapter 5.

Chapter 2

1. For more information on characteristics of import substitution development and export-led development, see Gillis et al. (1987), Chapters 16 and 17.

2. The export-led development strategy was formally initiated in 1958; however, it was not until the 1960s that it was actually launched. Examination of its impact on women's employment requires use of labor force information, which is only available from the *Census of Population* or *Labor Force Surveys* (taken in selected years). The most appropriate beginning date therefore is with the census of 1961. The 20-year period to 1981 is more than adequate to assess the impact of the process on female employment.

For more information on import substitution development in Ireland, refer to Chapter 4, note 6.

3. The Irish government had long been active in the economy with the *ad hoc* establishment in the years following independence (1922) of a sector of state-controlled industry that includes public transport (busses, the airline, railways, and some shipping), communications, electricity, and some basic industries.

During the period from 1961 to 1981, the role of the Irish state in the economy expanded in two ways: as a direct employer, with the increase in the public sector; and as administrator of the outward-looking development strategy, which has both dramatically reshaped the economy and led to an increasingly complicated and internationally focused macroeconomic policy.

4. This effort by the IDA has continued throughout the 1980s. The reader may often find a sizable advertisement by the IDA, promoting the Republic of Ireland as an attractive site in which to establish a production facility in the EEC, in the *Wall Street Journal* or weekly newsmagazines.

In addition, the IDA has expanded its horizons to include multinationals from the NICs (newly industrializing countries). According to the *Wall Street Journal*, June 27, 1989, Ireland has been actively encouraging South Korean firms interested in producing in Europe to locate within its borders.

5. Growth in each of these industries was 30 – 40 percent a year, compounded annually during the last decade.

6. According to Joseph Grunwald and Kenneth Flamm (1985), 82 percent of electronics production workers in Mexico in 1980 were female. Rachel Grossman (1980) indicates that 90 percent of assembly workers in electronics plants in Penang, Malaysia were women. Trends in the proportion female in foreign work forces in Ireland will be examined more fully in Chapter 4.

7. In addition, they offer a wide range of other subsidies or allowances such as 100 percent employee-training grants, complete freedom to repatriate profits, loan guarantees and interest subsidies, double taxation agreements, ad-

vance factory space, duty-free importation of capital equipment, and a variety of after-care support services.

8. For information on composition of exports in 1962 and 1981, see OECD, *Ireland* 1964 and 1982. Additionally, there was some change in the dependence of the Irish economy on the United Kingdom as a trading partner. Exports to the United Kingdom fell from 73 percent to 40 percent; however, the proportion of imports from there remained constant at one-half.

9. Data in Kennedy and Dowling (1975:20), shows how low Irish growth rates in the 1950s were relative to the other Western European countries. These relatively high growth rates were reduced when the recession began in 1979.

Additionally, long-standing trends of high emigration and negative growth of population were reversed. Over a century and a quarter of emigration, capped off by what were considered extraordinary levels of 43,000 a year emigrating in the 1950s, subsided in the 1960s. This trend was reversed in the 1970s when net immigration began to occur. The rate of growth of population, which had been decreasing almost continually since the turn of the century, began to grow after 1961 and in the early 1980s was growing at 1.3 percent a year, the highest in Europe (Minard, 1982).

10. However, even an economist like Dermot McAleese (1977a), who has long studied foreign direct investment in Ireland and believes it is favorable, is careful not to attribute all the changes to it. He says there is suggestive rather than compelling evidence regarding the causality between industrial policy and industrial growth.

The growing role of foreign firms in the Irish economy is not without controversy. There are substantial differences of opinion among these economists with regard to the net benefits and stability engendered by this process, particularly in light of the high costs of the incentives package and the limited change in total employment. (See Note 13, this chapter.)

11. It is hard to estimate closely the full extent of foreign presence in Ireland for two reasons. First, most of the data is categorized as New Industry or Grant-Aided Industry (these terms will be used here as synonymous although they are technically different). This terminology is misleading, perhaps deliberately so, and it obscures the full role of foreign investment in Ireland. The term New Industry includes (1) "domestic" industry ("established Irish and *overseas* firms plus new Irish firms") and (2) "new overseas investment" ("overseas firms which have just commenced operations") (McAleese, 1977b:13). Use of "new overseas investment" when discussing foreign direct investment clearly understates actual foreign investment by an amount equal to the overseas component in "domestic" industry.

Second, Sweeney's research revealed that, in 1972, foreign corporations owned over half of the fixed assets of Irish registered industrial and service companies. However, only 45 percent of these foreign-owned assets appeared in Industrial Development Authority (IDA) reports accounting for the role of foreign-owned corporations. Many British companies had subsidiaries in Ireland, but only one-third of them had a relationship with the IDA. Sweeney hypothesized that those not counted must have been in the older protected industry and were therefore termed "home" industry (National Economic and Social Council, 1980:35).

12. For the last half of the 1970s exports were still growing at 10 percent per year, pushed by the 13 percent yearly increase in industrial exports.

13. With regard to employment, however, the picture is mixed. The increasing numbers employed by foreign corporations have been counteracted by employment decreases in both agriculture and traditional industry. Total employment, allegedly a primary goal of the new development strategy, failed to show much growth (NESC, 1980:20–23).

Specifically, total employment, 1949–1961, was falling at an average annual rate of 1.3 percent; this was curtailed, 1961–1973, when employment gains in industry and services just offset declines in agriculture; it wasn't until the period 1973–1978 that average annual rates of growth of employment in industry and services offset the decreases in agriculture for a net overall growth in employment of 1 percent a year (Nolan, 1981:154).

The limited growth of total employment has been recognized. In light of the increasing costs associated with the development strategy, the benefits of attracting foreign direct investment have been questioned. This culminated in an extensive study of the strategy by an outside consultant, *A Review of Industrial Policy* (NESC 1982a and 1982b).

14. Census data (the source of information on labor force participation rates and female share of the labor force for all these countries) must be used with a full understanding of its limitations. The data does not distinguish between full-time and part-time workers. In addition, statistics regarding the numbers gainfully occupied may be inaccurate due to the self-reporting of one's principal economic status, the questions asked on census forms, and different conventions regarding inclusion of individuals in certain occupations as gainfully employed. Furthermore, there is widespread undercounting of women as unpaid family laborers (on family farms and businesses) and women in the informal sector. Activities in the underground economy are not picked up by census data and there is the additional problem that those in home duties are not considered among the economically active in spite of their various productive activities. (See Beneria, 1982; Standing, 1981:25–54; OECD, 1979:21, 23).

15. $\text{LFPR}_j = (f_j/F_j) \times 100$ where

LFPR is the labor force participation rate for women in category j
(a specified age and/or marital status grouping);
f_j is the number of women of category j who are gainfully
occupied (at work or unemployed);
F_j is the total number of women in category j; and

FEMALE SHARE$_i$ = $[f_i/(f_i + m_i)] \times 100$ where

f_i is the number of women at work in the ith sector of the
economy;
m_i is the number of men at work in the ith sector.

These statistics measure slightly different aspects of the labor force. The "share" approach uses "persons at work" whereas the labor force participation rate is those gainfully occupied ("persons at work" and those "unemployed, having lost or given up previous job"). The relation between the two measures can be expressed as follows:

$$\text{Female share} = \frac{[\text{LFPR}(F) \times (\# \text{ females}) - \text{UN}(F)]}{[\text{LFPR}(F) \times (\# \text{ females}) - \text{UN}(F)] + [\text{LFPR}(M) \times (\# \text{ males}) - \text{UN}(M)]}$$

where LFPR(F) is the aggregate labor force participation rate for women, UN(F) is the number of unemployed women; LFPR(M) and UN(M) are similar measures for men.

16. Of course, intergender comparisons can be made by comparing similarly defined labor force participation statistics for both genders.

17. The literatures examining the position of women in the labor market usually look at one of these types of data or the other. For example, the neoclassical human capital approach focuses mainly on variables affecting the supply of labor decision and utilizes labor force participation rate information. The neo-Marxist segmented labor market approach analyzes factors influencing the demand for labor and observes the female share of sectors or occupations.

Labor market decisions occur in both firms and in households. I will argue that a complete understanding of labor market outcomes requires understanding of gender-based inequalities in both firms and households and how these are influenced by state policies.

18. Irish Census of population and International Labour Organization (ILO) data on the female labor force participation rate and female share in Ireland differ slightly. Given the limited documentation accompanying each database it is not clear why. I have therefore chosen to use both, assuming that the census data is more accurate, but wanting to preserve as much comparability among the Western European countries as possible.

19. That this was not due to a demographic shift, such as a change in the structure of the population of working age, will be discussed in Chapter 3. For the first time in over a century, women's share of the total labor force in 1981 regained the level it had in 1861 (29 percent).

20. Another technique developed recently that provides a more detailed perspective on changes in women's age-participation patterns is cohort partic-

ipation rate analysis (see Lloyd and Niemi, 1979:72–73). It has been used to observe changes in labor force participation at each age in the life cycle of successive cohorts of women in the United States.

21. The chief trends in these age-specific labor force participation rates—the sharply falling participation of 15–19-year-olds, due to changes in state financing of public education and increased years spent in schooling; the declining labor force participation rate of women aged 65 and over attributable to decreases in the number of people engaged in farming and increases in social welfare provisions; the increasing rates for women aged 20–54—were all common to OECD countries during these years (OECD, 1979:25–31).

22. There are normally differences between male and female labor force participation rates within countries, although the size of this difference can vary substantially across countries. Typically, male rates are higher and falling (due to increased years in schooling by young men and increased coverage of pension programs) whereas female rates are low but rising (OECD, 1979:17–18; OECD, 1979:20; Lloyd and Niemi, 1979:17). The case of Ireland differs from this general profile because women's rates did not rise.

23. I use EEC data because data is not available for this entire period for all Western European OECD countries.

24. Divorce is illegal in Ireland and therefore neither "divorced" nor "separated and/or divorced" is an officially recognized census category. The number of separated couples rose in the late 1970s. Data on them was placed in the "married" census category, so there are no official statistics on the labor force participation patterns of divorced or separated women.

The *Census of Population 1979* sought information on marital status on the basis of present legal status with provision for four categories: "single," "married," "widowed," and "other." Of the 7,600 persons who returned themselves as "other," "many of these entered further information (e.g., 'separated,' 'deserted,' 'annulled') which indicated that the appropriate 'present legal status' was 'married.' It was therefore decided to include all persons returning themselves as 'other status' with the 'married' in the tabulations" (Vol. II, p. ix).

In the 1981 census 14,000 persons classified themselves as "other" and again were placed within the "married" category by the Central Statistics Office.

25. According to United Nations data for 1970, the labor force participation rates of divorced women in six European OECD countries had an unweighted average of 60 percent. This suggests that placing "other" women into the "married" category in Ireland inflated the actual labor force participation rates of gainfully occupied married women *living with spouse.*

For example, if one makes the following assumptions—that half of those self-reporting as "other" marital status were separated women; that they could therefore be more appropriately classified as single; that two-thirds of them would have been working in the late 1970s—and adjusts the labor force participation rates by marital status accordingly, the labor force participation rate of married women would fall to 14.9 percent in 1979 and 16.9 percent in 1981. Although these are only slight downward adjustments, it is also unlikely that those self-reporting as "other" fully represent persons separated in Ireland. Further downward adjustments would be necessary if complete information were available.

26. Although the participation rate of married Irish women was rising during this period, it remained at such low levels that its positive impact only just offset the downward trends in the participation of single women (teens and older women) and widows—declines that were typically occurring in Western European OECD countries because of increased years in schooling and the spread of old-age insurance.

27. Looked at from a slightly different perspective with OECD data, in 1979 married women constituted 61 percent of the total female labor force in Europe as a whole whereas in Ireland they were only 30 percent (OECD, 1984:32).

28. As will be shown in Chapter 3, the overall change in the female labor force was composed of diverse changes in these subsectors: combinations of declining and growth sectors as well as changes in the proportions of women within these subsectors.

29. There can and have been differences across countries or over time in the percent female in a sector, but for this period, "male" and "female" industries can be considered the same for these countries.

30. Data of this type is not available for Singapore.

31. The major changes in these two decades were alterations in the importance of these sectors, the addition of two sectors (metals rose from twelfth to seventh place, fire and insurance rose from eleventh to fifth) and the decline of two sectors (paper and other industry).

32. From the point of view of the ten largest employers of women in 1981, there were decreases in the share of women in five of them during this period.

33. Due to lack of data in comparable form, analyses by detailed sector are not possible for all Western European OECD countries throughout these two decades.

Walsh (1970–1971:89–91) studied the relationship between the sex ratios in detailed Irish industrial categories and similar categories for the United Kingdom, using 1966 data. His data revealed that there was a higher sex ratio in Great Britain than in Ireland. Out of 35 manufacturing categories, the female share in Britain exceeded that in Ireland in 24, was roughly equal in 4, and was larger in only 7.

34. As will be shown in Chapter 4, there are significant differences in the gender composition of the work forces of domestic-owned and foreign-owned firms in Irish industrial sectors, with foreign-owned firms hiring substantially larger proportions of women in eighteen out of twenty subsectors.

Chapter 3

1. Hirata's argument countered the expectations of Helieth Saffioti and Elsa Chaney and Marianne Schmink that industrialization would marginalize women because of the decline in sectors that traditionally employed women (textiles) and an increased demand for skilled workers. (See Humphrey, 1984 for a review of this controversy.)

2. These differing trends corresponded to periods of export-led and import substitution industrialization respectively.

3. As will be shown later in this chapter, there was a latent supply of female workers, interested in obtaining employment. Therefore, it was not a problem of supply constraints, and it is valid to investigate a demand side approach.

4. The decomposition analysis is an adaptation of shift-share analysis, often used in examining change in regional economies.

5. Calculations are available from the author upon request.

6. This result was obtained by recalculating the decomposition analysis with these assumptions: total employment increased as it did; sex ratios changed as they did; however, distribution of employment between sectors remained at the 1961 proportions. Computations available from the author.

7. See Chapter 4, note 17. See Mahon (1987) regarding the 1980s.

8. As adapted to this situation, the elasticity of substitution is the percentage change in the ratio of male employment to female employment divided by the percentage change in the ratio of female earnings to male earnings. According to neoclassical theory, it ranges in value from zero to positive infinity. Therefore, as the ratio of female earnings to male earnings increases, there would be an increase in the ratio of male employment to female employment. For a more detailed explanation of the elasticity of substitution, see Jones (1976), pp. 33–34.

9. They interviewed 5000 women in the age bracket 14–64 in early 1971 following the methodology of the Household Budget Inquiry 1965/66 (Central Statistics Office).

10. Ireland has been widely characterized in the Irish literature as a labor surplus economy (Walsh, 1978; *Second Programme for Economic Expansion, 1964–1970*:165; O'Neill, 1972:40).

11. The rate of growth of the population of working age (15–64) depends on the rate of growth of population and its age structure.
Labor force participation rates provide the link between the characteristics of the population of working age and those of the labor force. Therefore, the size and composition of the labor force are influenced by changes in the total population as well as by changes in labor force participation rates.

12. One of the two major components of the rate of growth of total population, the rate of natural increase, had been rising since the 1930s, based on a steadily falling death rate and a high and unchanging birth rate. This did not translate into a positive population growth rate before the 1960s because of trends in the other component, net outward migration.

Since the Great Hunger of the 1840s, emigration had been a primary method of dealing with the problem of providing a means to make a living for the population. It had increased from the 1930s, reaching twentieth-century highs in the 1956–1961 period. After the initiation of the export-led development strategy, this outflow diminished throughout the 1960s and was reversed, 1971–1979, when net immigration occurred.

13. Demographic variables have long been recognized as important factors which influence trends in labor force composition and the pattern of women's labor force participation (Durand, 1948/1968; International Labour Organization, 1981; Moore and Elkin, 1983). However, the interrelation between demographic variables, labor supply and labor force participation, and the structure of job availability has not been fully understood. According to the ILO, it is still not clear what the impact of policy is on this network of interaction (1981:2), and much recent research has been designed to decipher these relationships.

14. In addition, the rate of natural increase in Ireland is high relative to other Western European countries. This is because the Irish birth rate is higher than that of the other Western European OECD countries whereas its death rate is comparable, having fallen throughout this century as it did in the other countries.

To continue comparisons with Singapore, the rate of natural increase fell from 2.3 percent in 1966 to 1.2 percent in 1979, largely due to decreases in fertility (Wong, 1981:434).

15. The apparently paradoxical increase in real wages which accompanied this job scarcity has been discussed in Walsh (1978). Refer also to Chapter 2, note 13 for its discussion of the problem of employment generation and the controversy regarding the ability of the export-led development strategy to generate sufficient employment.

16. According to OECD projections for the 1975–1990 period, this pattern of divergence between the rate of growth of population of working age and the growth of employment was to continue, at higher levels of change. The population of working age was expected to grow by 24 percent and the labor force by 16 percent.

In comparing the projections for the 1975–1990 period with the 1960–1975 period, Ireland was the only country in the Western European OECD expected to have simultaneously an increase in the rate of growth of population, an increase in the growth rate of population of working age, *and* an appreciable fall in the overall labor force participation rate (OECD *Demographic Trends 1950 – 1990*, 1979:16,32–33).

17. The migration statistics utilized are "estimated" net migration rates because there are no direct measures of inward and outward flows of population in Ireland. Instead, net migration is the residual after the number of persons in the state on census night has been adjusted by the number of births and deaths occurring since the last census (known directly from vital records). The net migration figures therefore may include some effects of nonmigratory movements, such as a change between successive censuses in the number of Irish visitors abroad and/or the number of foreign visitors in the state.

18. Net migration was reversed again during the period 1979–1981 as the impact of the recession was felt in Ireland and unemployment rates increased.

19. In addition, the female share of net outmigration in the 15–29-year-old group increased, 1956–1979.

20. According to a study by anthropologist George Gmelch (1979) married Irish women immigrating back to the West of Ireland from outside the country were often unable to find jobs (25, 30).

21. More recent studies of émigrées were not possible at this writing. The mid-1970s Irish census had been cancelled and a detailed analysis awaits the publication of detailed results of the next Census of Population.

22. Feminist theory is a broad body of knowledge spanning a variety of viewpoints regarding the source of gender inequality in a society. Refer to Chapter 6 for a brief outline of these literatures or see Rosemary Tong (1989).

Although some feminists have argued that patriarchy is fundamentally reproduced in the firm (Hartmann, 1976), because of the low proportions employed in Ireland, I have focused primarily on the household in this section.

Emphasis on the importance of the household in perpetuating male dominance has come from a number of feminist perspectives. It began with the work of Costa and James and was expanded by the domestic labor debate (see Eisenstein, 1979, for a review of the major articles). It has been implicated by psychoanalytic studies of mothering (Chodorow, 1978). Analysis of time-budget surveys of household labor indicated its persistence (Hartmann, 1981a).

More rigorous analytical attention has been revived by the work of Nancy Folbre, who has used Marxian categories to analyze exploitation in the household (1982 and 1984). Ferguson develops a broader historical typology of forms of patriarchal domination based upon her "sex-affective production systems" approach. In advanced capitalist societies, she argues that the major labor exchanges and distribution of goods of this system occurs in the family-household.

In Britain, although Barrett (1980) analyzes the importance of numerous social institutions in reproducing patriarchy, these appear to be derivative of household relations. The critique of Barrett by Brenner and Ramas (1984) locates it basically in the household, based on biological reproduction.

Work incorporating households into the world systems analysis has been done by Spalter-Roth and Zeitz (1981) and Smith, Wallerstein, and Evers (1984). On a more general level (i.e., the citations just given refer to feminist perspectives on the household) for a review of attention given households in the development literature see Folbre (1986a).

It must be noted that the past decade has witnessed increasing interest in social relations in the household from a variety of theoretical points of view, with particular attention to relations of domination and structural conflict. Folbre succinctly reviews the neoclassical and Marxist perspectives and their revisions, which range from the assumption of altruism in the household to bargaining or conflict models of household inequality (1986b).

23. Although this explanation is totally distinct from the job-scarcity argument examined in the previous section and is based on a different theoretical framework, it may be used in conjunction with that analysis; that is, that patriarchy is the mechanism which ensures that in a labor surplus economy it is men who are allocated the jobs.

24. This analysis was based on the survey data described in the Walsh and O'Toole study (note 9).

25. R^2 is the proportion of the total variation in the dependent variable explained by the regression.

The continuing importance of the opinion of the husband throughout this period is suggested by the results of Fine-Davis's survey in 1981. "Husband's disapproval" was seventh on the list of reasons for why the nonworking mothers interviewed were not employed at present (*Working Party on Child Care Facilities for Working Parents*, 1983:146).

26. The total fertility rate for a given year is the number of live born children that hypothetically would be born to a woman if she were to live to the end of her childbearing years (15–49) and bear children at each age in accordance with age-specific fertility rates of that year (*World Tables*, 1983). It is considered representative of average completed family size.

The relationship between the birth rate and the total fertility rate is as follows: the birth rate depends on changes in the proportion of women of childbearing age in the female population and changes in the total fertility rate. As shown in Table 3.7, the Irish birth rate has varied only slightly during the past 80 years and remains at essentially the same level as at the turn of the century (22 live births per thousand). Its constituents changed slightly, 1961–1981. There was a slight increase in the proportion of women of child-bearing age relative to the total female population (from 43 percent to 46 percent) and a small decrease in the total fertility rate (the total fertility rate, 3.8 in 1961, fluctuated in the 1960s before declining slightly, 1973–1981, to 3.2).

Birth rates declined substantially in all other Western European OECD countries from 1960 to 1977; the level in Ireland became the highest in that region by 1970 and, over the period, exceeded the unweighted average by an increased amount.

27. There is some controversy over the direction of the relation and the source of causality, whether direct or indirect, via some other variable(s). Most industrialized countries exhibit an inverse relation between female labor force

participation rate and fertility, whereas the results are not so strong in low-income countries.

28. The degree of motivation of mothers to work is more difficult to assess. The surveys by Walsh and O'Toole in 1971 and Fine-Davis in 1981 indicate a substantial number of married women were interested in returning to work (Walsh and O'Toole, 1973; Fine-Davis, 1983a).

Chapter 4

1. There is considerable debate over the behavior of state personnel in the wider social sciences literature. Skocpol (1985) reviews the literature and analyses the major trends in the theory of the state, carefully providing an overview of the complexities involved in the theory of the state. Nevertheless, to assume state officials are interested in perpetuating their own tenure is a reasonable assumption. In fact, the notion of the self-interest of state officials is a basic assumption of a subdiscipline of economics, public choice theory. This approach has experienced tremendous growth and considerable impetus in recent years, especially with the awarding of the 1986 Nobel prize in economics to James Buchanan, who is considered the "father" of public choice theory.

Although not a public choice theorist, I feel there is legitimacy in assuming state officials are substantially motivated by perpetuating their own tenure, and securing votes and support by their performance to do so. To put this in terms of Appendix D and the figures in Chapter 4, they are interested in formulating a set of policies that will attain the highest iso-vote curve for them. However, they are constrained by limited resources and the trade-offs involved in facilitating employment growth while maintaining gender domination.

2. The marriage ban or marriage bar refers to the policy of compulsory retirement of women from employment upon marriage. It applied to females in clerical jobs in service industries, banks, local authorities, and semi-state bodies. It was phased out over a four-year period, 1973–1977. It will be discussed further in this chapter.

3. Not surprisingly, this legislation reflected the teachings and influence of the Irish Roman Catholic Church. Ireland is 97 percent Catholic, and the Church in Ireland has been an extremely important political force. It has been somewhat isolated from the erosion of importance that the Church has experienced during the twentieth century in other predominantly Catholic countries. For more information on the impact of the Church on women, see Beale (1987) and Mahon (1987).

The impact of Catholicism on women's labor force activity in the Western European OECD countries is investigated econometrically in Chapter 5 and found to lack significance.

4. Preliminary research by Mary Robinson (1979:62) regarding women's roles in this early period in the Republic of Ireland reveals no opposition by women to legislative changes such as prohibition of divorce, ban on the availability of contraceptives, and protective legislation. Even within the trade union

movement, there appeared to be virtually no support for the right of women to have access to employment or for equality of rights for women who were employed. Not surprisingly, many male trade unionists opposed female employment, reflecting conventional attitudes towards women and a fear of competition in a country of job shortages (Daly, 1979:77). Mary Daly (1979:75–78) cites weak opposition by trade unions to the marriage ban, and her initial research indicates that there was confusion within the ranks of the female trade union membership itself regarding (1) the appropriate roles for women, (2) access of women to work, and (3) equal pay.

There has been no comprehensive and satisfactory analysis of why there was no movement to ensure access to employment for women or equality of conditions; why opposition was weak; and what, if any, links there were between increased women's industrial employment in the 1930s and the enactments. Among important factors suggested by Daly, but unexplored, in considering why there were no advances for women are weak trade union response, the relative social stagnation in the 1930s and 1940s combined with high unemployment and emigration, and the harshness of women's lives. Although a part of the explanation, these reasons are inadequate; even when these conditions changed in the 1961 – 1981 period there was still little overall gain for women.

5. Information on migration is presented in Tables 3.5, 3.6, and C.1.

6. Import substitution strategy placed great importance on economic self-sufficiency. The state owned and ran industries in certain sectors of the economy unlikely to be developed by the private sector. The import substitution strategy was accompanied by an agenda promoting Irish nationalism (including the resurrection of the Irish language).

Import substitution had appeared successful at first with industrial employment increasing 50 percent in the mid-1930s. [Women's share of industrial employment rose to 22.4 percent in 1936 (from 20 percent in 1926) with the creation of much light industry (Daly, 1981b)—a higher proportion than women's share in 1981 (19.5 percent).]

However, by the early 1950s the failures of this strategy became increasingly evident and a shift toward increased exports occurred. The world's first free-trade zone had been established at Shannon, Ireland in the late 1940s (Stanton, 1979). Import substitution was limited by the small internal market in Ireland (Long, 1980) and by balance of payments deficits that arose when the level of exports couldn't support the increased demand for industrial and consumer imports (National Economic and Social Council, 1980:5). The government corrective in the 1950s, a deflationary policy, resulted in stagnation: decreased industrial employment, higher unemployment, and the highest rate of emigration since the 1880s (NESC, 1980:5). This contrasted sharply to the generally prosperous period of growth experienced in Western Europe. Social unrest increased.

Although much has been written about this policy shift, a clear analysis of the motivation behind the shift has not been constructed. Traditional economic analyses emphasize the need to rectify the balance of payments deficits, attract new technology, and provide employment. However, the choice of strategy was not unanimous. Others such as Stanton (1979) and Wickham (1980) seek an explanation in the motivations of particular classes.

With respect to women, job opportunities during the 1950s were very limited and organizations such as the Irish Women Workers Union declined. Protective legislation limiting the hours which women could work was enacted in 1955 (Robinson, 1979:67). Issues of equal pay or equal access to employment for women were never mentioned, apparently considered irrelevant in the face of recession and emigration. The number of women in farming areas declined and domestic service ceased to be the single most important source of employment for women. Large numbers of women emigrated.

7. Ireland had to conform to the Directive of 1975 (equal pay) and the Directive of 1976 (equal treatment for men and women as regards access to employment, vocational training, and promotion and working conditions). It implemented the latter in 1977. In addition a directive was passed in 1978 regarding changes in social security. Ireland was required to conform to it in the early 1980s.

8. Protective legislation in the 1950s. And, as will be reviewed in detail below, policies were established to provide largely male employment during export-led development.

9. The Irish women's movement, which had been revitalized in the mid-1960s over the issue of unequal pay, broadened in scope. The Commission on the Status of Women was appointed to assess the entire economic, legal, and social environment of women in Ireland. It published a comprehensive report in 1972, describing multifaceted discrimination against women and proposing a list of policy changes. It was instrumental in pressuring for social change and was joined by the efforts of numerous other groups founded in the early 1970s to promote equal rights for women.

For information on the women's movement in Ireland see Barry, 1988; Daly, 1979; Mahon, 1987; Prendiville, 1988; Robinson, 1988; Robinson, 1979 (both in MacCurtain and O'Corrain, 1979); Rose, 1975; and Smyth, 1988. The 1988 references are in a special issue of *Women's Studies International Forum* (1988). They provide information regarding the Irish women's movement in the 1980s and document the political controversies regarding abortion in 1983 and the divorce referendum in 1986. A personal account of an Irish feminist is available in Levine (1982).

10. For a more complete explanation of this type of analytical device, the reader could consult an introductory economics text under the topic of production possibilities curves (a similar construct).

11. Similarly, to obtain more complete information on the meaning and derivation of curves like the V curve, the reader can consult an introductory economics text under the topic of indifference curves.

12. This is a comparative statics model. Although the real world is dynamic, this type of model is often used to simplify understanding of the rela-

tionship between key variables. The curves in each graph in Figure 4.1, for example, are drawn with the assumption that other factors which could influence the relationship between the variables on the x and y axes are held constant. State policy is clearly such a variable and we have traced how changes in it can alter the position of some curves. Shifts can also occur if there is change in the way patriarchy is reproduced in a society (i.e., the particular set of social institutions that perpetuate it may change), the way capitalism and patriarchy interact, or the interactive human agents themselves.

13. For further information on employment policy, including up-to-date information, consult Smyth (1983) (chapters on education and training and work) or Working Party on Women's Affairs and Family Law Reforms, 1985 (chapters on employment and education) or contact the

Employment Equality Agency
36 Upper Mount Street
Dublin 2

or

Council for the Status of Women
64 Lower Mount Street
Dublin 2

14. With respect to the research mentioned in Chapter 2 on women, most papers in the latter part of this period simply described the position of women in the Irish labor market (Blackwell, 1982; Garvey, 1983; McLernon, 1980; Walsh, 1982). Although data has been collected on women in the labor force, it has never been analyzed in terms of how it compares to the experience of women in other countries (Western European or export-led) and in terms of the effect of economic development on women. Earlier work by Walsh and Whelan (1973–1974) applied the neoclassical labor supply work of Mincer and Cain to Irish women. These papers were of an academic nature. With the exception of one brief and cursory paper by Walsh (1982) discussing the impact of membership in the EEC on Irish women, there was virtually no analysis of the effect of the development program on women. In the 1980s some Irish women have begun to work along this line (Jackson, 1982; Jackson and Barry, 1983; Rudd, 1983).

It is the literatures for praxis (the planning of the development process and its strategies to alleviate the unemployment problem) that are most useful to examine in assessing the approach taken toward women. As mentioned in Chapter 2, the main documents establishing the export-led development plan were *Economic Development* and the first *Programme for Economic Expansion*, both published in 1958. Neither discussed the potential role of women in this development strategy.

15. These works are from, respectively, a respected research institute in Ireland (Economic and Social Research Institute) and a prominent Irish economist, Brendan Walsh. The ESRI conducts many research projects utilized in government policy-making. Walsh, a professor at University College–Dublin, has served on select government commissions.

16. Conclusions are couched in terms of males (Walsh, 1974:111, 113, 115).

17. Strategies ranged from ways to reduce the supply of labor (reduce the number of hours worked, early retirement, increased years in education, demographic policy, changes in the structures of tax and transfer policies) to policies designed to increase the demand for labor (public employment, subsidization of private sector employment).

18. This normative analysis contrasts sharply with his academic examination in the early 1970s of Irish female labor supply, using neoclassical analysis; he did not include taxes or welfare/pension systems and therefore did not account for their impact on female labor supply.

19. This disparity existed in the service sector also. According to the *Annual Report 1967–1968* of the Department of Education, from December 1964 salaries of national teachers were as follows:

for principals and assistants:
married men: £770 − £31 × 5, £41 × 5, £51 × 4, £52 × 3 − £1,490.
women/single men: £620 − £24 × 5, £32 × 5, £41 × 4, £42 × 3 − £1,190.

(in 1964 women were 40 percent of principals and 78 percent of assistants).

20. However, these enterprises constituted a small percentage of the total manufacturing labor force in these years and, therefore, the fact that the percent female in the foreign grant-aided was higher than the average could only have a minor impact on aggregate statistics. It was not until the 1970s when the proportion of total manufacturing employment provided by foreign firms increased, that this could have much impact on manufacturing statistics.

21. They also targeted specific industrial sectors for development and set up a worldwide network of offices to attract foreign investment with the desired qualifications.

22. The goals of the IDA (industries that employ predominantly men, have a low-capital intensity, low probability of technological obsolescence, and rapid growth potential) are typically incompatible. In general, the low-capital intense industries do not hire predominantly males and are vulnerable to technological change and foreign competition.
The contradictions between these criteria for new industries have been discussed by Charles Kindleberger. He assesses the IDA's wider criteria (looking for international companies whose subsidiaries have a high degree of independence) as having "something of a Utopian character" (124).

23. There are scattered references in the literature that there may have been a shortage of female workers (Walsh, 1970–1971; Wickham, 1982). For example, the Commission of the European Communities (1974) explains the position of the IDA thusly:

the recent increase in women's employment opportunities, combined with the apparent reduction in the availability of women for work, especially in production occupations, has led the IDA to stress male-employment creation in its efforts to attract foreign industries to Ireland. (49)

I argue that this was not a carefully researched assertion. As shown in Chapter 3, there was a latent supply of female workers available, as revealed by Walsh's own survey work (Walsh and O'Toole, 1973). There was not a shortage of female workers in Ireland because of emigration, but rather there was female emigration because of the lack of employment opportunities for women in Ireland.

24. Refer to IDA *Regional Industrial Plans 1973–1977, part 1* for a complete listing of two categories of IDA objectives:

A. Objectives deriving directly from the functions and responsibilities of the IDA with respect to industrial development.
B. Objectives deriving from the wider demographic, social and economic goals which are not within the direct and exclusive field of responsibility of the IDA but which, nevertheless, form part of the framework within which IDA activities are carried out. (39)

25. Efforts to obtain a copy of the evaluation forms met with no response.

26. They stopped publishing data by sex in these categories with the 1975 *Annual Report*.

27. The increase in total employment in the eighteen year period, 1952–1970, was only 87 percent of the increase in total employment in the five-year period 1970–1974.

28. The proportion of female workers by sector (or change in it) reflects not only this aspect of government policy but also the effect of legislation (i.e., protective legislation, training and apprenticeships) or its absence (i.e., lack of provision for child care, maternity leave, equal pay); however, because I am examining the female share (or change in it) in grant-aided or new industries vis-à-vis all industries, the effects of these other factors (with the possible exception of protective legislation) can be assumed to occur evenly over both sets of data. Variation between them can therefore be attributed to some other factor, for example, the ability of state policy to control access to employment opportunities in manufacturing by sex.

29. Refer to note 11 of Chapter 2 for information on new industry and grant-aided.

30. This is a set of unpublished IDA employment data for detailed industrial subsectors, 1973–1983. This information differs from previous data sets by: (1) the use of the NACE industrial classification, (2) the use of foreign and indigenous categories, and (3) the redefinition of "foreign" and "domestic" to solve the problem mentioned earlier in these definitions (see note 11 of Chapter 2).
 Understood as a unique database, it can be used to examine employment differences (and trends in them) between foreign firms (widely taken to desire

larger proportions of women in their work forces) and domestic (seen in the EEC perspective to have a smaller percent female than the EEC average in most sectors) in light of IDA desire to provide largely male employment in the new industries.

However, the survey has been changed retroactively to pick up companies that should have been included. Therefore, the file on 1974 is not the same data file used in the *Profile* by McAleese (1977b). Accordingly, this data set cannot be compared to the information regarding the percent female in grant-aided sectors in 1967 or in new industry in 1974.

31. There are 19 other sectors but all employ fewer than 1000 women.

32. These five sectors (in which the percent female in foreign grant-aided was less than the percent female for domestic grant-aided firms for any of the years) were ones in which more advanced technology and production processes, requiring shift work in many instances, were imported by the foreign firms. As will be discussed in the section of this chapter on protective legislation, it was largely due to protective legislation, which remained in effect until 1983 and restricted women from night work, that the female shares in these sectors of the foreign grant-aided firms were (or became) less than that in domestic grant-aided.

Additionally, there was also a tendency to define these more mechanized processes as "skilled" and therefore male. The validity of defining these processes as more skilled is questionable; so is the notion that it is men who are to be given skilled jobs. This invokes the recent debate over the alleged objectivity/subjectivity of skill classification. (See Phillips and Taylor, 1980, who suggest that skill classifications are often culturally determined.)

33. Ruane (1980) refers to a 1979 IDA publication as mentioning provision of male employment as an objective. My research could not verify this. And, in fact, in some instances I found the phrase "men and women" (IDA, 1979:17).

The IDA may have been under dual pressure to eliminate explicit references to this blatantly discriminatory policy regarding the sex of net new employment. The condition of joining the EEC—that Irish employment policy be changed to correspond with community equal employment legislation—may have also been a factor.

34. An accurate comparison requires employment of comparable industrial categories and data reflecting the type of production at that location.

35. Additionally, a survey of U.S. electronics firms in Malaysia reveals that 60 percent of the total work force is female, in comparison to the 51 percent in Ireland (Ramzi, 1983).

36. The marriage bar was established in Ireland in the 1930s. It had originally been proposed as applicable to teachers, although it was finally put into practice with the groups listed affected, teachers exempt.

37. Only nine had qualified by the end of that year (AnCO, 1980). For an update in the 1980s, see Mahon (1987:74).

38. In addition, it impeded the movement of women into higher levels of jobs. Women were restricted to the lowest levels within the organization because employers considered all women likely to marry.

Oppenheimer (1970) reports that negative attitudes toward the employment of married women existed in the United States in the 1930s and 1940s. It was feared that they would take employment opportunities away from married men and single women who were thought to need employment more. In two national samples in 1939, a majority indicated they would support legislation restricting employment of married women. Bills to this end were introduced in 26 states but passed in only one (to be repealed later) (127). For information regarding the marriage bar in the United States in the earlier part of this century, see Goldin (1988).

39. In the 1980s it made increased efforts to enroll women in traditionally male occupations.

40. Detailed information regarding each of the policies discussed in this section and progress, if any, that has been made in altering them can be obtained from (listed in chronological order) the Commission on the Status of Women, *Report to Minister for Finance* (1972) and the two progress reports which followed it in 1976 and 1978 (*Progress Report on the Implementation of the Recommendations in the Report of the Commission on the Status of Women*, 1976; *Second Progress Report on the Implementation of the Recommendations in the Report of the Commission on the Status of Women*, 1978). *The Essential Guide for Women in Ireland* by Martin (1977) is also useful. For information regarding the 1980s, see Smyth, 1983 (chapters on abortion, marriage, one-parent families, child-minding, and pre-school facilities) and Working Party on Women's Affairs and Family Law Reform (1985) (chapters on child care, social welfare, women in the home, issues related to single parenthood and family law reform). For a complete update on any issue, contact the Council for the Status of Women (64 Lower Mount Street, Dublin 2).

41. To provide another example of inequities in the law between husbands and wives: A husband can sue a person who had sexual relations with his wife; the wife cannot bring a similar suit against a sexual partner of her husband's (Martin, 1977:96).

42. This stance toward divorce and separation permeates government policy. For example, as shown in Chapter 2, the Irish government does not allow collection of census data listing people as separated and/or divorced. The census category "divorced" has become standard in most other industrialized countries.

43. Janet Martin (1977:133) reports, "According to the British Abortion Act 1967 two doctors must agree that: continuation of the pregnancy would involve greater risk to your life or injury to your physical or mental health if it was not terminated; or if continuation of the pregnancy would involve risk to the physical or mental health of any children you already have; or if there is a substantial risk that your unborn child would suffer from a serious physical or mental handicap."

44. "Illegitimate children, legally defined as 'bastards' are socially stigmatized and denied equality before the law. They are regarded in law as 'filius nullius'—the child of nobody. Their legal rights in relation to inheritance, property and maintenance are inferior to those of children born in wedlock." (*Singled Out*, 1983:41; see this publication for more complete details regarding the legal inequities.)

45. Comparisons drawn between women in Ireland and Western Europe and Singapore (Chapter 2) are not fully developed throughout the manuscript, because a complete study of such a nature is well beyond the scope of this book. These comparisons are the subjects of my ongoing research. This book was not designed to be a full-fledged comparative study, but rather to examine the Irish case and the lessons that can be drawn from it. Data on female participation in the labor force in Western Europe and Singapore was used to show that even though Ireland experienced similar types of economic changes (movement of employment from agriculture to industry and services and export-led growth, respectively) it had dramatically different changes in female economic activity. The objective was to determine why this happened in Ireland.

46. Referring again to Figure 4.2, the process occurring in other nations is the reverse of that shown. As policies that reinforced female subordination in the household were eliminated in other nations, a given growth of employment became asssociated with a higher labor force participation rate for women (leftward shift in part 1). This in turn meant that the given growth of employment was associated with a weaker form of male domination (leftward shift in *N-P*).

Chapter 5

1. I will argue later, utilizing the approach I suggest for understanding the reproduction of patriarchy (the social structure of patriarchy), that this is because male domination in these other societies is constituted and perpetuated by institutions that vary, including different roles for the state and policies less supportive of male domination. For example, in Italy state policy has been utilized to give women more options regarding exit from marriage and regarding biological reproduction, even though it too is a Roman Catholic country. Similarly, the Singapore state, in its desire to promote economic growth, established family planning programs that substantially reduced fertility, thereby diminishing this one dimension of male domination (Fawcett and Khoo, 1980).

2. The argument went as follows: the given sexual division of labor (male – wage-earner/female – homemaker) would tend to be undermined by the increased availability of jobs for women in an export-led development strategy. The types of industries that are part of an export-led growth are generally low-wage assembly jobs in electronics, textiles, or clothing, which hire workforces made up of large proportions of women.

The erosion of the traditional division of labor would be furthered by the fact that in joining the EEC (necessary to attract foreign capital to Ireland to produce for export) Ireland had to alter discriminatory employment legislation to correspond with EEC directives.

3. The explanation based upon patriarchy as reproduced in the household was explored in Chapter 3. The feminist literature exploring this line of reasoning was cited in Chapter 3, note 22.

4. These countries are Austria, Belgium, Denmark, Finland, Germany, Greece, Ireland, Italy, Luxembourg, Netherlands, Norway, Portugal, Spain, Sweden, Switzerland, and the United Kingdom.

5. Regressions on additional transformations of independent variables produced no significant results. I substituted $(GNP-C)^2$ and GNPPCTC (percentage change in GNP) for GNP-C, and LNURBAN-C (the change in the ln of proportion of the population living in urban areas) and $(URBAN-C)^2$ for URBAN-C.

6. The broad feminist literature is briefly outlined in Chapter 6. References to feminists arguing patriarchy is reproduced in the household are in Chapter 3, note 22. Reference to another line of reasoning, that male domination is reproduced basically in the firm, is in the introductory section of this chapter.

7. WAGE-C represents the change in the organization of economic activity as capitalist growth occurs; it was chosen as more representative of economic change experienced by large proportions of the population than GNP-C, which for decades was considered the key measurement of how a country had developed or modernized. I would argue against the use of GNP-C for that purpose on the grounds that changes in it may occur in the absence of fundamental changes in the relations of production. In addition, skewed distributions of income in a country can bias its level and can indicate more widespread change in living conditions than the general population has experienced.

8. URBAN-C is somewhat correlated with both other independent variables; therefore, it has been incorporated as an independent variable to avoid bias in their coefficients. It was also used as a modernization variable.

9. Both aspects of this line of argument were developed in Chapter 3 based upon Standing's (1981) work on the relationship between fertility and labor force participation rates and Folbre's (1983) on how male domination can affect fertility rates.

10. The log (ln) of change in fertility was regressed on the change in per capita GNP and the percentage change in real GNP per capita.

Appendix B

1. As adapted to this situation, the elasticity of substitution is the percentage change in the ratio of male employment to female employment divided by the percentage change in the ratio of female earnings to male earnings. According to neoclassical theory it ranges in value from zero to positive infinity. Therefore, as the ratio of female earnings to male earnings increases, there would be an increase in the ratio of male employment to female employment.

For a more detailed explanation of the elasticity of substitution, see Jones (1976:33–34).

2. Analysis of relative earnings in manufacturing involves about one-fifth of the female workforce. Only fragmentary data is available for other sectors of the Irish economy and is inadequate for analysis of responsiveness of male–female employment ratios to changes in relative earnings. See Blackwell (1982), Tables 6.7–6.10 for relative earnings data in wholesale and retail distribution, banking, and insurance for 1974.

In spite of these data limitations for an economywide analysis, the focus on manufacturing is fruitful. The female share in manufacturing and industry fell, 1961–1981 (and 1966–1981), and the relevance of the neoclassical argument should be examined in particular here.

3. Looking at an even broader region, *The Employment and Unemployment of Women in OECD Countries* (1984) reports that male–female earnings differentials have narrowed in all OECD countries in recent years. However, no evidence has been found that this had a negative impact on the growth of female employment. A rank correlation of twelve OECD countries with comparable data produced a low and statistically insignificant correlation coefficient when used to analyze relative changes in female employment shares and relative earnings (OECD, 1984:57).

4. Economywide analyses of the relation between the change in relative wages and changes in employment ratios of women and men are not possible due to data limitations. Adequate information is only available for the manufacturing sector; it is fragmentary for other sectors of the economy.

Furthermore, the data utilized in this analysis is relative hourly earnings rather than relative hourly wages. Earnings and wage data usually differ. Even in cases where relative wages may be the same in an industry or occupation, trends in relative hourly earnings could diverge because of the existence of overtime payments or shift premiums. As men are generally the recipients of such payments, a gap in addition to any wage-rate differential is likely. From the standpoint of the employer, the wage rate is the relevant concept in choosing between male and female workers; whereas, from the perspective of attaining equal access to earnings for women, earnings data is more relevant.

Earnings data used in time series must be interpreted with caution. Over the years, earnings data reflects changing occupational structures (particularly the growth of service-type occupations within the manufacturing sector) and changing skill levels.

Selected Bibliography

Abel, Marjorie R. 1987. "Women, Labor Force Participation and Economic Development: The Issue of Occupational Segregation." Unpublished doctoral dissertation. University of Massachusetts, Amherst.

Afshar, Haleh, ed. 1987. *Women, State, and Ideology: Studies from Africa and Asia.* Albany: State University of New York Press.

Agarwal, Bina, ed. 1988. *Structures of Patriarchy: State, Community and Household in Modernising Asia.* London: Zed Books.

"American Business Finds Ireland." (1983) *New York Times,* 21 August, sec. F, p. 8.

AnCO. 1980. "Training for Women, Progress Report—1980." Dublin: AnCO.

Barrett, Michele. 1980. *Women's Oppression Today.* London: Verso.

Barry, Bernadette. 1982. *Women At Home, A Report on Nationwide Get-Togethers of Women.* Dublin: Council for the Status of Women.

Barry, Ursula. 1988. "Women in Ireland." *Women's Studies International Forum* 11, no. 4:317–22.

Beale, Jenny. 1987. *Women In Ireland.* Bloomington: Indiana University Press.

Beneria, Lourdes. 1979. "Reproduction, Production and the Sexual Division of Labour." *Cambridge Journal of Economics* 3:203–25.

———. 1982. "Accounting for Women's Work." In *Women and Development—The Sexual Division of Labor in Rural Societies,* edited by Lourdes Beneria, 119–147. New York: Praeger.

Beneria, Lourdes, and Sen, Gita. 1981. "Accumulation, Reproduction, and Women's Role in Development: Boserup Revisited." *Signs* 7, no. 2:279–98.

———. 1982. "Class and Gender Inequalities and Women's Role in Economic Development — Theoretical and Practical Implications." *Feminist Studies* 8, no. 1:157–76.

Bergmann, Barbara R. 1986. *The Economic Emergence of Women.* New York: Basic Books.

Berk, Sarah Fenstermaker. 1985. *The Gender Factory: The Apportionment of Work in American Households.* New York: Plenum Press.

Blackwell, John. 1982. "Digest of Statistics on Women in the Labour Force." Dublin: Employment Equality Agency.

———. 1983. "Statistics on Women in the Labour Force and Related Topics: What Do We Need to Know?" Paper presented to the Employment Equality Agency seminar, Dublin, 23 February 1983.

Blackwell, John, and McGregor, John. 1982. *Population and Labour Force Projections by County and Region, 1979 – 1991.* Dublin: National Economic and Social Council.

Blau, Francine, and Ferber, Marianne A. 1986. *The Economics of Women, Men, and Work.* Englewood Cliffs, N.J.: Prentice-Hall.

Bose, Christine, and Spitze, Glenna, eds. 1987. *Ingredients for Women's Employment Policy.* Albany: State University of New York Press.

Boserup, Ester. 1970. *Women's Role in Economic Development.* New York: St. Martin's Press.

Bowles, Samuel, and Gintis, Herbert. 1981. "Structure and Practice in the Labor Theory of Value." *Review of Radical Political Economics* 12, no. 4:1–26.

———. 1982. "The Crisis of Liberal Democratic Capitalism." *Politics and Society* 11:51–93.

Bowles, Samuel; Gordon, David; and Weisskopf, Thomas. (1983) "Profits and Power — The Social Structure of Accumulation and the Profitability of the Postwar U.S. Economy." *Review of Radical Political Economy* 18, nos. 1 and 2:132–67.

Brady, Anna, compiler. 1988. *Women in Ireland: An Annotated Bibliography.* New York: Greenwood Press.

Brenner, Johanna, and Ramas, Maria. 1984. "Rethinking Women's Oppression." *New Left Review* 144 (March–April):33–71

Bristow, John. 1979. "Aspects of Economic Planning." *Administration* 27, no. 2:192–200.

Buckley, Peter J. 1974. "Some Aspects of Foreign Private Investment in the Manufacturing Sector of the Economy of the Irish Republic." *Economic and Social Review* (April):301–21.

Caldwell, Lesley. 1978. "Church, State, and Family: The Women's Movement in Italy." In *Feminism and Materialism*, edited by Annette Kuhn and AnnMarie Wolpe, 68–95. London: Routledge and Kegan Paul.

Central Statistics Office. *Census of Population of Ireland.* Dublin: CSO, various years.

———. Household Budget Inquiry. 1965–66. Dublin: Stationery office.

———. *Irish Statistical Bulletin*, various issues (quarterly).

———. 1981. *Labour Force Survey 1979 Results.* Dublin: Stationery office.

———. *Statistical Abstract of Ireland*, various years.

Charlton, Sue Ellen M. 1984. *Women in Third World Development.* Boulder: Westview Press.

Chodorow, Nancy. 1978. *The Reproduction of Mothering.* Berkeley: University of California Press.

Chubb, Basil, and Lynch, Patrick. 1969. *Economic Development and Planning.* Dublin: Institute of Public Administration.

Ciancanelli, Penelope. 1983. "Women's Transition to Wage Labor: A Critique of Labor Force Statistics and Reestimation of Labor Force Participation of Married Women in the United States 1900–1930." Unpublished doctoral dissertation. New School, New York.

Commission of the European Community. 1974. *Women and Employment in the United Kingdom, Ireland and Denmark.* Brussels: CEC.
————. 1980. *Women in the European Community.* Brussels: CEC.
————. 1982. *Women in Statistics.* Brussels: CEC.
————. *Women of Europe.* (various recent issues). Brussels: CEC.
Commission on the Status of Women. 1972. *Report to Minister for Finance.* Dublin: Stationery Office.
Cook, Alice H.; Lorwin, Val R.; and Daniels, Arlene Kaplan. 1984. *Women and Trade Unions.* Philadelphia: Temple University Press.
Coughlan, Anthony. 1980. "Ireland." In *Integration and Unequal Development,* edited by Dudley Seers and Constantine Vaitsos, 121–35. New York: St. Martin's Press.
Council for the Status of Women. 1981. *Irish Women Speak Out.* Dublin: Co-op Books.
————. 1982. *Newsletter* (July).
Cullen, L. M. 1972. *An Economic History of Ireland since 1660.* London: B. T. Batsford.
Dalla Costa, Mariarosa, and James, Selma. 1973. *The Power of Women and the Subversion of the Community* 2d ed. Bristol, England: Falling Wall Press.
Daly, Mary E. 1979. "Women, Work and Trade Unionism." In *Women in Irish Society,* edited by Margaret Mac Curtain and Donncha Ó Corráin. Westport, Conn.: Greenwood Press.
————. 1981a. *Social and Economic History of Ireland since 1800.* Dublin: The Educational Company.
————. 1981b. "Women in the Irish Work Force from Pre-industrial to Modern Times." *Journal of the Irish Labour History Society* 7:74–82.
Department of Education. *Annual Report, 1967–68.* Dublin.
Department of Labour. National Manpower Service *Reports* on Labour Availability, various areas, various years in the 1970s.
Development for Full Employment. 1978. Dublin: Stationery Office.
Dixon, Ruth B. 1978. "Late Marriage and Non-Marriage as Demographic Responses: Are They Similar?" *Population Studies* 32, no. 3:449–66.
Donaldson, Loraine. 1965. *Development Planning in Ireland.* New York: Praeger.
Dowling, B. R., and Durkan, J. 1978. *Irish Economic Policy: A Review of Major Issues.* Dublin: Economic and Social Research Institute.
Durand, John D. 1948–1968. *The Labor Force in the United States 1890–1960.* New York: Gordon and Breach Science Publishers.
Economic Development. 1958. Dublin: Stationery Office.
Economic and Social Development 1969–1972. 1969. Dublin: Stationery Office.
Economic and Social Development 1976–1980. 1976. Dublin: Stationery Office.
Economic and Social Position of Women in the Community. 1981. Luxembourg: Office of Official Publications of the European Community.
Eisenstein, Zillah. 1979. *Capitalist Patriarchy and the Case for Socialist Feminism.* New York: Monthly Review Press.
Elson, Diane, and Pearson, Ruth. 1981. "The Subordination of Women and the

Internationalisation of Factory Production." In *Of Marriage and the Market*, edited by Kate Young, Carol Wolkowitz and Roslyn McCullagh. London: CSE Books. pp. 144–66.

Employment Equality Agency. *Annual Report and Accounts*. (for the years 1978, 1979, 1980, 1981). Dublin: Employment Equality Agency.

———. 1978. *Review of the Ban on Industrial Nightwork for Women*. Report to the Minister for Labour. Dublin: Employment Equality Agency.

Engels, Frederick. 1972. *The Origin of the Family, Private Property and the State*. Introduction and Notes by Eleanor Burke Leacock. New York: International Publishers. (Original edition published 1942)

England, Paula, and Farkas, George. 1986. *Households, Employment, and Gender: A Social, Economic and Demographic View*. New York: Aldine De Gruyer.

England, Paula, and McCreary, Lori. 1987. "Gender Inequality in Paid Employment." In *Analyzing Gender: A Handbook of Social Science Research*, edited by Beth B. Hess and Myra Marx Ferree, 286–320. Newbury Park, Calif.: Sage.

Enloe, Cynthia. 1983. "Women Textile Workers in the Militarization of Southeast Asia." In *Women, Men and the International Division of Labor*, edited by June Nash and Patricia Fernandez-Kelly, 407–25. Albany: State University of New York Press.

———. 1984. *Does Khaki Become You?* Boston: South End Press.

Equal Opportunities and Vocational Training, Training and Labour Market Policy Measures for the Vocational Promotion of Women in Ireland. 1979. Berlin: European Centre for the Development of Vocational Training.

Equality for Women! 1980. Presented to 1980 Annual Delegate Conference of the Irish Transport and General Workers' Union. Prepared by the Research Department, Development Services Division Irish Transport and General Workers' Union.

Equality of Opportunity in the Public Sector, Report of a Seminar. 1982. Dublin: Employment Equality Agency.

European Foundation for the Improvement of Living and Working Conditions. 1982. *Shiftwork in the Textile Industry, Case Studies of Innovations, Ireland*. Dublin: Author.

Farley, Noel J. J. 1972. "Explanatory Hypotheses for Irish Trade in Manufactured Goods in the Mid-Nineteen Sixties." *Economic and Social Review* 4, no. 1:5–33.

———. 1973. "Outward-Looking Policies and Industrialization in a Small Economy: Some Notes on the Irish Case." *Economic Development and Cultural Change* 21, no. 4:610–28.

Fawcett, James T., and Khoo, Siew-Ean. 1980. "Singapore: Rapid Fertility Transition in a Compact Society." *Population and Development Review* 6, no. 4:549–79.

Ferber, Marianne A. 1987. *Women and Work, Paid and Unpaid: A Selected, Annotated Bibliography*. New York: Garland.

Ferguson, Ann. 1984. "On Conceiving Motherhood and Sexuality: A Feminist Materialist Approach." In *Mothering: Essays in Feminist Theory*, edited by Joyce Trebilcot, 153–84. Totowa, N.J.: Rowman and Allenheld.

Fernandez-Kelly, Maria Patricia. 1983. *For We Are Sold, I and My People*. Albany: State University of New York Press.

Fernandez-Kelly, M. Patricia, and Garcia, Anna M. 1989. "Power Surrendered, Power Restored: The Politics of Home and Work Among Hispanic Women in Southern California and Southern Florida." In *Women, Change and Politics*, edited by Louise Tilly and Patricia Guerin. New York: The Russell Sage Foundation.

Fine-Davis, Margret. 1983a. "Mothers' Attitudes Toward Child Care and Employment: A Nationwide Survey." In *Working Party on Child Care Facilities for Working Parents*, 73–168. Dublin: Stationery Office.

———. 1983b. "Social Attitudes and Beliefs in Ireland and Their Relationship to Women's Behavioural Intentions Regarding Employment." Paper presented at the Meetings of the International Society of Political Psychology, Oxford, July.

FitzGerald, Garret. 1968. *Planning in Ireland*. Dublin: Institute of Public Administration.

Folbre, Nancy. 1982. "Exploitation Comes Home: A Critique of the Marxian Theory of Labour Power." *Cambridge Journal of Economics* 6, no. 4:318–29.

———. 1983. "Of Patriarchy Born: The Political Economy of Fertility Decisions." *Feminist Studies* 9, no. 2:261–84.

———. 1984. "Household Production in the Philippines: A Non-Neoclassical Approach." *Economic Development and Cultural Change* 32, no. 2:303–30.

———. 1985. "The Pauperization of Mothers: Patriarchy and Public Policy in the United States." *Review of Radical Political Economics* 16, no. 4:72–88.

———. 1986a. "Cleaning House: New Perspectives in Households and Economic Development." *Journal of Development Economics* 22:5–40.

———. 1986b. "Hearts and Spades: Paradigms of Household Economics." *World Development* 14, no. 2:245–55.

———. 1987. "Patriarchy as a Mode of Production." In *Alternatives to Economic Orthodoxy*, edited by Randy Albelda, Christopher Gunn and William Walker. New York: M. E. Sharpe: 323–38.

Fuchs, Victor R. 1989. "Women's Quest for Economic Equality." *Journal of Economic Perspectives* 3, no. 1:25–41.

Fuentes, Annette, and Ehrenreich, Barbara. 1983. *Women in the Global Factory*. Boston: South End Press.

Gallin, Rita S.; Whittier, Patricia; and Graham, Margaret A. 1985. "Research and Policy: An Analysis of the Working Papers on Women in International Development." In *Women Creating Wealth: Transforming Economic Development*, edited by Rita S. Gallin and Anita Spring, 79–83. (Selected papers and speeches from the Association for Women in Development Conference, Washington, D.C., April 25–27, 1985.)

Garvey, Donal. 1983. "A Profile of the Demographic and Labour Force Characteristics of the Population—Sample Analysis of the 1981 Census of Population." Paper read to the Statistical and Social Inquiry Society of Ireland, Dublin, 28 April.

Geary, R. C., and Dempsey, M. 1977. *A Study of Schemes for the Relief of Unemployment in Ireland.* Dublin: Economic and Social Research Institute.

Geary, R. C., and Ó Muircheartaigh, F. S. 1974. *Equalization of Opportunity in Ireland: Statistical Aspects.* Dublin: Economic and Social Research Institute, Broadsheet No. 10.

Gillis, Malcolm; Perkins, Dwight H.; Roemer, Michael; and Snodgrass, Donald R. 1987. *Economics of Development.* 2d ed. New York: W. W. Norton and Company.

Gmelch, George. 1979. *Return Migration and Migrant Adjustment in Western Ireland.* Irish Foundation for Human Development.

Goldin, Claudia. 1988. "Marriage Bars: Discrimination Against Married Women Workers, 1920s to 1950s." Working Paper No. 2747. Cambridge, MA: National Bureau of Economic Research.

Gordon, David. 1980. "Stages of Accumulation and Long Economic Cycles." In *Processes of the World System,* edited by Terence Hopkins and Immanuel Wallerstein, 9–45. Beverly Hills, Calif.: Sage Publications.

Gordon, David; Edwards, Richard; and Reich, Michael. 1982. *Segmented Work, Divided Workers.* Cambridge: Cambridge University Press.

Grossman, Rachel. 1980. "Bitter Wages: Women in East Asia's Semiconductor Plants." *Multinational Monitor* 1, no. 2:8–11.

Grunwald, Joseph, and Flamm, Kenneth. 1985. *Global Factory: Foreign Assembly in International Trade.* Washington, D.C.: Brookings Institution.

Gunderson, Morley. 1989. "Male–Female Wage Differentials and Policy Responses." *Journal of Economic Literature* 27:46–72.

Hagen, Elisabeth, and Jenson, Jane. 1988. "Paradoxes and Promises: Work and Politics in the Postwar Years." In *Feminization of the Labor Force,* edited by Jane Jenson, Elisabeth Hagen, and Ceallaigh Reddy, 3–16. New York: Oxford University Press.

Hannan, Damian, and Breen, Richard. 1983. *Schooling and Sex Roles: Sex Differences in Subject Provision and Student Choice in Irish Post-Primary Schools.* Dublin: Economic and Social Research Institute.

Hannan, Damian, and Katsiaouni, Louise. 1977. *Traditional Families?* Dublin: Economic and Social Research Institute.

Harris, Lorelei. 1983. "Industrialization, Women and Working Class Politics in the West of Ireland." *Capital and Class* 19 (Spring):100–117.

Hartmann, Heidi. 1976. "Capitalism, Patriarchy, and Job Segregation by Sex." *Signs* 3, no. 2:137–69.

———. 1981a. "The Family as the Locus of Gender, Class, and Political Struggle: The Example of Housework." *Signs* 6, no. 3:366–94.

———. 1981b. "The Unhappy Marriage of Marxism and Feminism: Towards a More Progressive Union." In *Women and Revolution,* edited by Lydia Sargent, 1–41. Boston: South End Press.

Hazelkorn, Ellen. "Capital and the Irish Question." *Science and Society* 44, 3:326–56.

Heyzer, Noeleen. 1986. *Working Women in South-East Asia: Development, Subordination and Emancipation.* Milton Keynes, England: Open University Press.

Howenstine, Ned G. 1982. "Growth of U.S. Multinational Companies, 1966 – 77." *Survey of Current Business* 62, no. 4:34–46.

Hughes, J. G., and Walsh, B. M. 1976. "Migration Flows Between Ireland, the United Kingdom and the Rest of the World, 1966–1971." *European Demographic Information Bulletin* 7, no. 4:125–49.

Humphrey, John. 1984. "The Growth of Female Employment in Brazilian Manufacturing Industry in the 1970s." *Journal of Development Studies* 20, no. 4:224–47.

Industrial Development Authority of Ireland. *Annual Report.* (years 1970/71 to 1981). Dublin: IDA.

———. 1972. *Regional Industrial Plans 1973–1977. Part 1.* Dublin: IDA.

———. 1979. *IDA Industrial Plan 1978–82.* Dublin: IDA.

———. 1982. "Ireland—Consistently the Most Profitable Industrial Location in Europe." Dublin: IDA.

———. 1983. "Employment Survey." Unpublished.

"Industries Increase Overseas Investment." *Wall Street Journal,* 27 June, 1989, p. B13.

International Labour Organization. 1981. *Population and Development: A Progress Report on ILO Research.* Geneva: ILO. January, 1981.

———. *Yearbook of Labour Statistics.* Geneva: ILO. Various years.

Investment and National Development 1979–1983. 1980. Dublin: Stationery Office.

Investment Plan 1981. Dublin: Stationery Office.

"Ireland—Incentives for Industry in a Changing Land." 1975. *Fortune,* 91, no. 3 (March), 56–77.

"Irish Economy Dips After Big Decade." 1981. *New York Times,* 25 December, 37, 46 Section D.

Irish Times. 1981–1984. Various issues.

Jackson, Pauline. 1982. "An Outline of the Textiles Industry in the 26 Counties of Ireland." Paper for the Working Conference at the Transnational Institute, October.

———. 1983. "The Republic of Ireland — Europe's South East Asia?" Unpublished paper.

Jackson, Pauline and Barry, U. 1983. "Industries Without Industrialization — Technology Without Science: Some Implications For Women Workers in the 26 Counties of Ireland." Paper for the Annual Conference of the Sociological Association of Ireland, April.

Jacobsen, Kurt. 1978. "Changing Utterly?—Irish Development and the Problem of Dependence." *Studies: An Irish Quarterly Review* (Winter):276–91.

———. 1980. "The Republic of Ireland: Perils of Pragmatism." *Dissent* 27, no. 1:73–80.

Jaggar, Alison M. 1983. *Feminist Politics and Human Nature.* Totowa, N.J.: Rowman and Allenheld.

Jaquette, Jane S. 1982. "Women and Modernization Theory: A Decade of Feminist Criticism." *World Politics* 34, no. 2:267–84.

Jenson, Jane; Hagen, Elisabeth; and Reddy, Ceallaigh, eds. 1988. *Feminization of the Labor Force.* New York: Oxford University Press.

Jones, Gavin W. 1984a. "Economic Growth and Changing Female Employment Structure in the Cities of Southeast and East Asia." In *Women in the Urban and Industrial Workforce: Southeast and East Asia,* edited by Gavin W. Jones, 17–59. Canberra, Australia: Australian National University.

———. 1984b. "Introduction." In *Women in the Urban and Industrial Work Force: Southeast and East Asia,* edited by Gavin W. Jones, 1–14. Canberra, Australia: Australian National University.

Jones, Hywel G. 1976. *An Introduction to Modern Theories of Economic Growth.* New York: McGraw-Hill.

Katsiaouni, Olympios. 1977–1978. "Planning in a Small Economy: The Republic of Ireland." *Statistical and Social Inquiry Society of Ireland Journal,* 23:217–56.

Kennedy, Kiernan. 1975. "A Symposium on Increasing Employment in Ireland." *Statistical and Social Inquiry Society of Ireland. Journal.* (1975/76):37–50.

———. 1980. "Employment and Unemployment Prospects in Ireland." *Irish Banking Review.* (Sept.):15–23.

Kennedy, Kiernan, and Dowling, Brendan. 1975. *Economic Growth in Ireland: The Experience Since 1947.* Dublin: Gill and Macmillan.

Kennedy, Robert E., Jr. 1973. *The Irish: Emigration Marriage and Fertility.* Berkeley: University of California Press.

Kindleberger, Charles P. "Multinationals and the Small Open Economy." *Journal of Irish Business and Administration Research:* 115–28.

Lazear, Edward P. 1989. "Symposium on Women in the Labor Market." *Journal of Economic Perspectives* 3, no. 1:3–7.

Levine, June. 1982. *Sisters: The Personal Story of an Irish Feminist.* Dublin: Ward River Press.

Lewis, Jane. 1985. "The Debate on Sex and Class." *New Left Review* 149 (January/February):108–20.

Lim, Linda. 1983. "Capitalism, Imperialism, and Patriarchy: The Dilemma of Third-World Women Workers in Multinational Factories." In *Women, Men and the International Division of Labor,* edited by June Nash and Maria Patricia Fernandez-Kelly, 70–91. Albany: State University of New York Press.

Lloyd, Cynthia B., and Niemi, Beth T. 1979. *The Economics of Sex Differentials.* New York: Columbia University Press.

Long, Frank. 1976. "Foreign Direct Investment in an Underdeveloped European Economy—The Republic of Ireland." *World Development* 4, no. 1:59–84.

———. 1980. "Foreign Capital and Development Strategy in Irish Industrialization, 1958–70." *American Journal of Economics and Sociology* 39, no. 2:137–50.

"Luck, Chance, Skill Give Irish Premier a Good Week." (1985) *Boston Globe,* 24 February, p. 10.

McAleese, Dermot. 1976. "Industrial Specialisation and Trade: Northern Ireland and the Republic." *Economic and Social Review* 7, no. 2:143–60.

———. 1977a. "Outward-Looking Policies, Manufactured Exports and Economic Growth: The Irish Experience." In *Contemporary Economic Analysis,* edited by M. J. Artis and A. R. Nobay. London: Croom Helm.

———. 1977b. *A Profile of Grant-Aided Industry in Ireland.* Dublin: Industrial Development Authority.

McCarthy, Colm. 1979. "Economic Development and Economic Policy." *Administration* 27, no. 2:201–210.

McCarthy, Eunice. 1979. "Women and Work in Ireland: The Present and Preparing for the Future." In *Women in Irish Society,* edited by Margaret Mac Curtain and Donncha Ó Corráin, 103–12. Westport, Conn.: Greenwood Press.

McCrate, Elaine. 1985. "The Growth of Nonmarriage Among U.S. Women, 1954 –1983." Unpublished doctoral dissertation. University of Massachusetts, Amherst.

———. 1987. "Trade, Merger and Employment: Economic Theory on Marriage." *Review of Radical Political Economy* 19, no. 1:73–89.

Mac Curtain, Margaret, and Ó Corráin, Donncha. 1979. *Women in Irish Society.* Westport, Conn.: Greenwood Press.

McLernon, Douglas. 1980. "High-Level Conference on the Employment of Women. National Report, Ireland." Dublin, 16–17 April.

Mahon, Evelyn. 1987. "Women's Rights and Catholicism in Ireland." *New Left Review* 166 (November/December):53–77.

Maroney, Heather. 1983. "Feminism and Work." *New Left Review* 141 (September/October):51–71.

Martin, Janet. 1977. *The Essential Guide for Women in Ireland.* Galway, Ireland: Arlen House.

Minard, Lawrence. 1982. "Xenophobia Is Very Uncommon Here." *Forbes,* (February 1):50–54.

Mincer, Jacob. 1984. "Inter-Country Comparisons of Labor Force Trends and Of Related Developments: An Overview." National Bureau of Economic Research Working Paper No. 1438. Cambridge, MA: National Bureau of Economic Research.

Moore, Gary A., and Elkin, Randyl D. 1983. *Labor and the Economy.* Southwestern Publishing Co.

Morgan, Austen, and Purdie, Bob, eds. 1980. *Ireland: Divided Nation, Divided Class.* London: Ink Links.

Multinational Monitor 1983. Special issue on Women and Multinationals. 4, no. 8 (August).

Nash, June, and Fernandez-Kelly, Maria Patricia, eds. 1983. *Women, Men and the International Division of Labor.* Albany: State University of New York Press.

National Development 1977–1980. 1978. Dublin: Stationery Office.

National Economic and Social Council (NESC). 1980. *Industrial Policy and Development: A Survey of Literature from the Early 1960s.* (prepared by Eoin J. O'Malley). Dublin: NESC.

———. 1982a. *A Review of Industrial Policy.* Dublin: NESC No. 64.

———. 1982b. *A Review of Industrial Policy.* Summary of a Report Prepared by the Telesis Consultancy Group. Dublin: NESC No. 64.

Nolan, Sean. 1981. "Economic Growth." In *The Economy of Ireland.* 3d ed., edited by J. W. O'Hagan, 151–96. Dublin: Irish Management Institute.

Norton, Desmond. 1975. *Problems in Economic Planning and Policy Formation in Ireland, 1958–1974.* Dublin: Economic and Social Research Institute, Broadsheet No. 12.

O'Connor, James. 1973. *The Fiscal Crisis of the State.* New York: St. Martin's Press.

O'Donnell, Carol. 1984. *The Basis of the Bargain: Gender, Schooling and Jobs.* Sydney: George Allen & Unwin.

Offen, Karen. 1988. "Defining Feminism: A Comparative Historical Approach." *Signs* 14, no. 1:119–57.

O'Hagan, J. W. 1981. *The Economy of Ireland—Policy and Performance.* 3d ed. Dublin: Mount Salus Press.

O'Higgins, Kathleen. 1974. *Marital Desertion in Dublin, An Exploratory Study.* Dublin: Economic and Social Research Institute.

O'Neill, T. S. 1972. "Industrial Development in Ireland." *Administration* 20, no. 1:39–50.

Oppenheimer, Valerie Kincaide. 1970. *The Female Labor Force in the United States.* Westport, Conn.: Greenwood.

Organisation for Economic Cooperation and Development. *Ireland.* Approximately annually every year 1962 – 1982. OECD Economic Surveys. Paris: OECD.

———. 1974. *Educational Statistics Yearbook Vol. I.* Paris: OECD.

———. 1979. *Demographic Trends 1950–1990.* Paris: OECD.

———. 1980. *Women and Employment.* Paris: OECD.

———. 1981. *National Accounts of OECD Countries 1950–1979.* Paris: OECD.

———. 1984. *The Employment and Unemployment of Women in OECD Countries.* Paris: OECD.

O'Rourke, A. Desmond. 1978. "An Unofficial Reappraisal of the Irish Economic Dilemma—One Man's Opinion." *Studies: An Irish Quarterly Review:*164–82.

Overholt, Catherine; Anderson, M. B.; Cloud, K.; and Austin, J. E., eds. 1985. *Gender Roles in Development Projects.* West Hartford, Conn.: Kumarian Press.

Phillips, Anne, and Taylor, Barbara. 1980. "Sex and Skill: Notes towards a Feminist Economics." *Feminist Review* 6:79–88.

Prendiville, Patricia. 1988. "Divorce in Ireland: An Analysis of the Referendum to Amend the Constitution, June 1986." *Women's Studies International Forum* 11, no. 4:355–63.

Programme for Economic Expansion. 1958. Dublin: Stationery Office.

Programme for National Development 1978–1981. 1979. Dublin: Stationery Office.

Progress Report on the Implementation of the Recommendations in the Report of the Commission on the Status of Women. 1976. A Report by the Women's Representative Committee. Dublin: Stationery Office.

Ramzi, Anis Sabirin. 1983. "The Multinational Corporations and Employment Opportunities for Women in Malaysia." In *Women and Work in the Third World: The Impact of Industrialization and Global Economic Interdependence,* compiled by Nagat M. El-Sanabary, 99–100. Berkeley: Center for the Study, Education and Advancement of Women, University of California.

Randall, Vicky. 1987. *Women and Politics: An International Perspective.* 2d ed. Chicago: University of Chicago Press.

Reimers, Cordelia W. 1988. "*The Economic Emergence of Women:* A Review." CSWEP *Newsletter* (October):6–10.

Reskin, Barbara F., and Hartmann, Heidi I., eds. 1986. *Women's Work, Men's Work: Sex Segregation on the Job.* Washington D.C.: National Academy Press.

Review of the Ban on Industrial Nightwork for Women. 1978. Dublin: Employment Equality Agency.

Robinson, Mary. 1979. "Women and the New Irish State." In *Women in Irish Society,* edited by Margaret Mac Curtain and Donncha Ó Corráin, 58–70. Westport, Conn.: Greenwood Press.

———. 1988. "Women and the Law in Ireland." *Women's Studies International Forum* 11, no. 4:351–54.

Roos, Patricia A. 1985. *Gender and Work: A Comparative Analysis of Industrial Societies.* Albany: State University of New York Press.

Rose, Catherine. 1975. *The Female Experience, The Story of the Woman Movement in Ireland.* Galway, Ireland: Arlen House.

Ross, M., and Walsh, B. 1979. *Regional Policy and the Full-Employment Target.* Dublin: Economic and Social Research Institute.

Rottmann, David, and O'Connell, Philip. 1982. "The Changing Social Structure." *Administration* 30, nos. 2/3:63–87.

Ruane, Frances. 1980. "Optimal Labour Subsidies and Industrial Development in Ireland." *Economic and Social Review* 2, no. 2:77–98.

Rudd, Joy. 1983. "Economic Development in the 'Sixties in Ireland as It Affected Women." Paper read at the Tenth Annual Conference of the Sociological Association of Ireland, Wexford, Ireland.

Salaff, Janet W. 1985. "The State and Fertility Motivation in Singapore and China." In *China's One-Child Family Policy,* edited by Elisabeth Croll, Delia Davin, and Penny Kane, 325–57. New York: St. Martin's Press.

———. 1986. "Women, The Family and the State: Hong Kong, Taiwan, Singapore—Newly Industrialized Countries in Asia." In *Women in the World,* 2d rev. ed., edited by Lynn B. Iglitzin and Ruth Ross, 162–89. Santa Barbara, Calif.: ABC-CLIO.

Sandell, Steven H. 1980. "Monitoring the Labour Market Progress of Women in Ireland: Statistics Needed for Employment Equality." Dublin: Employment Equality Agency.

Schmitt, David E. 1973. *The Irony of Irish Democracy.* Lexington, Mass.: Lexington Books.

Second Programme for Economic Expansion, 1964–1970. Dublin: Stationery Office.

Second Progress Report on the Implementation of the Recommendations in the Report of the Commission on the Status of Women. (1978) Final Report of the Women's Representative Committee, December. Dublin: Stationery Office.

Sen, Gita, and Grown, Caren. 1987. *Development, Crises, and Alternative Visions.* New York: Monthly Review Press.

Sexton, J. J. 1981. "The Changing Labour Force." Paper presented at the 21st Anniversary Conference of the Economic and Social Research Institute, Dublin, October.

———. 1982. "Sectoral Changes in the Labour Force Over the Period 1961–1980 with Particular Reference to Public Sector and Services Employment." *Quarterly Economic Commentary* (August):36–45.

Sexton, J. J., and Walsh, B. M. 1982. "A Study of Labour Force Flows 1961–1981." *Quarterly Economic Commentary* (May):51–57.

Simms, Katharine. 1979. "Women in Norman Ireland." In *Women in Irish Society,* edited by Margaret Mac Curtain and Donncha Ó Corráin, 14–25. Westport, Conn.: Greenwood Press.

Signs 1981. (Special Issue). "Development and the Sexual Division of Labor." 7, no. 2.

Singled Out, Single Mothers in Ireland. 1983. Dublin: Cherish (in conjunction with Women's Community Press).

Skocpol, Theda. 1985. "Bringing the State Back In: Strategies of Analysis in Current Research." In *Bringing the State Back In,* edited by Peter Evans, Dietrich Rueschemeyer, and Theda Skocpol, 3–37. Cambridge: Cambridge University Press.

Smith, Joan; Wallerstein, Immanuel; and Evers, Hans-Dieter. 1984. *Households and the World Economy.* Beverly Hills, Calif.: Sage.

Smyth, Ailbhe. 1983. *Women's Rights in Ireland: A Practical Guide.* Dublin: Ward River Press.

———. 1988. "The Contemporary Women's Movement in the Republic of Ireland." *Women's Studies International Forum* 11, no. 4:331–41.

"Social Welfare—Discrimination Against Women." 1982. *Newsletter* (The Council for the Status of Women), July, p. 3.

Spalter-Roth, Roberta, and Zeitz, Eileen. 1981. "Production and Reproduction of Everyday Life." In *Dynamics of World Development,* edited by Richard Rubinson, 193–209. Beverly Hills, Calif.: Sage.

Standing, Guy. 1981. (1978) *Labour Force Participation and Development.* 2d ed. Geneva: ILO.

Standing, Guy, and Sheehan, Glen, eds. 1978. *Labour Force Participation in Low-Income Countries.* Geneva: International Labour Organization.

Stanton, Richard. 1979. "Foreign Investment and Host-Country Politics: The Irish Case." In *Underdeveloped Europe: Studies in Core-Periphery Relations,* edited by Dudley Seers, Bernard Schaeffer, and Marja Liisa Kiljunen, 103–24. Atlantic Highlands, N.J.: Humanities Press.

———. 1981. "The European Periphery as Export Platform: Metropolitan Firms and Local Class Relations in Ireland." Brighton, England: Institute of Development Studies. (Original edition published 1978)

Stewart, J. C. "Foreign Direct Investment and the Emergence of a Dual Economy." *Economic and Social Review:*173–97.

Survey of Grant-Aided Industry. 1967. Dublin: Stationery Office.

Tait, A. A., and Bristown, J. A. 1972. *Ireland—Some Problems of a Developing Economy.* New York: Barnes and Noble.

Tiano, Susan. 1981. "The Separation of Women's Remunerated and Household Work: Theoretical Perspectives on 'Women in Development.' " University of New Mexico, Working Paper No. 2.

———. 1987. "Gender, Work, and World Capitalism: Third World Women's Role in Development." In *Analyzing Gender: A Handbook of Social Science Research,* edited by Beth B. Hess and Myra Marx Ferree, 216–43. Newbury Park, Calif.: Sage.

Tong, Rosemarie. 1989. *Feminist Thought: A Comprehensive Introduction.* Boulder: Westview Press.

United Nations. 1980. *The Economic Roles of Women in the ECE Region.* New York: United Nations.

———. 1985. *The Economic Role of Women in the ECE Region: Developments 1975/85.* New York: United Nations.

Vasques de Miranda, Giaura. 1977. "Women's Labor Force Participation in a Developing Society: the Case of Brazil." *Signs* 3.

Walsh, Brendan M. 1970. *Migration to the United Kingdom from Ireland, 1961–1966.* Dublin: Economic and Social Research Institute. Memorandum Series No. 70.

———. 1970–1971. "Aspects of Labour Supply and Demand with Special Reference to the Employment of Women in Ireland." *Statistical and Social Inquiry Society of Ireland. Journal* 22, no. 3:88–123.

———. 1974. *The Structure of Unemployment in Ireland, 1964–1972.* Dublin: Economic and Social Research Institute.

———. 1978. *The Unemployment Problem in Ireland.* Dublin: Kincora Press.

———. 1982. "The Impact of EEC Membership on Women in the Labour Force." Policy Paper No. 1 of the Center for Economic Research, University College, Dublin. October.

———. 1983. "Vote of Thanks to Donal Garvey on his Paper: Sample Analysis of the 1981 Census of Population." Paper presented to the Statistical and Social Inquiry Society of Ireland. Dublin. 28 April.

Walsh, B. M., and Whelan, B. J. 1973–1974. "The Determinants of Female Labour Force Participation, An Econometric Analysis of Survey Data." *Statistical and Social Inquiry Society of Ireland* 23, no. 1:1–33.

Walsh, Brendan M., assisted by Annette O'Toole. 1973. *Women and Employment in Ireland: Results of a National Survey:* Dublin: Economic and Social Research Institute. Paper no. 69.

Ward, Kathryn. 1987. "Women in the Global Economy." In *Women and Work #3*, edited by B. Gutek, L. Larwood and Ann Stromberg, 17–48. Beverly Hills, Calif.: Sage.

Ward, Kathryn, and Pampel, Fred. 1985. "Structural Determinants of Female Labor Force Participation in Developed Nations, 1955–75." *Social Science Quarterly* 66:654–67.

Whelan, Brendan J., and Walsh, Brendan M. 1977. *Redundancy and Re-Employment in Ireland.* Dublin: Economic and Social Research Institute.

Whitaker, Jennifer Seymour. 1988. *How Can Africa Survive?* New York: Harper and Row.

Whitaker, T. K. 1973. "From Protection to Free Trade — The Irish Experience." *Administration* 21, no. 4:405–23.

White, Padraic A. 1981. "Ireland's Employment Needs in the 80s: The Nature of the Challenge and the Response." Paper presented Dublin, 30 September.

Wickham, Ann. 1982. "Women, Industrial Transition and Training Policy in the Republic of Ireland." In *Power, Conflict and Inequality,* edited by Mary Kelly, Liam O'Dowd, and James Wickham, 147–58. Dublin: Turoe Press.

Wickham, James. 1980. "The Politics of Dependent Capitalism: International Capital and the Nation State." In *Ireland: Divided Nation, Divided Class,* edited by Austen Morgan and Bob Purdie, 53–73. London: Ink Links.

Wickham, James, and Murray, Peter. "Women Workers and Bureaucratic Control in Irish Electronics Factories." Paper presented to the British Sociological Association, March 1983.

Women's Studies International Forum 1988. (Special Issue). "Feminism in Ireland." 11, no. 4.

Wong, Aline K. 1981. "Planned Development, Social Stratification, and the Sexual Division of Labor in Singapore." *Signs* 7, no. 2:434–52.

Working Party on Child Care Facilities for Working Parents. 1983. Report to the Minister for Labour. Dublin: Stationery Office.

Working Party on Women's Affairs and Family Law Reform. 1985. *Irish Women: Agenda for Practical Action*. Dublin: Stationery Office.

World Bank. 1983. *World Tables*, Vol. II, *Social Data*. 3d ed. Baltimore, Md.: Johns Hopkins University Press.

Index

General

Abortion, 8, 91, 93
  access to, 93
  policy on, 173n.43
Abuse. *See* Domestic abuse
Adultery, 93, 173n.41
Affirmative Action Program, 8, 127
Africa
  land titles, 13
  new technologies and men, 13
  patriarchy, 14
  the food crisis, 13
Agriculture, 13, 21, 127
AnCO, 88, 90
AnCO, 88, 172n.37
Annulment, 93. *See also* Divorce
Apprenticeships, 89
Asia, 46
  development similar to Ireland, 3
  export-led development, 4, 19, 46
  female labor force participation in,
    4, 25
  patriarchy, 14
  U.S. foreign direct investment in,
    19 (*See also* Singapore)

Baby bar, 88
Bastard
  legal definition of, 174n.44
Birth rate, 147
  compared to fertility rate, 165n.26
Brazil, 127
  Hirata's hypothesis, 40
Buchanan, James, 166n.1

Capitalism
  gender domination or patriarchy
    and, 134, 136, 139
  the working class and, 136 (*See also*
    Social structure of accumulation)
Catholic Church, 11, 55, 115, 166n.3,
  174n.1
  male dominance and, 135
Census data, 28, 173n.42
  cf ILO data, 159n.18
  limitations of, 158n.14
  undercounting women, 158n.14
  (*See also* Female share of the
    labor force; Labor force
    participation rate, women)
Chaney, Elsa, 162n.1
Childcare facilities, 96, 97
  lack of, 96
Childcare duties, 8, 61
  barrier to economic equality, 8
Children, 8, 60–62. *See also* Childcare
  duties
Class inequality, 131, 138–139
Clothing and footwear industry, 32,
  48, 52
Commission of the European Community,
  96, 170n.23
Commission on the Status of
  Women, 88–89, 168n.9, 173n.40
  economic roles of husband and
    wife, 91–92
Commission on the Status of Women, 68,
  87, 91, 92, 96

Authors